Tourism and the Creative Industries

This book focuses on the theoretical, policy and practice linkages and disjunctures between tourism and the creative industries. There are clear and strong connections between the sectors: for example, in the development and application of new and emerging media in tourism; festivals and cultural events showcasing the creative identity of place; tours and place identities associated with film, TV, music and arts tourism; as well as particular destinations being promoted on the basis of their 'creative' endowments such as theatre breaks, art exhibitions and fashion shows.

Tourism and the Creative Industries explores a variety of such relationships in one volume and offers innovative and critical insights into how creative industries and tourism together contribute to place identity, tourist experience, destination marketing and management. The book is aligned with the sectors that have been demarcated by the UK Government Department of Culture, Media and Sport as comprising the creative industries: advertising and marketing; architecture; design and designer fashion; film, TV, video, radio and photography; IT, software and computer services; publishing and music; and performing and visual arts. The title of this volume demonstrates how the exclusion of tourism from the creative industries is arguably perverse, given that much of the work by destination managers and of private sector tourism is characterised by creativity and innovation. Interdisciplinary research and international context bring a broader perspective on how the creative industries operate in varying cultural and policy contexts in relation to tourism.

This book brings together the parallel and disparate interdisciplinary fields of tourism and the creative industries and will be of interest to students, academics and researchers interested in tourism, creative industries, marketing and management.

Philip Long is a Principal Academic at Bournemouth University. His research interests include: relationships between tourism and popular culture; festivals; international film and television; diaspora communities; and social exclusion. He is a board member of the International Festivals and Events Association (Europe).

Nigel D. Morpeth is an academic and artist based at Leeds Beckett University. He has previously worked for UK local authorities in community-based leisure, festival and events organisation, and has worked in the field of Tourism Education over the last 26 years. His teaching and research is focused on diverse interdisciplinary academic approaches to Tourism, Cultural Studies, the Creative Industries, and Sport and Leisure. In a recent book, *Planning for Tourism: Towards a Sustainable Future*, he has written about the linkages between community initiatives and sustainability. He has delivered over 25 international conference papers including a keynote address on Tourism and the Arts at Ostfalia University in Germany and has delivered a presentation on public art at the Courtauld Institute, Somerset House, London.

Routledge Advances in Tourism

Edited by Stephen Page

Faculty of Management, Bournemouth University

Tourism and the Creative Industries

Theories, policies and practice

**Edited by Philip Long and
Nigel D. Morpeth**

Routledge
Taylor & Francis Group

LONDON AND NEW YORK

First published 2016 by Routledge

2 Park Square, Milton Park, Abingdon, Oxfordshire OX14 4RN
711 Third Avenue, New York, NY 10017

Routledge is an imprint of the Taylor & Francis Group, an informa business

First issued in paperback 2018

British Library Cataloguing in Publication Data
A catalogue record for this book is available from the British Library

Library of Congress Cataloging in Publication Data
A catalog record for this book has been requested

ISBN: 978-1-138-83270-1 (hbk)
ISBN: 978-1-138-59243-8 (pbk)

Typeset in Times New Roman
by Wearset Ltd, Boldon, Tyne and Wear

Contents

vi   *Contents*

Figures

Tables

Contributors

Charles Ambrosino is a Lecturer in Town Planning and Urban Design at the Grenoble Town Planning Institute, University of Grenoble, France. His research interests include: the social life of metropolitan creativity; cultural production of space and place; and international perspectives on culture-led regeneration.

Corinna Budnarowska is an academic at Bournemouth University, specialising in fashion retailing. Her research interests include: the relationship between fashion and place; fashion world cities and the role of flagship stores; pop-up retailing; online marketing tools for fashion; and the use of technology within retail and fashion.

Warwick Frost is Associate Professor in Tourism, Hospitality and Events at La Trobe University, Australia. His research interests are heritage tourism, tourism and the media, and events. He is the author (with Jennifer Laing) of *Imagining the American West through Films and Tourism* (Routledge 2015) and a convenor of the International Tourism and the Media conference series.

Vincent Guillon is Deputy Director, National Observatory of Cultural Policies, Grenoble, France. His research interests include: national, regional and local cultural policies; international perspectives on creative cities and culture-led regeneration and cultural participation.

Kevin Hannam is Professor of Tourism Mobilities at Leeds Beckett University, UK, and a research affiliate at the University of Johannesburg, South Africa. He is a founding co-editor of the journals *Mobilities* and *Applied Mobilities* (Routledge), co-author of the books *Understanding Tourism* (Sage) and *Tourism and India* (Routledge) and co-editor of the *Routledge Handbook of Mobilities Research* and *Moral Encounters in Tourism* (Ashgate). Forthcoming publications include the edited books *Event Mobilities* and *Tourism and Leisure Mobilities* (both Routledge). He has extensive field research experience in South and South East Asia and has collaborated with a number of artists with regard to his work on creative tourism mobilities. He has a PhD in Geography from the University of Portsmouth, UK, and is a Fellow of the Royal Geographical Society (FRGS), member of the Royal Anthropological

Institute (RAI) and Vice-Chair of the Association for Tourism and Leisure Education and Research (ATLAS). In 2015–2016 he was awarded a Vice-Chancellor International Scholarship to the University of Wollongong, Australia.

Sangkyun (Sean) Kim is a Senior Lecturer in Tourism at Flinders University, Australia. His research interests include: tourism and popular culture; film tourism; special interest tourism (e.g. intangible heritage); and research methods in tourism. He is on the editorial board of several international tourism journals including *Tourist Studies* and *Journal of Travel & Tourism Marketing*.

Jennifer Laing is a Senior Lecturer in Management at La Trobe University, Australia. Her research interests are travel narratives, tourism and the media and events. She is the author (with Warwick Frost) of *Imagining the American West through Films and Tourism* (Routledge 2015) and a convenor of the International Tourism and the Media Conference series.

Philip Long is a Principal Academic at Bournemouth University. His research interests include: relationships between tourism and popular culture; festivals; international film and television; diaspora communities; and social exclusion. He is a board member of the International Festivals and Events Association (Europe).

Ruth Marciniak is a Senior Lecturer at Glasgow Caledonian University who has over 20 years' experience of working as an academic. She completed her PhD in 2007; it explored strategy planning processes of UK fashion retailers for ecommerce. Her areas of teaching include fashion, digital marketing and strategy. Her research interests include 'selfies' and the use of the brand imagery in earned media, and post-purchase consumer behaviour, sustainability and fashion.

Nigel D. Morpeth is an academic and artist based at Leeds Beckett University. He has previously worked for UK local authorities in community-based leisure, festival and events organisation, and has worked in the field of Tourism Education over the last 26 years. His teaching and research is focused on diverse interdisciplinary academic approaches to Tourism, Cultural Studies, the Creative Industries, and Sport and Leisure. In a recent book, *Planning for Tourism: Towards a Sustainable Future*, he has written about the linkages between community initiatives and sustainability. He has delivered over 25 international conference papers including a keynote address on Tourism and the Arts at Ostfalia University in Germany and has delivered a presentation on public art at the Courtauld Institute, Somerset House, London.

Chanwoo Nam is Deputy Director of the Office for Tourism Industry at the Ministry of Culture, Sports and Tourism, Korea. His research interests include: tourism policy and regulation; stakeholders; tourism and popular culture; and tourism in Asia.

Mark Passera is a Lecturer in Communications and Media at the University of the Arts London. His research interests include: political economy; the public sphere; political marketing; design thinking; and communication theory. He is a member of the Political Studies Association.

Les Roberts is a Lecturer in Cultural and Media Studies in the School of the Arts, University of Liverpool. His research interests include: the cultural production of space and place; visual culture, tourism and mobility; urban cultural studies; spatial humanities; popular culture and cultural memory. He is the author of *Film, Mobility and Urban Space: A Cinematic Geography of Liverpool* (2012).

Dominique Sagot-Duvauroux is Professor of Economics at GRANEM (Research Centre in Economics and Management) at the University of Angers, France. Her research interests include: cultural economics; industrial organisations and clusters; and the economics of property rights.

Jacqueline Salmond received her PhD in Human Geography from the University of Kentucky in 2010. Her research focused on travel and tourism and their relationship with the environments and economies of developing countries, with a particular concentration on South East Asia. She is currently exploring how to reconceptualise new communities of tourism, reframing understandings of how tourism is practiced and understood by its participants. She is currently an academic adviser and instructor at Florida Gulf Coast University, teaching interdisciplinary studies with a focus on community participation and environmental humanities.

Michael Salmond is Associate Professor of Digital Media Design at Florida Gulf Coast University. He received his MFA in Electronic Media from the University of South Florida, Tampa, Florida. In 2013 his first book, *The Fundamentals of Interactive Media Design*, was published in the UK, USA and Australia. His second book, *Videogame Design; Practices and Principles from the Ground Up* will be published in 2016. Michael is currently researching videogames and their positive effects on cognition and ageing.

Ian Strange is Professor of Planning and Research Director, Faculty of Arts, Environment and Technology at Leeds Beckett University, UK. His research experience and activity lie in the areas of the politics of urban restructuring, urban governance, local economic policy, arts and cultural policy, and conservation and the planning and development process in historic cities.

James Whiting gained his PhD from the University of Sunderland in 2012 with a piece of research into the development of the Ouseburn Valley in Newcastle upon Tyne as an artists' quarter. This research focused on the development of this area as a tourism and leisure resource, as well as looking at the tourism habits of its artist residents. He has published articles in the *Annals of Tourism Research* and *Leisure Studies* and his current research interests include issues of tourism and gentrification and virtual tourism.

1 Introduction

Philip Long and Nigel D. Morpeth

This chapter discusses the relationships between tourism, creativity and the 'creative industries' in theory, policy and practice, and introduces the subsequent chapters that address these connections in various international sectorial contexts. Tourism, viewed in relation to creativity and what have become variously defined as the 'creative industries', involves intersecting and dynamic complex social systems, economic sectors, career prospects and professional practices which are subject to analysis through interdisciplinary fields of study though with parallel research agendas, academic publishing outlets, education and professional development programmes (Bouncken and Sungsoo, 2002; Cooper, 2006).

Seeking to understand the multiple, diverse and complex relationships between tourism and the creative industries includes study of the role of people as tourists (travelling individually and/or in 'packaged' groups) who are engaged in cultural consumption through participation (and at times 'co-creation') in the processes and outputs of component sectors of the creative industries. The links between creativity and tourism as 'industries' that are planned and promoted by national and local governments (and also by United Nations agencies and inter-governmental bodies such as the European Union) and identified as being located in particular and typically, though not exclusively, urban 'creative districts' that are attractive to tourists are further significant connections between these phenomena (Alvarez, 2010; Aquino *et al.*, 2012; Bell and Jayne, 2010; Evans, 2009; Landry, 2000).

As will be seen from the chapters in this volume, relationships between tourism and creative industry sectors are to varying extents explicit, complementary, synergistic and mutually constitutive but in some contexts they may be unacknowledged or competitive, in tension and contested. This duality and complexity offers rich territory for critical research that goes beyond advocacy for the creative industries and 'creative tourism'.

The emphasis in this introductory chapter is on creative industry studies and management concepts, policies and practices as these have only been applied to the field of tourism to a limited and fragmentary extent, with some of the sectors and domains defined as constituting the creative industries receiving significantly more attention than others in the tourism literature. However, there is increasing recognition of the strong and close theoretical connections between areas of creative practice and tourism. It is argued that there has been a 'creative turn' in tourism studies, tourist ('performative') practice and destination planning and development with some application of academic ideas from creative industries management, policy and consumption appearing in the tourism domain (Aitchison, 2006; Ateljevic *et al.*, 2007; Long and Morpeth, 2012; Richards, 2011). This 'turn' coincides with an increasing emphasis, in both theory and practice, on tourists being seen as 'co-creators' of experience rather than as passive consumers of fixed (cultural and heritage) tourism products (Richards and Wilson, 2006). However, there are problematic and controversial dimensions to 'creative tourism' which will be highlighted throughout this introduction.

In their influential 2006 work, Richards and Wilson argue that there has been a proliferation and 'serial reproduction' of generic built cultural attractions which are commonly associated with (usually urban) 'regeneration' programmes and that these have resulted in some bland developments driven by consumption and the commercial property market (typically retail, apartment and leisure projects). Critiques along similar lines have been noted in the work of architecture and planning commentators such as Owen Hatherley (2011) on the 'new ruins' of regeneration in British provincial cities and the vacuity of their claims for distinctiveness, quality, creativity and vibrancy. Alongside their argument concerning mediocre cultural attractions, Richards and Wilson also suggest that there is an ongoing turn towards more sophisticated, niche, fragmented and complex tourist markets as people (or at least those with the financial resources to do so) engage in discriminating and reflexive 'skilled consumption' or 'serious leisure' (Csíkszentmihályi, 1997; Gretzel and Jamal, 2009; Stebbins, 2007). Creative tourist practices may therefore provide opportunities for the building of personal identities, capacities and expertise involving the acquisition of 'cultural capital' through participation in *creative* pursuits and experiences (Bourdieu, 1993). The tourism industry internationally is increasingly developing and promoting packages, trails and products aimed at satisfying such demand. The implication of these arguments is that there is substantial scope for the tourism industry to work more closely with creative practitioners. However, positive working and strategic relationships across sectors must not be assumed, as contrasting educational, occupational and perhaps ideological backgrounds may militate against this, and some creative practitioners and neighbourhoods may resist being incorporated, packaged and presented as tourist attractions (Aoyama, 2009; Busa, 2009; Drake, 2003; Hughes, 1989; Maitland, 2010). These complexities and controversies indicate the need for a critical, theoretically informed approach to the study of creative tourism policy and practice.

1.1 Theorising creativity

'Creativity', like 'culture' (and indeed 'tourism'), is a complicated term which has profound philosophical antecedents (Bohm, 1996; Deleuze and Guattari,

1994; Habermas, 1987; Negus and Pickering, 2004; Sternberg, 1999). This section briefly considers interdisciplinary approaches to interpreting 'creativity' that may serve as a foundational set of concepts and perspectives for analysing the creative industries and their relationships with emerging and explicitly labelled models of creative tourism and with tourism more generally. Any critical discussion of the 'creative industries' should involve prior examination of diverse interpretations of creativity and the implications in theory and practice of linking the term with 'industries' involving political, economic and management connotations and conceptualisations of sectors, workers, markets, regulation and consumers (Oakley, 2009; Pratt and Jeffcut, 2009; Raunig *et al.*, 2011; Santagata, 2010; Schlesinger, 2007). Thus, before narrowing to this focus there is a need to look beyond corporatist, capitalist and industrial conceptualisations of creativity to consider its broader and diverse philosophical derivations and interpretations (Pope, 2005: 27).

Key definitions and connotations of creativity are associated first, with religion, the divine and cosmology (where a God-like figure Creates *ex nihilo*). Second, the 'creative arts' involve people creating *artistic* works either through the original, exhibited, critically acclaimed (or condemned), socially valued (or contested) and aesthetically pleasing (or challenging) works of 'geniuses' or in the everyday artistic expressions produced by *all* people individually and collectively in *crafting* works (Sennett, 2008). Third, the natural sciences typically interpret 'creation' as involving the physical transformation of material that previously existed, or that is discovered and adapted in industry and society through the development, application and social use of technologies (Pope, 2005). More recently, and controversially, associations are made in theory, policy rhetoric, media discourse and professional practice between creativity and the manipulation of signs and imagery through fashion, media, public relations and advertising, with practitioners working in these sectors deemed to be 'creatives' [*sic*] (Beck, 2003; Caves, 2000; Comunian *et al.*, 2011; Craik, 2009; McRobbie, 1998).

The fostering of creativity may also of course be considered to be a prime purpose of education at all stages of 'lifelong learning' from playwork in primary school to creative writing and arts courses in adult education classes for retired people such as those provided by the University of the Third Age in the United Kingdom (Ashton and Noonan, 2013; Fisher, 2012). Education theorist Sir Ken Robinson, for example, is a leading proponent of encouraging creativity through curriculum innovation and pedagogic development (Robinson, 2001). These ideas may usefully be applied to Tourism Studies, professional development curricula for tourism and creative industries practitioners and in pedagogy and also in considering what and how *tourists* learn. We will return to this in our consideration of the *practice* of creative tourism in section 1.4 below and in the conclusions to this book.

Also related to practice and in commercial contexts, synonyms for creativity are reflected in *entrepreneurialism* and *inventiveness* through product, distribution and market *innovations* and also as regards tourist practice through the '*co-creation*' of experience and in people's engagement with social media as tourists (Banks, 2012; Bilton, 2007; Caves, 2000). This interpretation of creativity is closest to an applied industry perspective, though this managerialist conceptualisation is not sufficient in the critical examination of the foundations, extent and implications of the creative tourism phenomenon.

The suggestion that creation needs to be recognised as taking place, at least potentially, in all areas of life and not just narrowly conceived as being exclusively the domain of supremely talented individuals is important (Deleuze and Guattari, 1994). Creativity may be viewed as chaotic, complex and emerging and concerns human *becomings* rather than a more static sense of *being* (Pope, 2005: 5). The ability to be creative *and* the capacity to appreciate aesthetic qualities are not solely the preserve of those who are somehow divinely inspired and/or endowed with unique, inherent talents and capabilities (Robinson, 2001). There is a risk of assigning the capacity to be creative exclusively to an elite, educated and privileged class possessing the requisite refinement of taste and talent. Our observations highlight that creative tourism should not be viewed as exclusive to elite, niche tourist market segments but may be applicable across all tourist markets and behaviour (Novelli, 2005).

'Creativity' also needs to be conceived within particular international linguistic, social, cultural, historical and political contexts as the term may not readily be translated, or share interpretations and modes of expression in different cultural settings. The contributions in this volume are primarily from English-language, North American and European contexts. Interpretations of creativity presented here may therefore not necessarily apply in other linguistic and cultural settings, for example in Asia, Latin America and Africa (Catalani, 2013; Flew, 2013; Li, 2011; Ooi, 2007; Rogerson, 2006; Sasaki, 2010; see also Chapter 7 in this volume by Kim and Nam).

McIntyre (2012) emphasises that it is a daunting task to theorise creativity comprehensively because of a lack of a common understanding as to how it is defined and interpreted and also because creativity pervades every area of life from the arts to business and the sciences. He argues that in many cultures there is commonly a conflation between the words 'artistic' and 'creative' which historically has been informed by the Renaissance and Romantic traditions, particularly through the work of philosophers such as Rousseau (Russell, 1946), and that creativity became synonymous with the metaphysical and the transformation of base metal into gold. This is perhaps a useful metaphor in terms of the contemporary application of creativity and its utility as a guiding principle for tourism and the creative industries in the 'regeneration' of post-industrial urban areas where creativity is assigned and promoted in cities and neighbourhoods which possess or may develop and transform exploitable *genius loci* as brands to attract footloose tourists (Alvarez, 2010; Bianchini and Parkinson, 1993; Landry *et al.*, 1996). We will return to this interpretation in our review in section 1.3 of policies that seek to promote creativity (and tourism) at local, national and international levels.

1.2 Creative industries and tourism

Creative industries are a burgeoning but contested interdisciplinary field of academic research, cross-departmental government policy-making, occupational categorisation and (co-creative) consumer (tourist) practice at a global scale (see O'Connor, 2011, for an excellent critical history of the conceptualisation of the cultural and creative industries and the development of associated theory and policy). This section first outlines the background to the delineation of the creative industries as an area of government industrial policy before turning to the critical debates that characterise the academic field of creative industries studies.

The definition of the 'creative industries' has its origins in policy discourse following earlier antecedents in the development of national and international cultural policy and also in policies and programmes to promote regeneration in post-industrial urban districts from the 1970s and 1980s (Flew, 2013, 2012; Hartley, 2005; Hesmondhalgh, 2013; Higgs and Cunningham, 2008; Miller, 2009). Connections between creative industries and tourism policies are considered in section 1.3 below. In the United Kingdom, the 'New Labour' government of the late 1990s/early 2000s was influential in the formal definition and 'mapping' of the 'creative industries'. A Department of Culture, Media and Sport (DCMS), replacing its predecessor Department of National Heritage, was founded in 1997 and charged with mapping, evaluating and developing a set of economic indicators for sectors related to arts, media, culture and digital technology. Effectively, this remit reconceptualised the arts as being, at least potentially, beyond reliance on public subsidy and emphasised their direct and indirect economic contributions through intellectual property, media, markets and technology (including implicitly the arts' value for shaping a 'Cool Britannia' national image and in the attraction of international investment and tourism) (DCMS 2001a, 2001b, 2004; Smith, 1998).

The DCMS mapping exercise resulted in sectors being identified as comprising the creative industries in the UK. These were rationalised by sector training agency Creative and Cultural Skills (CCS) in 2013 to include:

- advertising and marketing
- architecture
- design and designer fashion
- film, TV, video, radio and photography
- IT, software and computer services
- publishing
- music, performing and visual arts (DCMS, 2001a; revised by CCS, 2013).

The exclusion of tourism from the formal definition of the component sectors of the creative industries in the UK is notable (though this is not the case in United Nations and government definitions elsewhere). A justification of this is that the creative industry sectors as defined in the UK are all characterised by the possession of copyright and intellectual property rights, which are less applicable in the tourism industry where many products and destinations are replicable and/or substitutable.

The argument from governments past and present is that the UK 'excels' (Britain is 'Great' across all of the creative industry sectors in a current national advertising campaign) in a highly competitive global marketplace in the development, production, commercialisation and export of all these spheres of artistic, technological and design creativity and that these have considerable value as economic sectors and are pre-eminent contributors to national image-making and also in the attraction of inward investment and tourists (Aronczyk, 2013; Smith, 1998). It is notable that government rhetoric and strategies in support of the creative industries and creative economy in the UK have persisted beyond the demise of 'New Labour' (Bakhshi *et al.*, 2013; Hewison, 2014). Also notable is that the UK creative industries model was itself exported through the work of the British Council, cultural policy advisers and consultants, with comparable models being mapped and government ministries provided with 'toolkits' for policy intervention along similar lines in Europe, Asia, Australia, New Zealand and Latin America from the late 1990s (Australian Government, 1998; Flew, 2013; Taiwan Institute of Economic Research, 2012).

Creative industries have also been promoted as a vehicle for development globally by UN agencies for trade and development and also for education, science and culture (UNCTAD, 2010; UNESCO, 2009) and across member states of the European Union. UNCTAD claims that 7 per cent of world GDP and 14 per cent of annual growth rates globally were contributed by the creative industries throughout the 2000s and that this impressive performance of the 'creative economy' in tradable, intangible goods based on intellectual property had been relatively resistant to the global economic crisis of 2007–2008 (UNCTAD, 2010). In its 2010 report on the creative economy, UNCTAD provided an extended definition of the creative industries, suggesting that they:

- are cycles of creation, production and distribution of goods and services that use creativity and intellectual capital as primary inputs;
- constitute a set of knowledge-based activities, focused on but not limited to the arts, potentially generating revenue from trade and intellectual property rights (IPR);
- comprise tangible products and intangible intellectual or artistic services with creative content, economic value and market objectives;
- are at the crossroads among the artistic, services and industrial sectors (including tourism as a key related sector).

The UNCTAD model (Figure 1.1) includes the sectors incorporated by DCMS but also captures tangible and intangible heritage, cultural sites and 'recreational services', thus relating the creative industries to tourism more explicitly than does the UK framework.

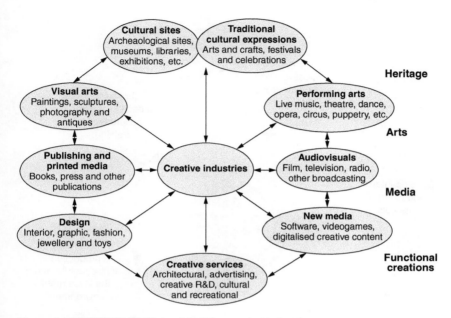

Figure 1.1 UNCTAD (2010) model of the creative industries.

UNESCO (2009) conceives the creative industries as operating across six direct domains:

- cultural and natural heritage: museums; archaeological and historical places; cultural landscapes;
- performance and celebrations: performing arts; music; festivals; fairs and feasts;
- visual arts and crafts: fine arts and photography;
- books and print media: virtual publishing; libraries; book fairs;
- audio-visual and interactive media: film and video; TV and radio; internet; video games;
- design and creative services: fashion design; graphic design; interior design; landscaping; architecture; advertising.

UNESCO identifies tourism and hospitality and also sport and recreation, including amusement parks, theme parks and gambling as being domains that are related to the core creative industries. It proposes, to national governments a 'circuit' of policy and market interventions for their development, as shown in Figure 1.2.

It is notable that the creative industries combine science with art in their embrace of digital, design and architectural technologies alongside the performing, literary and visual arts. Creative industries are also often conflated by policy-makers with the *cultural* industries, though these typically also focus on heritage, the arts and 'traditional' culture, whereas creative industries are usually seen as being more contemporary.

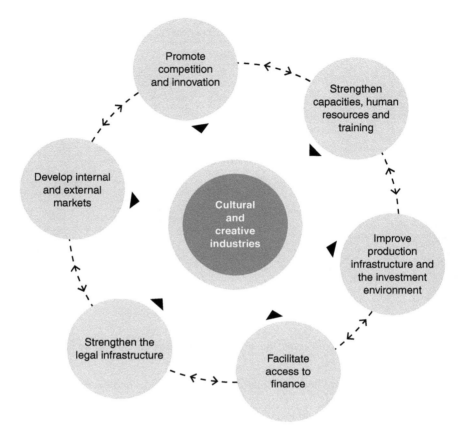

Figure 1.2 UNESCO (2009) creative industry circuits.

A further conceptualisation of the creative industries as businesses identifies four overlapping sub-groups that are concerned with the production and distribution of:

- *Originals*, trading on the production of unique, scarce and collectible works that are judged to possess aesthetic value as well as use and market exchange value, for example fine art;
- *Content* where, in contrast, mass media are produced and distributed and aimed to be as widely consumed as possible, for example popular cultural forms of visual and music entertainment;
- *Services* such as advertising, public-relations and architecture which are business-business, not final consumption or retail focused; and
- *Experiences* that attract people/tourists to live events such as music festivals and also to theme parks, museums, galleries, retail etc.

(Hartley *et al.*, 2013: 60)

As regards theoretical debates, for some critics the term 'creative industries' contains a dissonant association of two conflicting words, with Hartley suggesting that these 'two elements are crash-merged', adding that the word 'creative' seems to preclude organisation on an industrial scale, emphasising instead the centrality of individual creative talent. 'Industries seems to preclude much individual human creativity from consideration. In short, if creativity is part of human identity, then what has it got to do with industries?' (2005: 106).

Hartley considers the definition and application of creativity within different levels of society from the lead taken by policy-makers and taste-makers (Millard, 2001) in establishing policy that emphasises and seeks to direct the industrialisation of creativity. In contrast, at an individual level he describes 'DIY creativity', as an extension of 'DIY citizenship' ('people making themselves up as they go along', Millard, 2001: 111). The contrast between these interpretations is expressed in the elite strategies of high culture juxtaposed with the 'everyday actions' of citizens being creative as part of the everyday life of being human within mainstream and sub-cultural society (see Chambers *et al.*, 2013: 13–17 on performance studies in this context). What constitutes creativity is therefore extensive and inexhaustible in its possibilities. These sharp distinctions are important in providing a starting point for understanding the significance of the ways in which the creative industries as a concept are utilised academically and also in policy and practitioner terms.

The conflation of the 'cultural' and 'creative' with 'industry' is therefore a source of considerable controversy and academic debate. Some critics argue that the 'creative industries' definition values culture primarily or even solely for its economic role, rather than for its much wider contribution to radical ideas, aesthetics and social change. In particular, the related term 'culture industry' has negative connotations for some theorists who draw on the work of the Frankfurt School in their critique of the influence of the mass media in post-war Western society (Adorno, 1991; Habermas, 1987; Hesmondhalgh, 2013). For such critics, new and emerging media and technology organisations possess far too much power to shape socio-cultural change, particularly given their capacity for surveillance, their impact on the young, poor and vulnerable, and the alienation of society at large. For such critics, a defining feature of a creative industry market system-based economy is the search for constant innovation, production and consumption of disposable consumer goods and images. Negus and Pickering characterise this as an 'ever-rolling mobility of pleasure, frustrated desire, obsolescence and new desire rationally incorporated into a commodity system maintained by the techniques of advertising, publicity and marketing' (2004: 11).

There is therefore a sharp disjuncture between viewing creativity as Kantian aesthetics and the associated ideal type of the 'creative genius' creating order and beauty out of chaos and seeing creativity as paired with 'industry', indicating a utilitarian production line, obsolescence and commercial exploitation. Furthermore, an industrial association suggests a need for constant innovation and disposable fashion and novelty, yet, 'the adjective "creative" is liberally applied to products or works that involve negligible amounts of novelty. Alternatively, the term "creativity" ends up within a closed system as a completely self-referential concept.' Constant emphasis is placed on originality and novelty, implying opposition to anything deemed to be 'old-world', 'old-economy'; e.g. manufacturing and processing, are polluting while *design* is clean (Hartley *et al.* 2013: 67). This polarisation of views characterises debate in the field, particularly when tourism enters the frame, whether at the level of creative tourism as industry and/or as creative tourist practice.

1.3 Creative industries policy and tourism

This section addresses the cross-cutting agenda of government policies that are focused on culture and the creative industries and their associations with tourism. Policies and strategies for fostering creativity are derived from and are primarily related to the realm of cultural/arts policy though they also have increasingly strong industrial, economic and even foreign policy emphases (Bianchini and Parkinson, 1993; Flew, 2012; McGuigan, 1996; O'Brien, 2014; Scott, 2000). The focus and levels of cultural and creative industries policies and their explicit and implicit connections with tourism are summarised in Table 1.1. This table sets out the typical major goals of such policies, the mechanisms, agencies, actors and policy instruments by which they are to be implemented, how 'success' may be recognised, the associated level of government policy-making, the ways in which such policies engage with creative industry practitioners and examples suggesting the extent to which tourism is an explicit policy priority.

There are typically three key domains of *cultural policy* which possess explicit and implicit links with tourism. These are, first and most obviously, attention to the arts including direct funding to cultural producers (such as 'national' and regional performing arts companies – theatre, dance, music, etc.), support for cultural institutions (including museums and galleries) and the funding of agencies whose remit is the development of artistic culture, such as the Arts Councils in the UK. Such arts and culture institutions and agencies have clear and at times explicit interests in working strategically, if selectively, with the tourism sector as a vehicle for audience development and source of revenue, though this is often not articulated in policy statements as being a priority (Jenkins *et al.*, 2011).

Second, cultural policies typically attend to communications and media, including support for national film and broadcast media organisations such as the BBC and British Film Institute (BFI) which involve both publicly funded activity and also support for commercial ventures. Examples include providing tax incentives for attracting film makers to locate and produce their work and also to promote tourism associated with film and TV releases and their settings (see for example the work of national film agencies such as Film France in this context). Policies relating to the development and regulation of new media technologies, publishing and intellectual property are also typical components of cultural policies which have strong commercial dimensions (McIntyre, 2012; O'Brien, 2014; Scott, 2000).

Third, cultural policies are usually underpinned by a central emphasis on patrimony, citizenship and identity including language policy, cultural development and education, multiculturalism, democratisation and questions of national symbolic identity. These core cultural concerns are also expressed through policies for the development of community culture at local spatial levels, including urban and regional culture and planning, cultural heritage management, and cultural tourism, leisure and recreation. The projection of images of local, regional and national identity is central to the work of tourism boards and destination marketing organisations (Jenkins *et al.*, 2011; Voase, 2012; Wang and Pizam, 2011). Policies that are explicitly focused on the development and support of the *creative industries* are unsurprisingly more explicitly economic in emphasis than cultural policies. However, there are clear linkages regarding, for example, the promotion of film and media as creative industry sectors with the projection of an official version of national identity (such as the 'Britain's Great' campaign) and by extension into foreign policy as a major component of symbolic 'soft power' (Aronczyk, 2013).

There are, however, difficulties in devising, implementing, monitoring and evaluating creative industry policies. These include, first, the complex and fragmented nature of creative industry sectors and their close economic relationships with firms in the wider economy, meaning that it is difficult to distinguish them from other industries (including tourism) (Campbell, 2011b; McRobbie, 2004; Mato, 2009). Logically, all industries are or should be creative if they are to survive. A further definitional issue is that many of the creative industries (beyond major media and technology organisations) are characterised by large numbers of micro-businesses (firms employing fewer than 10 people) and, in the UK for example, businesses below the value added tax threshold (CCS, 2013; DCMS, 2004). Self-employment (and high rates of business failure and churn) also means that official data do not capture the extent of the creative industries accurately (Bakhshi and Windsor, 2015).

Furthermore, devising policies for the creative industries involves the complexity and incongruity of trying to connect two key contemporary policy clusters: the 'hard science' of high-growth information and communications technologies and research and development-based sectors (*production*); and the less readily quantifiable 'experience' economy, cultural identity, social networking and empowerment (*consumption*). Creative industries policies can present a simplistic narrative of the seamless merging of the arts and culture with science and economics and may represent incoherent policy-making with data sources often complex and possibly suspect, incommensurable, subject to hype and underdeveloped (Hartley *et al.*, 2013: 59). Creative industries are therefore a contested domain for economists and policy-makers. Knowledge, product and 'network spill-overs' between creative sectors and practitioners and tourism are very important here, with tourism being a key route to markets (and employment) for some creative industry practitioners. These network spill-overs can take the form of 'creative milieux' in particular neighbourhoods with a clustering of significant numbers of creative businesses, residents and activities

Table 1.1 Creative industries strategies as forms of policy

Policy focus	Major policy goals	Policy instruments	Success indicators	Level of government	Engagement with creative producers	Examples
Cultural policy	Artistic excellence; cultural heritage; access and participation	Public subsidy; art-form based expert advisory boards	Audience growth for arts and culture; public participation; international recognition	National	Direct – support for particular individuals and cultural institutions	National cultural policies; EU culture programmes *Tourism implicit or secondary*
Creative industries	Economic, employment and export growth in defined 'creative' sectors; new forms of intellectual property	Mapping of creative industries; sectorial development policies; training programmes; export promotion	Economic, employment and export growth; new forms of copyrighted product; linkages to other sectors	National/regional	Indirect – engages with industry bodies to promote policy networks	UK DCMS Mapping documents and other national strategies and policies *Recognition of tourism variable*
Creative clusters/ districts/quarters	Innovative city-regions; social cohesion and jobs	Local infrastructure investment (e.g. broadband and education); developing local/ regional networks	Inward migration of cultural producers; job growth; enhanced role of culture in city-region image	Local/sub-regional	Direct – government brokers collaboration; clusters may form independently of government but support generally a condition for sustainability	Hollywood/Los Angeles film cluster; Milan fashion district; Shanghai creative clusters; UK Northern 'Powerhouse' *Recognition of tourism variable*

Creative economy	Economy-wide application of creativity; human capital development	Promotion of creativity across all activities (e.g. through education); encouraging entrepreneurship and innovation	Linkage of creative industries to other sectors (e.g. manufacturing and services); collaboration between arts and sciences; improved educational outcomes	National	Indirect – impact on creative industries inputs (e.g. creative talent) and outputs (social network markets)	UNCTAD *Creative Economy Reports*; UK Creative Economy strategy *Recognition of tourism limited*
Creative cities	Global city-brands; tourism and inward investment; attracting talented professionals	Investment in cultural infrastructure; promotion of cultural amenities, usually inner-city; promotion of 'night-time economy'; marketing	Hosting major international festivals and events; growth of tourism and inward migration of skilled professionals	Local	Indirect- facilitate a 'creative environment' by reducing barriers to engagement and through an open, tolerant local culture	Numerous 'creative city' strategies, e.g. Rotterdam; Berlin; Bristol; Manchester; Sheffield; European Capitals of Culture

Source: adapted from Flew, 2013: 138–139.

influencing tourism, property values, the presence of specialist retail, food and drink outlets, etc. (Fleming, 2002; Pappalepore *et al.*, 2010; Roodhouse, 2010). This observation leads to consideration of policies that seek to advance the development of such *creative clusters*, *districts* and *quarters*.

With antecedents in 'industrial districts' and regional economic development, creative clusters, districts or quarters are commonly associated with post-industrial urban and regional regeneration programmes in North American and European cities where cultural/creative industries (and tourism) are key elements in area development and planning strategies (Chapain and Comunian, 2009; Fleming, 2002). Creative clusters also exist in emerging/developing economies, most notably in Asia and in some African and Latin American cities. There are also small town, coastal community and rural examples such as in St Ives, Cornwall, and Staithes, North Yorkshire, which are associated with 'schools' of visual art, both historic and contemporary (Bell and Jayne, 2010).

Creative cluster/district/quarter designations and *creative cities* of which they are part are often associated with advocacy from 'scholar-consultants' advising city governments on regeneration and cultural planning strategies. There is now a rampant and highly influential quasi-academic consultancy sector promoting audits, strategies and policy interventions in this domain of planning, architecture and regeneration (see for example Fleming and Erskine, 2011; Florida, 2010; Landry, 2000). There is much competitiveness rhetoric between places as city government politicians and marketing officers seek to put 'their' city (and also rural districts) on the map in order to secure a competitive position in a 'global marketplace' to attract inward investment, new professional classes and upmarket cultural tourism (Bagwell, 2008; Bell and Jayne, 2010; Chapain and Comunian 2009; Scott, 2000). As the examples in Table 1.1 suggest, such city marketing and 'creative tourism' branding may be associated with particular creative industry sectors such as fashion, film and music or are cross-cutting and focused on events such as those in the European Capitals of Culture programme (Campbell, 2011a).

Tourism in the UK and elsewhere is often referred to by economists and policy-makers as comprising the 'visitor economy' encapsulating balance of payments, externalities and value added associated with tourist spending along with investment by the private sector and by the state in tourism-related infrastructure (Coles *et al.*, 2012). Less recognised officially is that tourism is also a significant contributor to the *creative economy*, with parallels and overlaps also with notions of the 'knowledge economy' embracing education at all levels, though primarily the university and college sector (Bakhshi and Windsor, 2015; Chapain and Comunian, 2010; Cooke, 2002; Potts, 2011; Pratt and Jeffcut, 2009). There are issues of boundaries here between economic sectors as defined by Standard Industry Classifications (SICs) and what is admissible in terms of 'spill-over effects' and 'value chains' (CCS, 2013; DCMS, 2004; Fleming and Erskine, 2011; Throsby, 2010; see also Lash and Urry, 1994, on the 'culturisation of the economy'; and Howkins, 2001, on the 'economics of the imagination'). To stretch the '-economy' suffix even further, creative practitioners and destination marketing agencies also seek to attract recognition on the basis of their creative 'offer' as a core element of the '*attention economy*' where industry and destinations jostle to capture the attention (and spending) of audiences through multiple online and offline media channels (Davenport and Beck, 2001).

A central concept underpinning the creative economy which is also applicable in tourism is Joseph Schumpeter's notion of *creative destruction* involving linked processes of the accumulation and annihilation of wealth under capitalism (Hartley *et al.*, 2013: 51), reflecting extraordinary levels of technological and social change in the *creative economy* including new business start-ups and failures along with unpredictable emerging, ephemeral and declining markets with the stress on creative human agency through the figure of the *entrepreneur*. Hartley *et al.* (2013) identify four types of creative destruction where, first industry structures are transformed through lowered entry barriers; government regulatory approaches are adapted and usually lowered and made more flexible; competitive positioning strategies in complex business environments emerge; and last, technological assumptions evolve including product piracy and challenges to corporate control and structures.

Linking cultural and creative policies with tourism is becoming increasingly important as tourism destination management organisations (DMOs) and arts and cultural agencies in the UK and elsewhere face deep cuts in their funding under widely adopted government austerity programmes that are rolling back the role of the state in discretionary areas of public spending (Coles *et al.*, 2012). There are growing expectations that tourism, arts and cultural agencies will work more closely together and be increasingly (co-)funded by the private sector. Destination managers and arts/cultural officers in the UK are particularly vulnerable as many have been employed in local government where deep budgetary cuts have exposed discretionary activities such as tourism and the arts. Both tourism and arts/cultural sector practitioners therefore have shared experiences of the 'changing landscape' regarding public funding of their work, a consequence of which is some pooling of resources and the emergence of closer working relationships between tourism and cultural agencies at national and local levels.

In the UK government, ministries of tourism and the arts and cultural sectors currently 'reside' within DCMS (in England) as the 'home' of national tourist boards VisitBritain and VisitEngland (VE). DCMS also hosts cultural agencies which have strong relationships with tourism, including Arts Council England (ACE), English Heritage, Historic Royal Palaces, and Museums, Libraries and Archives. DCMS also leads on the creative industries. As previously noted, tourism is not recognised officially as being a component sector of the creative industries although much of the work of destination managers (tourism development officers) draws on, packages and promotes the creative industry milieu and outputs as major elements of many, particularly urban, destinations' tourism 'offer'.

An example of this closer and more strategic working relationship between tourism and the creative industries emerging in the UK is VE and ACE's

(VE/ACE, 2013) joint statement noting that 'the cultural sector – museums, art galleries, theatres and festivals – are a crucial part of England's visitor economy'. A specific initiative from the ACE/VE collaboration from 2014 was an invitation for consortia involving cultural and destination management organisations to tender for 'Cultural Destination' status. Successful bids needed to demonstrate that they will build capacity in the cultural and visitor economy sectors in their defined geographical area (which may transcend local government boundaries) and work to reposition cultural organisations to be more prominent in the local visitor economy (VE/ACE, 2013). The Arts Council/VisitEngland 2013 Cultural Destinations funding and development programme aimed to build capacity in the cultural and visitor economy sectors to achieve the following outcomes:

- more people experience the arts and culture in a way that contributes to the growth of the local visitor economy
- increased income leading to greater sustainability and resilience for cultural organisations and tourism businesses in local destinations
- the repositioning of cultural organisations to be more prominent in the local tourism offer
- a long term commitment from public and private sector partners to continue to support the growth of the local visitor economy through cultural tourism beyond the life of this project

(VE/ACE, 2013)

This programme, though nominally concerned with 'cultural tourism', provides a link to creative practice through its seeking to increase joint working between policy-makers and practitioners across sectors. Creative practice is the subject of the next section of this chapter and leads us to consider Richard Florida's (2002, 2010) contentious but highly influential conceptualisation of the *creative class* as exemplary practitioners and harbingers of the future.

1.4 Creative practice and tourism

Creative ways of 'doing tourism' by people travelling as tourists and also by tourism and creative industry workers is of increasing interest to researchers, policy-makers and practitioners in search of new, 'creatively destructive' and innovative models of creative tourism (see for example Ashton and Noonan, 2013; Bilton, 2007; Bouncken and Sungsoo, 2002; Comunian *et al.*, 2011; Fujiwara *et al.*, 2015). However, tourism and the creative industries as sectors inhabit parallel if increasingly intersecting worlds of education, professional practices and industry associations, government departments, training and development agencies, etc. This section considers theoretical ideas, drawn mainly from creative industry studies, and also examples of practice that connect tourism and the creative industries.

The most influential and widely recognised conceptualisation of creative industry practitioners is their grouping within a socio-economic '*creative class*' defined by its originator Richard Florida (2002) as comprising a new class of labour that reflects creative industry occupations and heralds the future of working (and social) life. Florida divides the creative class into two broad sections derived from standard industrial classification codes, with a 'Super-Creative Core' group including a wide range of occupations (e.g. science, engineering, education, technology and research), in which arts, design and media workers form an important sub-set. The primary job function of its members is to be creative and innovative. The super-creative core is described by Florida as being innovative and dynamic, creating commercial products and consumer goods; people in this group are fully engaged in creative processes (Florida, 2002: 69). Second, a 'Creative Professionals' group is deemed to be comprised of knowledge-based workers and includes those working in health-care, business and finance, the legal sector and education (again!). These workers 'draw on complex bodies of knowledge to solve specific problems', using higher degrees of education to do so (Florida, 2002: 70). The 'creative class' has achieved recognition in wider public discourse alongside a plethora of related terms that have been assigned by media pundits and marketing commentators to its members, including: 'symbolic analysts', 'netizens', 'digerati', 'immaterial labourers', 'new independents' and the 'cognitariat', along with the much derided or celebrated 'hipster'.

The creative class is therefore an extremely wide-ranging category of very mixed occupations, organisational structures, public and private sector employment, educational backgrounds, income levels, job security and more or less autonomous working practices. This huge diversity renders the label arguable at best in describing a coherent 'class'. Other critiques centre on an assumption that

> the creative class of the skilled, educated and hip would remake and revive American cities. The idea, packaged and peddled by consultant Richard Florida, had been that unlike spending public money to court Wall Street fat cats, corporate executives or other traditional elites, paying to appeal to the creative would truly trickle down, generating a widespread urban revival.
>
> (Kotkin, 2013: 1)

For such critics, the creative class is a chimera and stereotype and does not extend to those who are not in a position to participate in (and afford to inhabit) Florida's vision of inner-city, on-trend, hand-made bike-riding connoisseurs of craft ales and 'gastro-pubs', the night-time economy and urban street life (Campbell, 2011b; Comunian *et al.*, 2010; Hartley *et al.*, 2013; McRobbie, 2004; Peck, 2005). However, as noted in section 1.3 above, the creative class concept with all its flaws has received considerable traction among city politicians and marketing officials in devising policies, plans and strategies aimed at attracting such apparently desirable communities and their associated economic activity (including the attraction of tourists).

Whether one accepts the creative class as a coherent category or not, it is evident that arts, design and media practitioners acting as *entrepreneurs* who are alert to the opportunities that tourism may represent can and do realise and create new sources of value via tourism, while perhaps also disturbing and critiquing the existing order of commercial tourism. The English artist Banksy exemplified this with his dystopian theme park, 'Dismaland', which attracted thousands of tourists to the seaside resort of Weston-Super-Mare during the summer of 2015.

> There is an innate similarity between the artist and the entrepreneur as both are engaged in the creation of novelty in the face of fundamental uncertainty about notional value and they are often portrayed as 'outsiders', highly independent, self-actualising, imaginative, tolerant of ambiguity, risk-takers etc.'
>
> (Hartley *et al.*, 2013: 92)

A further observation is that tourism and creative industry structures alike tend to have large numbers of micro and small–medium-sized enterprises with a tendency to compete on entrepreneurial endeavour as they are unable to benefit from economies of scale and scope.

The realm of *co-creation* (*including user-created* or *user-generated content*) is increasingly fashionable in tourism, leisure and festivals studies as core to the 'experience economy' (Pine and Gilmore, 1999). Co-creation may be defined as 'consumers contributing a non-trivial component of the design, development, production, marketing and distribution of a new or existing product' (Hartley *et al.*, 2013: 21). Creative consumers thus generate value in this process through complex interactions between market and cultural domains. Conceptual related ideas to co-creation from the creative industries literature are *produsage* [*sic*] (Bruns, 2008) and also *crowd-sourcing* (Howe, 2008; Shirky, 2008). Issues include the extent of co-creation which may range from contributing an occasional blog or tweet through to the radical redesign of a product or process and how far this may involve the exploitation of *creative labour.*

Tourism and creative industries practice combined also exemplify *participatory* or *convergence culture*, where media, communication and tourism industries merge, intermediate and form alliances typically to extend their brand across media platforms and destinations/markets (Banks, 2012). Notable examples include Disney and Universal Studios combining film and television production, distribution, publishing and merchandising with theme parks and resorts. Technological convergence and the flow of content across media platforms therefore also represent a cultural shift as consumers/tourists seek new information and connections across dispersed media content.

A focus on creative *tourist* practice requires attention to the capacity of individuals (travelling and experiencing the world as tourists) to act independently and autonomously through their possession and desire to acquire, develop and deploy reflexive knowledge about creative (artistic) expressions and practices. This relates to the notion of *agency* (i.e. the capacity of individuals to act independently and to make their own free choices). For Hartley *et al.* (2013: 8), creative industries may also be conceived as 'social network markets' where a new kind of *collective* agency is emerging: that of the 'entrepreneurial consumer/ tourist, where consumers/tourists are risk-taking "novelty bundlers", choosing ensembles and situations in which to create new meanings using both emulation and innovation'. Specific illustrations of this phenomenon may be found in tourism located in the 'creative milieux' of fashionable city neighbourhoods or through tourist participation in diverse creative practices and emerging technologies. A 'Creative Tourism Network' online includes many such examples.

The notion of *audience(s)* is employed widely in media and arts theory and practice (and also in festival and event studies), but much less in the context of tourism studies and management where 'markets' and 'consumers' are more commonly used. Topics addressed in audience research include issues of participant choice (agency), control, composition and response ('effects'). Other terms may also be deployed for people participating in audiences, of course including: the 'consumer', 'public', 'user', 'citizen', 'visitor', 'spectator' or 'tourist' though these terms do have contrasting connotations. Audiences are an ideal type or abstraction but remain the subject of much academic and consultancy research by arts and cultural agencies such as The Audience Agency UK and the European Audiences Network. Audiences for film and TV genres and specific releases are commonly targeted as potential tourist markets. Tourist motivations, experience and behaviour in film locations have been widely covered in the 'screen tourism' literature (Beeton, 2005; Reijnders, 2011).

Fans as tourist market niches and sub-cultural audiences may contribute to the production as well as the consumption of artistic productions (for example as embodied in tourist 'performances' at festivals, the development of plotlines in TV series, online game conventions and presence at sites associated with the celebrity subjects of the audience gaze and veneration). Audiences are thus emerging, fragmented, complex, expert and specialised, with participants, no longer passive consumers, but engaged as active, creative co-producers with identities, relationships and meanings increasingly shared through social media and through their physical presence as tourists. This extension of the concept of audience into neighbouring domains is not confined to fans and (digital) gamers. In the leisure field, audience-hood and tourism are increasingly interdependent in the growth of 'experience-based' tourism, with certain places attracting visitors because of their associations with charismatic screen experiences. But this phenomenon also carries over to the realms of citizenship and global politics, when certain cultural *values*, for instance ideological, environmental and human-rights consciousness, are brokered into niche businesses, for example in 'extreme' and 'dark' tourism (Hartley *et al.*, 2013: 16). Such a focus also extends into so-called 'slum tourism' (Frenzel *et al.*, 2012) and politically activist volunteer 'tourism' (e.g. environmental campaigning and activist tourism in Palestine, Cuba, etc.).

Underlying the policy rationale for supporting and developing the creative industries and culture more broadly are value judgements ascribed by 'experts', the media and wider society that the attraction of high-spending cultural tourists may justify government funding of the 'public good' of cultural and creative sites and productions that are deemed to be of *aesthetic value* and intrinsic interest to discerning tourists. Questions arise as to who is qualified and empowered to ascribe aesthetic value and to define its relationship with economic interpretations of use and exchange values for the ideal-type creative tourist. There are issues concerning the criteria that are employed by experts in judging aesthetic quality and also implications for international relations in the context of the ownership, conservation and interpretation of aesthetic artefacts (e.g. World Heritage Sites) that are contested and/or 'at risk' and the role of tourism in these processes. These observations highlight that the creative industries overlap heritage and are indeed combined under UN definitions, as we noted above (UNDP-UNCTAD, 2010; UNESCO, 2009).

1.5   Chapter overviews

All of the chapters that are included in this book present critical analyses of the relationships between tourism and the creative industries as sectors and in relation to creative tourism policy and practice.

While the contributions cross-cut the themes of sectors, policies and practice, those chapters that are concerned mainly with the relationships between tourism and the creative industries as sectors include Chapter 2 by Roberts, who considers film-related tourism 'On location in Liverpool'. He notes an emphasis and established approach by policy makers and many researchers of conceptualising film tourism in relation to place-marketing and economic impacts and he advocates adopting more socio-cultural perspectives on the film tourism phenomenon as situated in particular locations/cities. Specifically this perspective is rooted in a spatial anthropology of film-related tourism which is positioned within wider considerations of the consumption of space and place in an urban context. Roberts focuses on the UK city of Liverpool to chart historically the role of film and television productions or, in his words, a 'cinematic geography' as a constituent part of the place-branding of Liverpool. Film and TV are viewed as part of the cultural production and consumption of space and as a way of communicating the intangible heritage of the city to an international audience. He identifies how a low-budget film, *Letter to Brezhnev*, led to the city council's intervention in establishing the Liverpool Film Organisation which provides a liaison service to the TV and film industries and how this was followed in 2002 by a film and TV trail in the city. Roberts argues that the slogan 'World in One City' which accompanied the 2008 European Capital of Culture celebration was yet another perennial example of how localised representations of the real, vernacular city can be 'masked out' in a globalised discourse.

Also focused primarily on a creative industry sector, in Chapter 5 Budnarowska and Marciniak consider the relationships between fashion and tourism principally within a UK context while acknowledging that there are international variations with different national connotations as to what constitutes the fashion design industry. They establish that whereas the UK Department of Culture, Media and Sport (2015) considers the fashion industry to be defined by specialised design activities, the British Design Council emphasises the importance of the retail element in promoting and selling designer fashion. In considering the scope of fashion tourism they identify the hospitality, attractions and retail dimensions as well as events and festivals, providing a diversity of elements for the fashion tourist to experience. Furthermore, they distinguish between the ubiquity of the fashion product and fashion-themed destinations as places to consume (luxury) experiences and locate the broader scope of these experiences beyond London as a global 'fashion capital' location. In profiling the fashion tourist they apply a theoretical review of the central tenets of the experience economy in relation to fashion.

In Chapter 4, 'Tourism and advertising as a creative industry sector', Mark Passera explores the significance of contemporary post-modern advertising and marketing practice which incorporates the concepts of design thinking, behavioural economics and digital technologies. He emphasises that 18 per cent of people employed in the creative industries in the UK work in advertising, emphasising that this 'class' of 'creatives' tends to be highly educated, white, middle class and male. He underpins his analysis with the 'Florida thesis', characterising creative clusters of advertising workers who are colonising proto-Silicon valley spaces or zones of creativity within the creative city. Passera provides examples of co-creative advertising in which interdisciplinary advertising has applied innovative IT technology to (rather sinisterly!) interpret heart rates and pulses as data improving understanding of emotional responses to products and events within the creative economy. In focusing on the case study of London he links observations on advertising, place branding and tourism and provides examples of experiential brand constructs such as the role of film in place advertising a 'world city'.

Chapters that primarily address policy relationships between the creative industries and tourism include Ian Strange's Chapter 6 on the reconfiguring relationship between planning, architecture and the creative industries. This chapter traces the development of policy in the UK and provides a framework in which the development and construction of creative spaces of quality design are promoted and established. The chapter offers a narrative that reveals the tensions and conflicts inherent in the management and regulation of urban planning and architecture and their relationship with tourism and the creative economy. The chapter also links with themes of creative industry sectors and practice in its discussion of architecture as a creative occupation. The chapter also examines some of the issues inherent in the interrelationships between architecture and the planning of creative spaces in the context of urban tourism and place promotion. Although it uses examples related to the experience of England and the rest of the UK, the chapter also considers the relationships between the development of architecture, urban planning and the creative economy internationally.

Ambrosino, Guillon and Sagot-Duvauroux's Chapter 8 on the creative renaissance of Nantes and Saint-Etienne emphasises how, in contrast to Anglo and Asian models of governments guiding national strategies for the creative industries, in France despite the innovative 1980s creation of a Minister for Culture, there has not been a similar ministerial designation for the creative industries. They describe how 'the French way' encapsulates a post-industrial narrative for cities as creative industries centres and/or cultural tourist destinations. They demonstrate how 'urban renaissance' in the cities of Nantes and Saint-Etienne has integrated social policy, the creative economy and tourism. Saint-Etienne has organised a recovery from industrial and demographic crises through a project centred on design and Nantes has used original events aimed at offering an alternative city narrative to that of a past dominated by the shipping industry. They suggest that the *genius loci* for these cities is located in the timely interventions of individual politicians and creative *animateurs* responsible for harnessing ideas and resources to realise city-wide initiatives for creativity.

In Chapter 7 Kim and Nam also provide an international policy perspective in their discussion of the opportunities and challenges facing tourism and the creative industries in South Korea, offering a very useful overview of the nascent relationships between creativity and tourism in an Asian context. They emphasise how the Korean government is harnessing the *Hallyu* phenomenon as a uniquely Korean mix of highly commercialised cultural products including music (K-pop), computer games, traditional and contemporary fashion and food as a huge attraction for inbound tourism primarily from Asian markets through the stewardship of the Ministry of Culture, Sports and Tourism which was established in 2006. Kim and Nam also provide a historical overview of *Hallyu* tourism and the development of 41 *Hallyu*-related tourism programmes that were launched between 2007 and 2011 through the auspices of Korean government agencies, principally as an instrument of economic growth. Despite these interventions they advocate a more co-ordinated government long-term development strategy for the tourism and creative industries rather than implementing improvised or one-off responses to market changes.

Whiting and Hannam connect policy with creative practice in Chapter 9 on 'bohemias' and the creation of a cosmopolitan tourism destination in the Ouseburn Valley, Newcastle upon Tyne, UK. Whiting and Hannam are consistent with the observations of Ambrosino, Guillon and Sagot-Duvauroux in their profiling the capacity of post-industrial cities to establish new *genius loci* through the more or less planned emergence of creative spaces which are a meeting place for both residents and visitors to consume creative experiences. In focusing on the UK city of Newcastle upon Tyne they highlight how visual and performing artists have colonised the depopulated Ouseburn Valley on the edge of the city to create a bohemia of creative production and also a zone of leisure and tourist consumption in cultural attractions, festivals and heritage trails. The local authority views these community-orientated creative enterprises as an important element in a citywide strategy for economic regeneration and the repopulation of the Ouseburn Valley through residential expansion. An interesting dimension to this chapter is its demonstration of how the bohemians of the Ouseburn Valley seek out similar creative experiences as acts of tourist consumption in bohemias in other urban centres globally.

Focusing primarily on creative tourist practice, in Chapter 10 Salmond and Salmond consider The gamer as tourist: the simulated environments and impossible geographies of videogames'. Here they identify how continuing advances in virtual reality technologies have opened up new (virtual) worlds for tourists. They elaborate on the parallels in the creation of both visual and physical spaces for tourism and the new hybrid spaces which are part real and part virtually altered realms that are either designed for the benefit of tourists explicitly or that possess tourist appeal incidentally. Their central thesis is that videogames enable their players to be creative and generate new or unique virtual experiences and allow the gamer to enact a touristic lifestyle both simultaneously and separately between physical and virtual realities. In taking part in these activities they have become and adopt the sobriquet of the 'gamer tourist' with the player enacting the modality of a tourist seeking quests and mini-quests, fantasy fulfilment and self-transformation, and more recently avatar customisation of the new self. They highlight the emergence of *unreality* characterised by the creation of digital spaces which include a floating archipelago within the online space of Sony's PlayStation home, 'Aurora', which digital tourists repeatedly visit and colonise, creating communities and going from enacting tourism to becoming migrants. Salmond and Salmond identify socio-cultural cross-overs in, for example, Japan-centric games which provide opportunities for Western players to explore Japanese culture virtually and touristically.

With parallels to Salmond and Salmond's chapter, Frost and Laing in Chapter 11 'Travel and transformation in the fantasy genre', demonstrate the power of mixed fantasy genres of creative fiction to construct heroic narratives of adventure and quest and portray the act of travel as both transformative and inspiring through the multimedia examples of *Dr Who*, *Game of Thrones* and *The Hobbit*, all of which have reached huge global audiences and possess strong associated fan cultures involving co-creative tourist practice. The sites and locations that feature in *Game of Thrones* and *The Hobbit* have been extensively packaged and promoted by national tourism organisations and tour organisers as 'screen tourism' destinations though this has been less so in the case of *Dr Who*.

Morpeth and Long in Chapter 3 consider the relationships between creativity and visual arts practice and their linkages with tourism from historical depictions and popularisation of destinations for tourism through the artistic representations of landscapes by artists painting in situ. Furthermore, the colonisation of artistic communities within different parts of the UK and elsewhere in Europe in the nineteenth and twentieth centuries served as a pull factor for tourists, whether welcome or otherwise, hoping to watch artists paint, and for place associations with and exhibitions of 'schools' of art. Train travel in the mid-twentieth century was promoted by artwork commissioned by holiday resorts which depicted destinations in stylised forms beyond their physical embodiments (an approach also adopted in early airline advertising posters in their artistic representations of the national identities of 'flag carrier' airlines and destinations served). The chapter also includes an exploration of the role of the celebrity artist in acting as a draw for tourists, exemplified in the work of highly popular contemporary

British artists David Hockney and 'Banksy'. A central part of the chapter highlights the application of the visual arts through paintings, installation, public sculpture and objects which increasingly have been used in an attempt to regenerate and promote cities (and also some rural locations) as destinations for tourism. Case study examples are used of post-industrial urban destinations in the UK which have been partially reimaged through the visual arts. As a counterpoint to the use of visual arts as a means of attracting tourists is the example of Rachel Whiteread's *House*, symbolising a challenge to gentrification and the replacement of established communities with gentrified zones for tourists and new residents. The commitment of the DCMS and the English Arts Council to the visual arts is evaluated in an age of austerity with the re-emergence of museum and gallery entrance charges and the transformation of cultural facilities into competing tourist attractions, raising important issues of access to creative tourism resources and opportunities.

References

Adorno, T. (1991). *The Culture Industry: Selected Essays on Mass Culture*, London: Routledge

Aitchison, C. (2006). The critical and the cultural: explaining the divergent paths of leisure studies and tourism studies, *Leisure Studies*, 25 (4): 417–422

Alvarez, M.D. (2010). Creative cities and cultural spaces: new perspectives for city tourism, *International Journal of Culture, Tourism and Hospitality Research*, 4: 171–175

Aoyama, Y. (2009). Artists, tourists and the state: cultural tourism and the flamenco industry in Andalusia, Spain, *International Journal of Urban and Regional Research*, 33: 80–104

Aquino, J., Phillips, R. and Sung, H. (2012). Tourism, culture and the creative industries: reviving distressed neighbourhoods with arts-based community tourism, *Tourism, Culture and Communication*, 12: 5–18

Aronczyk, M. (2013). *Branding the Nation: The Global Business of National Identity*, New York: Oxford University Press

Ashton, D. and Noonan, C. (eds) (2013). *Cultural Work and Higher Education*, Basingstoke: Palgrave Macmillan

Ateljevic, I., Pritchard, A. and Morgan, N. (eds) (2007). *The Critical Turn in Tourism Studies*, Amsterdam: Elsevier

Australian Government (1998). *Creative Australia: National Cultural Policy*, Canberra: Australian Government Office of the Arts

Bagwell, S. (2008). Creative clusters and city growth, *Creative Industries Journal*, 1 (1): 31–46

Bakhshi, H. and Windsor, G. (2015). *The Creative Economy and the Future of Employment*, London: NESTA

Bakhshi, H., Hargreaves, I. and Mateos-Garcia, J. (2013). *A Manifesto for the Creative Economy*,. London: National Endowment for Science, Technology and the Arts

Banks, J. (2012). *Co-creating Videogames*, London: Bloomsbury Academic

Banks, M., Lovatt, A., O'Connor, J. and Raffo, C. (2000). Risk and trust in the cultural industries, *Geoforum*, 31: 453–464

Beck, A. (2003). *Cultural Work: Understanding the Cultural Industries*, Routledge: London

Beeton, S. (2005). *Film-induced Tourism*, Clevedon: Channel View

Bell, D. and Jayne, M. (2010). The creative countryside: policy and practice in the UK rural cultural economy, *Journal of Rural Studies*, 26: 209–218

Bianchini, F. and Parkinson, M. (eds) (1993). *Cultural Policy and Urban Regeneration*. Manchester: Manchester University Press

Bilton, C. (2007). *Management and Creativity: From Creative Industries to Creative Management*, Oxford: Wiley Blackwell

Bohm, D. (1996). *On Creativity*, London: Routledge

Bouncken, R. and Sungsoo, P. (eds) (2002). *Knowledge Management in Hospitality and Tourism*, New York: Haworth Hospitality Press

Bourdieu, P. (1984). *Distinction: A Social Critique of the Judgement of Taste* [1979], trans. R. Nice, Cambridge, MA: Harvard University Press

Bourdieu, P. (1993). *The Field of Cultural Production*. Cambridge: Polity Press

Bramwell, W., Henry, I., Jackson, A.G., Briguglio, L., Archer, B., Jafasi, J. and Wall, G. (1996). *Sustainable Tourism Development: Principles and Practice*, Tilburg: Tilburg University Press

Bruns, A. (2008). *Blogs, Wikipedia, Second Life, and Beyond: From Production to Produsage*, New York: Peter Lang

Busa, A. (2009). The right to the city: the entitled and the excluded, *The Urban Reinventors Online Journal*, 3(9): 1–13

Campbell, P. (2011a). Creative industries in a European capital of culture, *International Journal of Cultural Policy*, 17 (5): 510–522

Campbell, P. (2011b). You say 'creative' and I say 'creative', *Journal of Policy Research in Tourism, Leisure and Events*, 3 (1): 18–30

Catalani, A. (2013). Integrating Western and non-Western cultural expressions to further cultural and creative tourism: a case study, *World Leisure Journal*, 55 (3): 252–263

Caves, R. (2000). *Creative Industries, Contracts between Art and Commerce*. Cambridge, MA: Harvard University Press

CCS (2013). *Classifying and Measuring the Creative Industries*, London: Creative and Cultural Skills

Chambers, C.M., Du Toit, S.W. and Edelman, J. (2013). *Performing Religion in Public*, Basingstoke: Palgrave Macmillan

Chambers, D. (2007). An agenda for cutting-edge research in tourism, in J. Tribe and D Airey (eds) *Developments in Tourism Research*, Oxford: Elsevier, pp. 233–246

Chapain, C.A. and Comunian, R. (2009). Creative cities in England: researching realities and images, *Built Environment*, 35 (2): 212–229

Chapain, C.A. and Comunian, R. (2010). Enabling and inhibiting the creative economy: the role of the local and regional dimensions in England, *Regional Studies*, 43 (6): 717–734

Coles, T., Dinan, C. and Hutchison, F. (2012). May we live in less interesting times? Changing public sector support for tourism in England during the sovereign debt crisis, *Journal of Destination Marketing and Management*, 1: 4–7

Comunian, R., Chapain, C. and Clifton, N. (2010). Location, location, location: exploring the complex relationships between creative industries and place, *Creative Industries Journal*, 3 (1): 5–10

Comunian, R., Faggian, A. and Jewell, S. (2011). Winning and losing in the creative industries: an analysis of creative graduates' career opportunities across creative disciplines, 'A Golden Age?' Reflections on New Labour's cultural policy and its post-recession legacy, *Cultural Trends*, 20 (3–4) Special Issue: 291–308

Comunian, R., Faggian, A. and Li, Q. (2010). Unrewarded careers in the creative class: the strange case of Bohemian graduates, *Papers in Regional Science*, 89 (2): 389–410

Connell, C. and Gibson, C. (2004). Vicarious journeys: travels in music, *Tourism Geographies*, 6 (1): 2–25

Cooke, P. (2002). *Knowledge Economies: Clusters, Learning and Cooperative Advantage*, London: Routledge

Cooper, C. (2006). Knowledge management and tourism, *Annals of Tourism Research*, 35 (1): 47–64

Craik, J. (2009). *Fashion: The Key Concepts.* Oxford: Berg

Csíkszentmihályi, M. (1997). *Creativity: Flow and the Psychology of Discovery and Invention*, New York: Harper

Csíkszentmihályi, M. (1999). Implications of a systems perspective for the study of creativity, in R.J. Sternberg (ed.) *Handbook of Creativity*, Cambridge: Cambridge University Press, pp. 313–339

Davenport, T. and Beck, J. (2001). *The Attention Economy: Understanding the New Currency of Business*, Cambridge, MA: Harvard Business School Press

Davies, R. and Sigthorsson, G. (2013). *Introducing the Creative Industries: From Theory to Practice*, Los Angeles: Sage

DCMS (2001a). *The Creative Industries Mapping Document 2001*, London: Department of Culture, Media and Sport

DCMS (2001b). *Culture and Creativity*, London: Department of Culture, Media and Sport

DCMS (2004). *Government and the Value of Culture*, London: Department of Culture, Media and Sport

DCMS (2015). *Creative Industries Economic Estimates*, London: Department of Culture, Media and Sport

Deleuze, G. and Guattari, F. (1994). *What is Philosophy?*, trans. G. Burchell and H. Tomlinson, London: Verso

Drake, G. (2003). 'This place gives me space': place and creativity in the creative industries, *Geoforum*, 34: 511–524

Evans, G. (2009). Creative cities, creative spaces and cultural policy, *Urban Studies*, 46: 1003–1040

Fisher, S. (2012). The cultural knowledge ecology: a discussion paper on partnerships between HEIs and cultural organisations, working paper, London: Arts Council England

Fitzgibbon, M. and Kelly, A. (eds) (1997). *From Maestro to Manager: Critical Issues in Arts and Cultural Management*, Dublin: Oak Tree Press

Fleming, T. (2002). Supporting the cultural quarter? The role of the creative intermediary, in D. Bell and M. Jayne (eds) *City of Quarters: Urban Villages in the Contemporary City*, Aldershot: Ashgate, pp. 94–106

Fleming, T. and Erskine, A. (2011). *Supporting Growth in the Arts Economy*, London: Arts Council England/Tom Fleming Creative Consultancy

Flew, T. (2012). *The Creative Industries, Culture and Policy.* London: Sage

Flew, T. (2013). *Global Creative Industries*, Cambridge: Polity Press

Florida, R. (2002). *The Rise of the Creative Class: And How It's Transforming Work, Leisure, Community and Everyday Life*, New York: Basic Books

Florida, R. (2010). *The Great Reset: How New Ways of Living and Working Drive Post-Crash Prosperity*, New York: Harper

Frenzel, F., Koens, K. and Steinbrink, M. (eds) (2012). *Slum Tourism: Poverty, Power and Ethics*, London: Taylor and Francis

Fujiwara, D., Dolan, P. and Lawton, R. (2015). *Creative Occupations and Subjective Wellbeing*, London: NESTA

Garnham, N. (1990). *Capitalism and Communication*, London: Sage

Garrett, B. (2014). *Explore Everything: Place Hacking the City*, London: Verso

Gibson, C. and Connell, J. (2005). *Music and Tourism: On the Road Again*, Clevedon: Channel View

Gretzel, U. and Jamal, T. (2009). Conceptualizing the creative tourist class: technology, mobility, and tourist experiences, *Tourism Analysis*, 14: 471–481

Habermas, J. (1987). *The Philosophical Discourse of Modernity: Twelve Lectures*, trans. F. Lawrence, Cambridge, MA: MIT Press

Hager, M. and Sung, H. (2012). Local arts agencies as destination management organizations, *Journal of Travel Research*, 51 (4): 400–411

Hall, S. and Jefferson, T. (eds) (1976). *Resistance Through Rituals*, London: Routledge

Hartley, J. (ed.) (2005). *Creative Industries*, Blackwell: Oxford

Hartley, J., Potts, J., Cunningham, S., Flew, T., Keane, M. and Banks, J. (2013). *Key Concepts in Creative Industries*, London: Sage

Hatherley, O. (2011). *A Guide to the New Ruins of Great Britain*, London: Verso

Hesmondhalgh, D. (2013). *The Cultural Industries*, London: Sage, 3rd edition

Hewison, R. (2014). *Cultural Capital: The Rise and Fall of Creative Britain*, London: Verso

Higgs, P. and Cunningham, S. (2008). Creative industries mapping: where have we come from and where are we going?, *Creative Industries Journal*, 1 (1): 7–30

Howe, J. (2008). *Crowdsourcing: Why the Power of the Crowd Is Driving the Future of Business*, New York: Random House

Howkins, J. (2001). *The Creative Economy: How People Make Money from Ideas*, London: Allen Lane

Hudson, S. and Brent Ritchie, J.R. (2006). Promoting destinations via film tourism: an empirical identification of supporting marketing initiatives. *Journal of Travel Research*, 44: 387–396

Hughes, H.L. (1989). Tourism and the arts: a potentially destructive relationship?, *Tourism Management*, 10: 97–99

Jenkins, J., Dredge, D. and Taplin, J. (2011). *Destination Planning and Policy: Process and Practice*, Wallingford: CABI

Jenks, C. (2005). *Subculture: The Fragmentation of the Social*, London: Sage

Kim, S., Long, P. and Robinson, M. (2009). Small screen, big tourism: the role of popular Korean television dramas in South Korean tourism, *Tourism Geographies*, 11 (3): 308–333

Kotkin, J. (2013). Richard Florida concedes the limits of the creative class, *The Daily Beast* www.thedailybeast.com/articles/2013/03/20/richard-florida-concedes-the-limits-of-the-creative-class.html#

Landry, C. (2000). *The Creative City: A Toolkit for Urban Innovators*. London: Earthscan Publications

Landry, C., Greene, L., Matarasso, F. and Bianchini, F. (1996). *The Art of Regeneration: Urban Renewal through Cultural Activity*, London: Comedia

Lash, S. and Urry, J. (1994). *Economics of Signs and Space*, London: Sage

Li, W. (2011). *How Creativity is Changing China*, London: Bloomsbury Academic

Long, P.E. (2014). Popular music, psychogeography, place identity and tourism: the case of Sheffield, *Tourist Studies*, 14 (1): 48–65

Long, P.E. and Morpeth, N. (2012). Critiquing creativity in tourism, in M. Smith and G. Richards (eds) *Routledge Handbook of Cultural Tourism*, London: Routledge, pp. 304–311

McGuigan, J. (1996). *Culture and the Public Sphere*, London: Routledge

McIntyre, P. (2012). *Creativity and Cultural Production: Issues for Media Practice*, Basingstoke: Palgrave Macmillan

McKee, A., Collis, C. and Hamley, B. (eds) (2011). *Entertainment Industries: Entertainment as a Cultural System*, London: Routledge

McRobbie, A. (1998). *British Fashion Design; Rag Trade or Image Industry?*, London: Routledge

McRobbie, A. (2004). Everyone is creative?, in T. Bennett and E. De Silva (eds) *Contemporary Culture and Everyday Life*, London: Routledge, pp. 106–109

Maitland, R. (2010). Everyday life as a creative experience in cities, *International Journal of Culture, Tourism and Hospitality Research*, 4: 176–185

Marletta, D. (2011). 'Sharing bits': creating sociability in the age of the digital agora, unpublished PhD thesis, Leeds Metropolitan University, UK

Mato, D. (2009). All industries are cultural, *Cultural Studies*, 23 (1): 70–87

Millard, R. (2001). *The Tastemakers: UK Art Now*, London: Thames and Hudson

Miller, T. (2009) From creative to cultural industries, *Cultural Studies*, 23 (1): 88–99

Mould, O., Roodhouse, S. and Vorley, T (2009). Realising capabilities – academic creativity and the creative industries, *Creative Industries Journal*, 1: 137–150

Muggleton, D. and Weinzierl, R. (eds) (2003). *The Post-Subcultures Reader*, Oxford: Berg

Negus, K. and Pickering, M. (2004). *Creativity, Communication and Cultural Value*, London: Sage

Novelli, M. (ed.) (2005). *Niche Tourism: Contemporary Issues, Trends and Cases*, Oxford: Elsevier

Oakley, K. (2004). Not so Cool Britannia: the role of the creative industries in economic development, *International Journal of Cultural Studies*, 7 (1): 67–77.

Oakley, K. (2009). The disappearing arts: creativity and innovation after the creative industries, *International Journal of Cultural Policy*, 15 (4): 403–413

O'Brien, D. (2014). *Cultural Policy: Management, Value and Modernity in the Creative Industries*, London: Routledge

O'Connor, J. (2011). The cultural and creative industries: a critical history, *Ekonomiaz*, 78: 25–45

Ooi, C.S. (2007). Creative industries and tourism in Singapore, in G. Richards and J. Wilson (eds) *Tourism, Creativity and Development*, London: Routledge, pp. 240–251

Packard, V. (1960). *The Wastemakers*, London: Verso

Pappalepore, I., Maitland, R. and Smith, A. (2010). Exploring urban creativity: visitor experiences of Spitalfields, London, *Tourism, Culture and Communication*, 10: 217–230

Peck, J. (2005). Struggling with the creative class, *International Journal of Urban and Regional Research*, 29: 740–770

Pine, B.J. and Gilmore, J.H. (1999). *The Experience Economy*, Boston: Harvard Business School Press

Pope, R. (2005). *Creativity: Theory, History, Practice*, London: Routledge

Potts, J. (2011). *Creative Industries and Economic Evolution*, Cheltenham: Edward Elgar

Pratt, A. and Jeffcut, P. (eds) (2009). *Creativity, Innovation and the Cultural Economy*, London: Routledge

Raunig, G., Ray, G. and Wuggenig, U. (eds) (2011). *Critique of Creativity: Precarity, Subjectivity and Resistance in the Creative Industries*, London: Mayfly Books

Reijnders, S. (2011). *Places of the Imagination: Media, Tourism, Culture*, Farnham: Ashgate

Richards, G. (2011). Creativity and tourism: the state of the art, *Annals of Tourism Research* (38): 1225–1253

Richards, G. and Wilson, J. (2006). Developing creativity in tourist experiences: a solution to the serial reproduction of culture?, *Tourism Management*, 27: 1209–1223

Robinson, K. (2001). *Out of our Minds: Learning to be Creative*, Chichester: Capstone

Rogerson, C.M. (2006). Creative industries and urban tourism: South African perspectives, *Urban Forum*, 17 (2): 149–166

Roodhouse, S. (2009). Universities and the creative industries, *The Journal of Arts Management, Law and Society*, Fall: 187–199

Roodhouse, S. (2010). *Cultural Quarters: Principles and Practices*, Bristol: Intellect Books, 2nd edition

Russell, B. (1946). *History of Western Philosophy*, Oxford: Unwin University Books

Santagata, W. (2010). *The Culture Factory: Creativity and the Production of Culture*, Heidelberg: Springer

Sasaki, M. (2010). Urban regeneration through cultural creativity and social inclusion: rethinking creative city theory through a Japanese case study, *Cities*, 27: 53–59

Schlesinger, P. (2007). Creativity: from discourse to doctrine?, *Screen*, 48 (3): 377–387

Scott, A. (2000). *The Cultural Economy of Cities: Essays on the Geography of Image-Producing Industries*, London: Sage

Sennett, R. (2008). *The Craftsman*, New Haven, CT: Yale University Press

Shaw, G. and Williams, A. (2009). Knowledge transfer and management in tourism organisation: an emerging research agenda, *Tourism Management*, 30: 325–335

Shirky, C. (2008). *Here Comes Everybody: The Power of Organizing Without Organizations*, London: Penguin

Smith, C. (1998). *Creative Britain*, London: Faber and Faber

Stebbins, R.A. (2007). *Serious Leisure: A Perspective for Our Time.* New Brunswick, NJ, and London: Transaction

Sternberg, R. (ed.) (1999). *The Handbook of Creativity*, Cambridge: Cambridge University Press

Stockton, A. (2003). *Rudolf Steiner: Art: An Introductory Reader*, Forest Row: Rudolf Steiner Press

Storry, M. and Childs, P. (1997). *British Cultural Identities*, London: Routledge

Taiwan Institute of Economic Research (2012). *Cultural and Creative Industries*, Taipei: Taiwan Industry Reports

Throsby, D. (2010). *The Economics of Cultural Policy*, Cambridge: Cambridge University Press

UNDP-UNCTAD (2010). *The Creative Economy Report*, Geneva and New York: UNCTAD/UNDP

UNESCO (2009). *UNESCO Framework for Cultural Statistics*, Montreal: UNESCO

VE/ACE (2013). *Partnership Statement: Supporting and Creating Economic Growth through Culture and the Visitor Economy*, London: VisitEngland, Arts Council England

Voase, R. (2012). Recognition, reputation and response: some critical thoughts on destinations and brands, *Journal of Destination Marketing and Management*, 1: 78–83

Wang, Y. and Pizam, A. (eds) (2011). *Destination Marketing and Management: Theories and Applications*, Wallingford: CABI

Xiao, H and Smith, S. (2007). The use of tourism knowledge: research propositions, *Annals of Tourism Research*, 34 (2): 738–749

2 On location in Liverpool

Film-related tourism and the consumption of place

Les Roberts

Liverpool is a great place. The people are so cool.... The town is so much fun.
(Samuel L. Jackson, quoted in 'Boomtown! Liverpool Movie and
Television Map', 2002)

Introduction: on 'location'

To date, research into the field of what might provisionally be termed 'film-related tourism' has remained uneven, fragmented and, in disciplinary terms, strongly weighted towards economic and marketing perspectives. Despite an extensive and growing literature in the areas of tourism and marketing, coupled with a more general proliferation of film tourism media (e.g. film/television location guides, film tourism websites, movie maps, locative media apps and so on), there have been surprisingly few critical interventions that have more explicitly focused attention on the socio-cultural value of 'location': the common denominator that underscores all film-related tourism practices.

In this chapter, which bases its analysis on the case study of the city of Liverpool in North West England, I set out some preliminary steps towards the development of what might be referred to as a 'spatial anthropology' (Roberts 2015) of film-related tourism. This takes as its modus operandi the need for a more holistic and anthropologically grounded approach to film and media tourism practices which critically foregrounds the role of film and television locations in the wider production and consumption of space and place in an urban context (Lefebvre 1991). A related aim of the chapter is to highlight the ways in which film tourism might instructively be approached less in terms of direct 'inducements' to travel (the consumption of a cinematic or televisual simulacrum of place as the principal motivational factor) and more in terms of the role film and television locations play in place branding and marketing initiatives more generally (e.g. the discursive framing of a city's place-image). While the implications of both may of course be comparable in terms of their underlying economic objectives (the growth in local and regional tourism markets), by placing critical emphasis on the spatialities of location-based consumption rather than the instrumental 'pull factors' by which film tourism practices are otherwise transacted, the focus of discussion is shifted towards analyses that extend beyond the disciplinary confines of more narrowly framed tourism or film studies perspectives. To these ends, the arguments presented in this chapter might be considered as interventions in broader urban cultural studies debates on the cultural production and consumption of space in cities, and the social and cultural value of 'location' more specifically (Fraser 2015).

From a place marketing perspective, the appeal of a 'hyperreal post-tourist experience of place' (Schofield 1996: 335) is that it makes possible the capacity to harness the symbolic potential of virtual geographies and mediated representations. As a consequence, what might potentially constitute the 'tourist gaze' (the dominant visual index by which a place is discursively constructed) is rendered that much more malleable and plastic. As Urry notes, there is 'much less sense of the authentic, the once-in-a-lifetime gaze, and much more of the endless availability of gazes through a frame at the flick of a switch' (1990: 100). The post-touristic appeal of cinematic representations of place is thus one that has generated considerable interest among policy-makers and practitioners in the cultural, tourism and heritage industries. This is matched by a growing multidisciplinary field of scholarship, much of which, as previously noted, has been dominated by tourism management and marketing perspectives focused on the economic and instrumental value of film and television tourism (see, for example, Riley and Van Doren 1992; Tooke and Baker 1996; Riley *et al.* 1998; Busby and Klug 2001; Morkham and Staiff 2002; Kim and Richardson 2003; Beeton 2005; Roesch 2009; Connell 2012). These more industry-based studies sit alongside a more narrowly refined body of work in which discussions on film and tourism straddle perspectives variously reflective of debates in, for example, cultural sociology, media and cultural studies, cultural geography and film studies (e.g. Edensor 2002; Crouch *et al.* 2005; Mazierska and Walton 2006; Tzanelli 2007; Roberts 2010a, 2010c, 2012; Reijnders 2011; Leotta 2013; Martin-Jones 2014).

Broaden this out to take account of the growing number of film tourism/film location guide books (e.g. the Intellect World Film Locations series), and we begin to glimpse the breadth of interest and debate that coalesces in some shape or form around discussions of film *locations*. Given this, the absence of research focused more squarely on organisations such as film offices, whose remit is to oversee the production, consumption and commodification of location sites, becomes all the more evident. Moreover, take into consideration the growing patterns of convergence that position the role of film offices alongside that of tourist and place-marketing bodies, and the increasingly synergistic relationship between the film and tourism industries is found to be similarly wanting in terms of sustained academic scrutiny.

In this regard, analyses drawn from ongoing research into the cultural and symbolic economy of film locations in Liverpool – and the important role played by the Liverpool Film Office – can offer some tentative insights into the ways that a spatial anthropology of film-related tourism might frame new perspectives on the relationship between moving image cultures and the consumption of place. The aim of this chapter is therefore to sketch out some provisional

reflections on the production and consumption of 'location' in the cinematic geography of Liverpool. As I go on to explore in the next section, a focus on
location can throw a spotlight as much on the heterotopic configuration of the
city in film (location as a semiotic marker of 'other' places and spaces) as on
issues of place specificity and vernacular cultural spaces (the cinematic city
'playing itself'[1]). Viewed thus, the marketing tagline 'The World in One City'
(which was conceived as part of endeavours to brand Liverpool as a cosmopolitan city in its early running as a contender for status of European Capital of
Culture in 2008) conjures a new set of meanings linked to the 'generic' and delocalised cultural value that can be attributed to the city's landscapes and locations
(Roberts 2012: 162–189).

Liverpool: world in one city

I came looking for a beach and they sold me the whole city. International
concert halls, Moscow hotels, Parisian apartments, golden synagogues, civic
buildings, sand dunes and stately homes.
(Andy Patterson, producer of *Hilary and Jackie*, quoted in 'Boomtown!
Liverpool Movie and Television Map', 2002)

This quote provides a good illustration of the ways in which the idea of a 'world
in one city' has been productively harnessed to boost economic activity in the
Merseyside area, and attests to the success of bodies such as the Liverpool Film
Office (LFO) in promoting the city as a centre of film and television production
in the UK. *Hilary and Jackie* (Anand Tucker 1998) is a biopic based on Hilary
and her brother Piers du Pré's memoir *A Genius in the Family*, which chronicles
the life of Hilary's sister, the celebrated cellist Jacqueline du Pré who died from
multiple sclerosis in 1987 at the age of 42. Most of the film was shot in and
around Liverpool, with buildings such as St George's Hall, the Blue Coat School
in Wavertree, the Philharmonic Hall, the Adelphi Hotel, the Princes Road Syna-
gogue, the Walker Art Gallery and the George's Dock Building standing in for
locations in a number of international cities, including London, Berlin, Madrid
and Moscow. As well as featuring on a film and television map of the city produced in 2002 by Liverpool council, *Hilary and Jackie* also appears on a map of
North Wales film and television locations compiled by Wales Screen Commission (the regional equivalent of the Liverpool film office, now called Wales
Screen) in partnership with tourism businesses in the region. Brithdir Mawr, a
Grade II-listed farmhouse near the small village of Cilcain in Flintshire, was
used as a location for the country home of Hilary and her husband Christopher
Finzi, which Jackie visits at one point in the film. Erected at the entrance to the
White Horse Inn in Cilcain is a heritage plaque marking the fact that scenes from
the film were shot in the village. Unveiled in 2005 by the local MP David
Hanson, the plaque has no 'authentic' significance in terms of representing local
cultural heritage in Cilcain, serving merely as a tangible reminder that for a few
days in the late 1990s a film crew visited the area (presumably making use of the

White Horse Inn while they were there), and that a movie that in all other respects has no connection with Cilcain whatsoever, and which was received with moderate critical acclaim and commercial success, was eventually released. Moreover, as few people who watched the film would have known that the scenes in question had in fact been shot in Cilcain (a place they probably had never heard of anyway), any cultural significance suggested by the plaque would be limited to those who live in the area, perhaps reflecting local pride that *their* village had been chosen. That such a marker of intangible local heritage should be the basis for attracting visitors to the area highlights the ways in which local authorities and destination marketing organisations (DMOs) are exploiting to the hilt the potential benefits of film-related tourism, even in circumstances where the degree of local cultural resonance is comparatively low.[2]

Similar arguments could be made in relation to the Liverpool locations used in the film. Although, unlike North Wales, there are (as yet) no heritage plaques linked to this, or indeed any other, film shot in Liverpool, the inclusion of a selection of the locations on the Liverpool Film and Television Map suggests that it is less the influence these cultural markers may have in terms of attracting visitors to the city that determines the function of marketing devices such as movie maps (those visitors to Britain interested in Jacqueline du Pré would presumably seek out the actual locations associated with her life and career), but rather the importance in acknowledging and promoting the fact that Liverpool is suitably equipped to offer a location service to relatively high-profile film productions. As such, it is again a largely local constituency that the movie map is directed towards in recognition that the city's landscapes convey an appeal and significance that extend beyond the local, offering an image of the city that counters that which has long dogged perceptions of Liverpool in the national media as a place wracked by crime, unemployment and social unrest. As well as highlighting the cultural and economic well-being of Liverpool, the movie map is also a means by which the LFO can promote its services to the wider film industry, whether nationally (and the city's capacity to double up as London has served Liverpool particularly well in this respect) or at international trade expos such as the annual Association of Film Commissioners International (AFCI) Locations Show.

Hollywood on the Mersey

Buoyed by the unexpected success of the low-budget film *Letter to Brezhnev* (Chris Bernard 1985), in 1989 the city council set up the LFO which was the UK's first city film commission. The overall remit of the LFO has been to provide a film liaison service to the film and television industry and to stimulate demand for local production skills. As Lynn Saunders, manager of the LFO, has pointed out, the marketing of Liverpool and Merseyside as a site of film tourism is recognised by council leaders as an increasingly important part of the wider promotional strategies focused around the Liverpool brand.[3] The development of movie maps, both in printed form and as part of online marketing campaigns, has been at the forefront of on-going initiatives surrounding film-related tourism in Merseyside. Published in 2002 by Liverpool City Council's tourism unit and film office, 'Boomtown! Liverpool Movie and Television Map' was less far-reaching in its scope as a place-marketing tool, and as a consequence met with limited success. This was prior to the spotlight that was soon to be cast on the city, however. The designation of European Capital of Culture status which was to follow a year later was instrumental in positioning the Liverpool brand within a more global consumer marketplace.

As sites of film-related production and consumption, Liverpool's cinematic geographies reflect a heterotopic configuration of urban space in which markers of place denote a fragmentary and increasingly delocalised topography defined by style and genre rather than local urban specificity. Liverpool's status as the UK's second most filmed city (after London) has meant that many of its most popular locations (of which films such as *Hilary and Jackie* provide a fairly representative spread) have featured in hundreds of productions, although in only a small percentage of these can Liverpool be said to be 'playing itself'. Promising a 'world in one city', Liverpool's success as a location base is therefore founded on its ability to 'mask out' the real city and exploit the semiotic value attached to a handful of key locations, each of which is designed to convey a particular style, setting or 'sense of place' in some way evocative of the diegetic world imagined by the film maker, writer or audience. The production of these post-industrial spaces of representation developed out of initiatives begun in the late 1980s which sought to build on the city's new-found role as a film set:

> When the Victorian and Edwardian merchant princes laid the cornerstones of Liverpool's imperialistic heyday, little did they know that they were building some of the best film sets of the late twentieth century. Focus a camera on the architecture, landscape or seascape of this city, and you can still be anywhere from pre-revolutionary France to post-revolutionary Romania.
>
> (*Liverpool Echo*, 21 February 1991: 6–7)

Headlines in the local press such as 'Hollywood on the Mersey' or 'Hollywood Dream: it's a big Scouse drive for new film industry' (*Liverpool Echo*, 21 February: 6–7; 10 October 1988: 8) captured the sense of optimism felt by those involved in the development of a film industry in Liverpool in the early 1990s. Behind the 'Hollywood Dream' rhetoric lay the more sober reality of an industry that relies little on local talent and production skills, and whose main contribution to the local economy is in the form of 'business tourism' (Channon [*sic*] 1996: 180). While these short-term economic benefits are of importance to the hotel and catering businesses in the city, and job opportunities are often available for film extras, in terms of 'trapping' (Channon [*sic*] 1996: 180) expenditure in the region, and channelling investment towards the development of local film production in Merseyside, 'Hollywood on the Mersey' this most certainly is not. Commenting on the Liverpool 'boom town' tag, the actor Ricky Tomlinson likens the US studios which film in the city to 'seagulls': 'They fly in, shit all over you, and fly out again. None of this is any good unless it helps the people of Liverpool.' Conditional to Tomlinson's involvement in a big-budget studio production is that the foreign film crews make an effort to hire local people ('Boom town', *Guardian*, 15 December 2000).[4]

As well as its capacity to look like somewhere else, the desirability of Liverpool as a film location was based on its cheapness and accessibility (Brown 1995: 10), not to mention, in comparison to cities such as London, its relatively traffic- and crowd-free streets. A consequence of years of depopulation and economic decline, this somewhat down-at-heel urban situation (which the LFO initiatives were designed to address) was, ironically, one of the key selling points for attracting prospective film makers to the city.

In addition to the obvious economic benefits, it was also felt that Liverpool's increased screen presence would have a positive psychological impact on the city. As Paul Mingard, the LFO's first film liaison officer, suggests, 'Imagine – you see your city, this derided place, up there on the screen, again and again, and it tells you that Liverpool is special.... It tells you that faith in this city is justified' (Gilbey 1995). However, as we have seen, how much of itself Liverpool does in fact see up there on the screen is a moot point. While in *Letter to Brezhnev* Liverpool was uncharacteristically (and unflinchingly) 'playing itself', the industry it helped to spawn is one in which, typically, locations count only insofar as they are able to enhance another city's screen presence, or to sustain the production of 'generic' spaces and narratives. Although, as Mingard suggests, the on-screen visibility of the city's urban landscapes may, from a local perspective, boost confidence and pride in terms of countering negative perceptions of Liverpool, that many viewers from outside the city would not necessarily know that specific productions had been filmed there means that local film production alone would have had little direct impact on the enhancement of the city's overall place-image. The subsequent growth in film-related place-marketing discourses of Liverpool and Merseyside can thus be seen as an attempt to make that crucial geographical connection much more explicit, bringing a greater level of awareness to the fact that Liverpool, as a much-visited site of *virtual* tourism, has also much to offer as an actual tourist destination, providing an experience where 'the imagined journey of movie watchers' is made complete through the act of travelling to the spaces previously seen on screen (Tzanelli 2007: 3).

Themed city tours: Holmesian Liverpool

The marketing surrounding the release of the films *Sherlock Holmes* (Guy Ritchie 2009) and *Harry Potter and the Deathly Hallows Part 1* (David Yates, 2010) provides a good illustration of the way Liverpool film locations are currently being promoted as visitor attractions. Visit Britain's marketing evaluation report for *Sherlock Holmes* outlines the rationale for launching a high-profile global campaign based around the film, stating that Sherlock Holmes, according to the Guinness World Records, is the 'most portrayed movie character' and as such represents 'a powerful brand not only in the UK, but also internationally' (Visit Britain 2010). The international success of the BBC television drama series *Sherlock* (2010–) is cited as an illustration of the further reach of the Sherlock Holmes brand, which thus provides a good indicator by which to gauge the likely success of the film *Sherlock Holmes* in the global marketing of Britain as a tourist destination. The film was shot on location in London, Liverpool and Manchester, and as part of Visit Britain's campaign the organisation ran a competition called Discover Sherlock Holmes' Britain. Promoted in 30 countries, two winners from each country enjoyed a prize of a tour around locations linked to the film and to Arthur Conan Doyle who wrote the original stories. The marketing campaign and the competition promotion was the result of a partnership between Visit Britain and Warner Bros Pictures, with additional sponsorship from Radisson Edwardian Hotels, as well as other promotional partners including Visit Liverpool, Visit Manchester, St Paul's Cathedral, Peckforton Castle in Cheshire and the Sherlock Holmes Museum in London. The competition was promoted via online advertising in 13 countries, print advertising in 12 countries, and television advertising in six. Using stills and marketing imagery from Warner Bros, additional promotional activities included a dedicated website and a British Film Locations iPhone app, as well as a range of other marketing devices and literature. Visit Britain's stand at the annual London-based World Travel Market in 2009 featured *Sherlock Holmes* and film tourism more generally as its main theme. Visit Britain's campaign material was also exhibited and distributed at local premiere screenings of the film. In short, the use of the film in UK place marketing was extensive. The choice of the film's locations was thus the principal factor underpinning the rationale and overall effectiveness of the global campaign.

Visit Britain's dedicated *Sherlock Holmes* web page provides information about each of the locations featured in the film, with suggested itineraries for those planning a trip to London, Liverpool or Manchester. The Liverpool itinerary invites visitors to '[t]ake a stroll through Liverpool's historic Georgian Quarter…. The houses around the Canning area with blackened ironwork and cobbled streets are much the same today as they were in Arthur Conan Doyle's time'. It then suggests a visit to Croxteth Hall which was used as a location in the Granada television series *Sherlock Holmes* (1984–1994). After lunch in a restaurant set in an 'elegant Georgian house' in Falkner Street, visitors are invited to visit Albert Dock which is located near to disused Stanley Dock where an action scene from Ritchie's *Sherlock Holmes* was filmed. Ironically, the only Liverpool location that is actually used in the film is off-limits to tourists who are only able to see it from the road. In the evening after dinner (in another restaurant set in a Georgian house), visitors are encouraged to have a pint in the famous Philharmonic Dining Rooms, described as 'a Holmesian pub with antique charm in buckets'.[5]

What is clear from this example is that it is not so much the capacity of the film *text* to 'induce' tourists that underpins the effectiveness of the campaign, but rather the ways in which the film functions as a mechanism by which DMOs can tap into a wider cultural imaginary that is resonant with consumers in the global marketplace. The role of DMOs and place-marketing discourses that surround the film text is therefore of crucial importance in 'directing' the film-related tourist gaze. In the Liverpool *Sherlock Holmes* itinerary it is not the actual locations that appear in the film that are of importance. It is the associative meanings that attach themselves to the text (or rather the character of Holmes) that demand attention. In this example the evocation of a certain imaginary of place conjures an 'idea' of Liverpool as a 'Holmesian' period theme park. Although the Holmes stories were set in the Victorian era, and tropes associated with the character such as pea-souper fog have remained popular metonyms of Victorian London (Brunsdon 2007: 45–47), the emphasis placed on Liverpool's Georgian buildings in the Liverpool itinerary plays on the 'authenticity' of the period architecture, steering its semiotic connotations towards the creation of a setting (or set) that is in some way reminiscent of the symbolic landscapes evoked by the Holmes character and stories.

Tunnel vision: Harry Potter and the magic of CGI

The *Sherlock Holmes* example illustrates the growing importance placed on film-related tourism by the travel industry and the role of the film text as part of the arsenal of place-marketing tools at the disposal of DMOs such as Visit Britain. Another example worth briefly mentioning here is the hugely successful series of Harry Potter films. Film-related Harry Potter tourism dates back to the release in 2001 of the first in the series, *Harry Potter and the Philosopher's Stone*. Visit Britain (or the British Tourism Authority as it was then) produced a movie map to accompany the film, and the Potter brand has since gone on to play an increasingly important role in film-related tourism marketing and consumption in the UK. Although much could be said about the Potter phenomenon and its value to the UK tourism market, for the purposes of the present discussion I want to limit my analysis to the Liverpool location used in the seventh film in the series, *Deathly Hallows Part 1*.

On Visit Britain's web page detailing 'a roster of "not-to-be-missed" locations throughout the UK for Harry Potter fans wishing to experience the magic up close', Great Britain is divided into four sections: 'London in Lumos', 'Enchanted England', 'Sorcerer's Scotland' and 'Wizardly Wales'. The page also gives information on a range of Potter-themed tours available in different parts of the country. The entry under 'Enchanted England' begins with a reference to Liverpool and *Deathly Hallows*: 'In the new film fans will see the Mersey Tunnels of Liverpool during a scene where Hagrid and Harry flee from the pursuit of some Death Eaters.... *Fans can visit the tunnels and other great sites Liverpool offers.*'[7] 'Compared to some of the other locations on offer to visitors of 'Enchanted England', such as Christchurch College, Oxford, Gloucester Cathedral, and Alnwick Castle in Northumberland, the 'pull factor' (Riley and Doren 1992) of a busy road tunnel underneath the Mersey is likely to be minimal. Even if a die-hard Potter fan were motivated to visit the actual location (i.e. the interior of the tunnel), in most cases s/he could only 'experience the magic up close' by driving or getting a bus through the tunnel and hoping that something meaningful might offer itself up along the way. The scene in question, a chase sequence involving Harry and Hagrid, is brief and involves extensive use of computer-generated imagery (CGI), so the likelihood that (1) the location could accrue sufficient cultural resonance to 'induce' visits to Liverpool, or (2) Potter tourists, were they to visit the tunnel, would be able to identify anything directly recognisable from the film (other than the tunnel wall more generally), would appear to be small. That said, reports in the *Liverpool Echo* that 'film fans rushed to snap up one-off Harry Potter Mersey tunnel tour tickets' suggest that there is some degree of interest in the film location.[7] However, the tour is run by Merseytravel which already organises regular tours of the tunnel and ventilation tower for visitors interested in the history and engineering of the tunnel system. The publicity generated by the release of *Deathly Hallows* thus served to enhance the profile of an existing Liverpool tourist attraction. The special one-off tour that took place in December 2010, as well as allowing visitors to see the workings of the tunnel (as in the usual tour), provided a rare opportunity to walk out onto the tunnel roadway where filming had taken place.[8] Tickets for the tour quickly sold out, the overwhelming majority, according to Merseytravel, were bought by people from the Merseyside area.[9]

There is, as Paul Swann has observed, 'a postmodern inexorability in valuing cities as images rather than as sites of production' (2001: 96). Indeed – and as is increasingly the case – from a studio perspective it may be that the 'site' of production is such that it is the virtual architectures of digital space rather than the material landscapes of the city that offer the more favourable creative environment. Access to blueprints of buildings, or measurements and dimensions of a specific architectural space, allow the possibility for film makers to digitally recreate the landscape or building in question without the inconvenience (and cost) of filming in the actual location. Not surprisingly, the use of computer-generated imagery to render virtually the one commodity upon which screen agencies are dependent – *location* – is a practice that is looked upon rather less favourably by those local authorities, businesses and communities which have benefited from income generated from productions based in real geographies and real spaces. By way of illustration, LFO manager Lynn Saunders describes a location recce in the pre-production stage of *Harry Potter and the Deathly Hallows Part 1*. Having taken members of the production crew to view a 'typical' northern terraced house, Saunders watched as they crawled around the building taking measurements: 'We knew they had no intention of filming there', she recalled. 'It's just impossible for a huge Hollywood production to film in a small terraced house. But that is the reality and local authorities need to be aware of that.'[10]

Conclusion: location, location, location

The kind of semiotic bargain sale which sees a city's urban landscape virtually harvested for CGI reconstruction, reduced to a categorical typology of topographic forms in a film and television locations database, or reimagined as a period theme park, has shaped a cultural economy in which *location, location, location* is the guiding mantra. Refashioned by the virtualising logic of the global sign industries (Tzanelli 2007), cities and other landscapes become stages or sets where imaginaries and narratives can be played out in ways that demand little if any intrinsic connection with 'real' geographies of place and identity. If, as Tzanelli suggests, 'there is a danger that tourist consumption of simulatory landscape and cultures will overwrite specific histories of actual places and cultures' (2004: 38), then it is one that is weighed against the many instrumental benefits offered by film-related place-marketing strategies. The fetishisation of place and space which underpins the cultural economics of film tourism has laid the foundations for a growing convergence between the film, tourism and marketing industries and the development of a 'new, differentiated heritage [product]' (Schofield 1996: 339). While it is the case that films such as those discussed in this chapter may exert something of a 'pull factor' in terms of influencing film-related tourism practices, there is little evidence in support of the claim that the film text alone directly 'induces' tourists to visit city locations previously seen on screen. The effectiveness of film-related tourism can be attributed instead to the capacity of high-profile film productions to shape and manipulate the dominant place-image attached to a given destination. In this respect, the film text (and the cinematic geographies therein) functions as part of a wider integrated marketing campaign centred on the film and its locations. Film-related tourism, in other words, is an increasingly powerful engine in the cultural production of space and place in cities and other destinations. As the case of Liverpool shows, mapping a city through the heterotopic prism of its cinematic geographies both reveals and reinforces the schizophrenic patterning of the city's symbolic landscapes. As part of an image-based economy, the cinematic production and consumption of urban architectural simulacra enable cities to assume (or accommodate) preordained identities and narratives (e.g. a nineteenth-century 'Holmesian' period setting), yet often does little to project a more socially embedded sense of history, place and urban identity. The 'place' of Liverpool in these heterotopic landscapes of consumption therefore becomes ever less certain; less geographically 'concrete'.

While, from an economic vantage point, the competitive cut and thrust of place-based location filming policies may out-trump the significance otherwise afforded critically to issues of authenticity, habitus and identity, the degree to which a city's cinematic geographies contribute to the further virtualisation or 'cinematisation' of urban space is nevertheless of not inconsiderable import. In this respect, the Liverpool case study might productively be considered alongside examples of other cities or regions that have sought to harness the economic opportunities offered by location-based filming, whether from a tourism or a film industry perspective. If the mainstay of extant research into film-related or film/movie-induced tourism has been oriented towards analyses of the economic and marketing potential of location-based filming, then approaches that cast a more critical or anthropological lens on these practices remain comparatively underdeveloped. Building on existing research conducted into film, place and intangible cultural heritage in Liverpool (Roberts 2010a, 2010b, 2010c, 2012, 2014; Hallam and Roberts 2011), studies that examine the spatial anthropology of film-related tourism in the city can sharpen critical insights into the production and consumption of cinematic geographies of place in a post-industrial region. But equally they can cast into sharper relief the ways in which film and archival film practices (Roberts 2014) might conceivably bolster rather than overwrite a city's embedded geographies of place, history and identity.[11] It is not that cinematic geographies of cities project an irredeemably 'inauthentic' or 'pseudo' layering of image on place. It is rather that, by developing more of a holistic understanding of film-related tourism practices it is possible to graft a more detailed map of a city's symbolic spaces of representation onto an urban landscape otherwise rendered mute. After all, cities in film rarely 'play themselves', however correspondingly 'real' they may be in terms of their projected on-screen identity. Cinematic geographies should be looked upon not as a priori bearers of signification but as markers of place whose meanings are more productively harvested from the lived spaces and symbolic practices that constitute the anthropological – and contested – field of film- and media-related tourism consumption.

Notes

1 As a 'cinematic city', Liverpool's on-screen identity has been shaped by a number of key films and locations (not least iconic landmarks such as the Liver Building and River Mersey). But the extent to which the city gets to 'play itself' is far outweighed by the number of productions that use the city's locations in more generic terms. Not surprisingly, it is this latter, more heterotopic conception of Liverpool as a 'cinematic city' that has informed the development of film and media tourism initiatives in the city. That said, with the release of Terence Davies's celebrated 'cine-poem' *Of Time and the City* (2008) and a greater awareness of Liverpool's film and television heritage, there remains significant scope for capitalising on this heritage as part of future film tourism and place-based marketing activities. The proposed Liverpool Film Posters exhibition, scheduled for opening at the Museum of Liverpool in 2017, is one example of endeavours to put the city's film heritage more firmly on the map (see Conolly and Whelan 2013; for online resources see the British Film Institute's Screenonline website: www.screenonline.org.uk/liverpool; see also the University of Liverpool's *Mapping the City in Film* project: www.liv.ac.uk/communication-and-media/research/cityfilm).

2 This is, however, an area of analysis which will benefit from more detailed ethnographic research into local and visitor perceptions of film heritage plaques, movie maps and cinematographic tourism.

3 Although, as she also notes, the redevelopment and transformation of parts of the city centre can impact on the availability of attractive film location sites (interviews with Lynn Saunders conducted by the author, June and November 2009).

4 www.guardian.co.uk/film/2000/dec/15/culture.features2 (accessed 7 May 2008).

5 www2.visitbritain.com/en/campaigns/sherlock-holmes/Locations-itineraries/itineraries/index.aspx (accessed 9 December 2010).
6 www.visitbritain.us/campaigns/film/deathly-hallows/deathly-hallows-locations.aspx (accessed 10 December 2010).
7 'Harry Potter fans snap up Mersey tunnel tour tickets', 7 December 2010, www.liverpoolecho.co.uk/liverpool-entertainment/harry-potter/2010/12/07/harry-potter-fans-snap-up-mersey-tunnel-tour-tickets-100252-27779372/ (accessed 10 December 2010).
8 www.bbc.co.uk/news/uk-england-merseyside-11921779 (accessed 10 December 2010).
9 Merseytravel, personal communication, 10 December 2010.
10 Interview with Lynn Saunders, manager of Liverpool Film Office, November 2009.
11 The University of Liverpool's *Mapping the City in Film* project (on which the author was lead research associate) is one such initiative that has sought to put the city's film history and heritage more firmly on the map (in this case, quite literally, information on over 1,700 archive films of the city were mapped by location using geographical information system (GIS) tools to create a comprehensive interactive heritage map of Liverpool in film. The map, along with related project data as well as a selection of digitised film clips, can be accessed on-line at: www.liv.ac.uk/communication-and-media/research/cityfilm.

References

Beeton, S. 2005. *Film-Induced Tourism*. Clevedon: Channel View Publications.
Brown, T. 1995. 'Everytown, Nowhere City: Location Filming and the British City', unpublished MA dissertation, Birkbeck College, University of London.
Brunsdon, C. 2007. *London in Cinema: The Cinematic City Since 1945*. London: BFI.
Busby, G. and J. Klug. 2001. 'Movie-Induced Tourism: The Challenge of Measurement and Other Issues', *Journal of Vacation Marketing* 7 (4): 316–332.
Channon [Shannon], R. 1996. 'Moving Image Development Agency in Liverpool', *Local Economy* 11 (2): 179–181.
Connell, J. 2012. 'Film Tourism: Evolution, Progress and Prospects', *Tourism Management* 33 (5): 1007–1029.
Conolly, J. and C. Whelan (eds) 2013. *World Film Locations: Liverpool*, Bristol: Intellect.
Crouch, D., R. Jackson and F. Thompson. 2005. *The Media and the Tourist Imagination*. London: Routledge.
Edensor, T. 2002. *National Identity, Popular Culture and Everyday Life*. Oxford: Berg.
Fraser, B. 2015. *Toward an Urban Cultural Studies: Henri Lefebvre and the Humanities*. New York: Palgrave.
Gilbey, R. 1995. 'Cut and Print: Tales of the Celluloid City', *Independent*, 19 April 1995, p. 20.
Hallam, J. and L. Roberts. 2011. 'Mapping, Memory and the City: Archives, Databases and Film Historiography', *European Journal of Cultural Studies* 14 (3): 355–372.
Kim, H. and S. Richardson. 2003. 'Motion Picture Impacts on Destination Images', *Annals of Tourism Research* 30 (1): 216–237.
Lefebvre, H. 1991. *The Production of Space*. Oxford: Blackwell.
Leotta, A. 2013. *Touring the Screen: Tourism and New Zealand Film Geographies*. London: Intellect.
Martin-Jones, D. 2014. 'Film Tourism as Heritage Tourism: Scotland, Diaspora and *The Da Vinci Code* (2006)', *New Review of Film and Television Studies* 12 (2): 156–177.
Mazierska, E. and J.K. Walton (eds) 2006. Special issue on 'Tourism and the Moving Image', *Tourist Studies* 6 (1).

Morkham, B. and R. Staiff. 2002. 'The Cinematic Tourist: Perception and Subjectivity', in G. Dann (ed.), *The Tourist as Metaphor of the Social World*. Wallingfold, UK: CABI Press, pp. 297–316.

Reijnders, S. 2011. *Places of the Imagination: Media, Tourism, Culture*. London: Ashgate.

Riley, R. and C.S.V. Doren. 1992. 'Movies as Tourism Promotion: A "Pull" Factor in a "Push" Location', *Tourism Management* 13 (3): 267–274.

Riley, R., D. Baker and C.S.V. Doren. 1998. 'Movie Induced Tourism', *Annals of Tourism Research* 25 (4): 919–935.

Roberts, L. 2010a. 'Dis/embedded Geographies of Film: Virtual Panoramas and the Touristic Consumption of Liverpool Waterfront', *Space and Culture* 13 (1): 54–74.

Roberts, L. 2010b. 'Making Connections: Crossing Boundaries of Place and Identity in Liverpool and Merseyside Amateur Transport Films', *Mobilities* 5 (1): 83–109.

Roberts, L. 2010c. 'Projecting Place: Location Mapping, Consumption and Cinematographic Tourism', in R. Koeck and L. Roberts (eds), *The City and the Moving Image: Urban Projections*. Basingstoke: Palgrave, pp. 183–204.

Roberts, L. 2012. *Film, Mobility and Urban Space: A Cinematic Geography of Liverpool*. Liverpool: Liverpool University Press.

Roberts, L. 2014. 'Navigating the "Archive City": Digital Spatial Humanities and Archival Film Practice', *Convergence: The International Journal of Research into New Media Technologies* 21 (1): 100–115.

Roberts, L. 2015. 'Mapping Cultures: A Spatial Anthropology', in L. Roberts (ed.), *Mapping Cultures: Place, Practice, Performance*. Basingstoke: Palgrave, pp. 1–25.

Roesch, S. 2009. *The Experience of Film Location Tourists*. Bristol: Channel View.

Schofield, P. 1996. 'Cinematographic Images of a City: Alternative Heritage Tourism in Manchester', *Tourism Management* 17 (5): 333–340.

Swann, P. 2001. 'From Workshop to Backlot: the Greater Philadelphia Film Office', in M. Shiel and T. Fitzmaurice (eds), *Cinema and the City: Film and Urban Societies in a Global Context*. Oxford: Basil Blackwell, pp. 88–98.

Tooke, N. and M. Baker. 1996. 'Seeing is Believing: the Effect of Film on Visitor Numbers to Screened Locations', *Tourism Management* 17 (2): 87–94.

Tzanelli, R. 2004. 'Constructing the "Cinematic Tourist": The "sign industry" of *The Lord of the Rings*', *Tourist Studies* 4 (1): 21–42.

Tzanelli, R. 2007. *The Cinematic Tourist: Explorations in Globalization, Culture and Resistance*. London: Routledge.

Urry, J. 1990. *The Tourist Gaze: Leisure and Travel in Contemporary Societies*. London: Sage.

Visit Britain. 2010. *Visit Britain and Warner Bros. Pictures Partnership – Global Evaluation Report, Nov. 09–Feb. 10*. London: Visit Britain.

3   Creativity, the visual arts and tourism

Nigel D. Morpeth and Philip Long

Introduction

The role of the visual arts in society predates by far the very recent emergence of the creative industries as an 'official' term, now commonly used to characterise the industrialisation of economic sectors of creativity which became prominent after 1998 in the UK (DCMS, 1998) and subsequently internationally, as reviewed in the introductory chapter above. Historically, the visual arts have had a significant and central place within society both aesthetically and commercially, as a symbol of power, taste and wealth but also as distinctive artistic forms of creativity. Within this context, the role of the artist as a creative artisan has been a mainstay of Western society (and societies elsewhere) from medieval times to the present day and arguably artists and their creative outputs are representative of an early example of a key part of what is now characterised as the creative industries. Artists have created images to symbolise, in particular, the ubiquitous power of the church and to convey the wealth of rich benefactors such as the Medici family in sixteenth century Italy. Now artists are used to promote the commercial potential of international fashion brands and to represent, market and enhance the visual image of destinations designed to attract tourists. The combination of the celebratory artist and the citing of their work, in established and 'would be' tourist destinations, adds further credence to the argument that artists, as a contemporary representation of the creative industries, have not only retained a significant place in society but have in the case of internationally renowned artists such as Tracey Emin and Banksy, become creative taste-makers. Furthermore, the challenging nature of their work about contemporary society can serve as a powerful attractor for some tourist visitation. As Rakic and Lester (2013: 1) identified, 'Art in its many forms has long played an important role in people's imagination, experiences and remembrance of places.'

This chapter initially considers the connections between creativity and visual arts and their significance in society. Broad consideration is given to the linkages between the visual arts and tourism before specifically highlighting the development of destinations particularly through a focus on different manifestations of the visual arts, in particular painting, installation, public art and sculptural form or 'objects', as attractions for tourism.

Creativity and the visual arts

In trying to define what is art Freeland (2001: 206) highlights that a myriad of creative processes are involved in the production of art and a confluence of disciplinary traditions is used to theorise about it. Nevertheless, she conceded, despite this search for meaning, that art may be interpreted in so many ways that it might ultimately be rendered meaningless. Additionally, the search for meaning requires the application of theories related to complex and intersecting notions of ritual, communication, aesthetics and taste. Freeland also postulates that art has been a central part of societies from the ancient world onwards and has been used as an expression of religious and political power, and in a contemporary sense is used both to challenge and to endorse ideological crosscurrents in society. Freeland (2001) also reminds us that culturally for certain societies, the concept of art might be inseparable from the notions of ritual and artefact and that the reification of art might be most prevalent in Western cultural mores and tastes.

Joseph Beuys's mantra, 'society into art, art into society', highlighted in his view how symbolically we are all artists all of the time (Michely, 2007: 95). In a sense there is a parallel with John Urry's (1992) notion that we are all tourists all of the time. These ideas on the blurring of the boundaries between art and society were shared by the artist Conrad Atkinson (1981), who talked of the role of the artist as an activist, with his work mirroring Beuys's in documenting perceived social issues through conceptual art in exhibitions, using a multiple of different sources of information and images. In a contemporary sense, to paraphrase Rosie Millard (2001), visual artists, curators, sponsors and buyers have continued to be taste-makers, defining and establishing creative trends within society. In this respect Charles Saatchi was viewed by Jardine (1997) as a modern Medici in terms of his patronage of artists. Millard (2001) argued that artists had sought fame and celebrity status through their work and in her view there has been a cross-fertilisation of the visual arts into other areas of creativity: 'Top of the Pops. Advertising. Food. Fashion. Film. Brands. Not since David Hockney painted the fashion guru Ossie Clark have artists fused their traditional world of private creativity with such a popular market of commerce and publicity' (2001: 73).

Mcintyre (2012: 43), in postulating about the phenomenon of creativity and the production of art, argues that it is important to consider the social and cultural context of the societies in which this ubiquitous human activity takes place. He advocates the application of a sociological perspective in which artwork is viewed as the product of social institutions, ideological factors and institutionalised sub-cultures. Furthermore, Chandler reminds us in his treatise on semiotics that 'there are no neutral sign-systems, signs function to persuade as well as refer' (2002: 214) and that the visual arts have an important role in the communication of these signs, in particular, within the context of media and tourism. In the early 1970s John Berger's *Ways of Seeing*, a book and a UK TV series, was credited with enabling people to engage with and to see visual art in its many forms from photography and graphic art to painting in new ways. He argued that with the increasing reproducibility of art in its multiple forms, consistent with the work of Chandler (and Walter Benjamin), semiotics could be used to decode an array of signs and symbols embodied within visual art.

These broader considerations of the position of art within society provide an important dimension in locating the historical significance of the creative output of artists and the so-called epochs of artistic expression (while it is not possible within the scope of this chapter to review each of these epochs, examples are drawn from different artists within these periods that have stimulated tourism). For example, in relation to this the art historian Pevsner used the phrase the 'Englishness of English Art', locating both a geography and a history of art in England, and highlighted the creativity of artists such as Hogarth and the impact of his visual story-telling, moralising and caricature to chronicle life in eighteenth century England, particularly scenes of 'common' life in London (1955: 37). He contrasts this artwork of observation of people and society with the later work of artists such as Constable, Cotman and Cox and their pursuit and representation of nature and landscape and with Turner's ability to capture a fusion of the ethereal qualities of both landscape and architecture, in what Pevsner describes as visionary work.

As regards 'official' understanding of the arts and their role (including in tourism), the Arts Council (2015), the main public sector funding body for the arts in the UK, highlights how the

> visual arts is a dynamic art form which seeks constantly to reinvent itself. It embraces a range of media such as painting and moving image work, but it is notable for blurring boundaries and for collaborating with other social practices and creative disciplines.

Its 2013 revised 10-year strategic framework, 'Great Art and Culture for Everyone', highlighted how 'the arts and culture play an important role in local regeneration, in attracting tourists, in the development of talent and innovation, in improving health and well-being, and in delivering essential services' (2013: 12).

The visual arts and tourism

Arguably, Turner is an early example of an artist who, in part through his prolific travels, provided a chronicle of places that became recognised as tourist destinations both within the UK and in continental Europe. Through his paintings he was able to enhance and embellish the dramatic qualities of places such as Venice and provide a visual and romanticised narrative that stimulated tourist visitation. Turner's work in a creative sense could be viewed as an early example of 'photo-shopping', fusing different images of Venice's architectural landmarks into single paintings to add or create a sense of wonder, awe and anticipation to potential tourist audiences (though this would not have been his purpose or intention). The visual arts emerge as a motivator for travel from a variety of sources, not least the Grand Tour (see Towner, 1985), with English aristocrats seeking out (and bringing home in some cases) 'great' works of art in cultural centres in Europe. Turner in his depiction of the landscapes painted in his travels in continental Europe drew particular inspiration from the seventeenth-century French landscape painter Claude Lorrain who, Gombrich argues, was the first painter to create a faithful representation of nature and who 'first opened people's eyes to the sublime beauty of nature' (1972: 309). The Grand Tour is seen as the origin of cultural tourism as an elite pursuit and also as a forerunner of mass visitation of art housed in high cultural institutions of museums, galleries and stately homes. An example of this is the eternal scrum of tourists around Da Vinci's *Mona Lisa* in the Louvre in Paris, as a 'must-see' attraction.

Within the pantheon of art history in a UK context in the early twentieth-century artists' communities or enclaves emerged in coastal areas such as St Ives in Cornwall, Staithes in North Yorkshire; and Betws-y-Coed, in North Wales, as well as in the urban centres of, for example, Glasgow, Norwich and London. Art in these locations has provided a lasting historical legacy and painterly tradition for tourists to enjoy as a pictorial and historical archive encapsulated through the eyes of the artist. It is clear that art is viewed as an important sub-set of culture and as a major stimulus for travel, with tourists going to watch or be portrayed by artists working in situ (such as 'street artists' painting portraits of more or less artistic quality of tourists in European cities). The artist has thus become a performer and an act of spectacle rife for tourist observation.

This emergence of creative and artistic communities based largely in coastal locations paralleled in tourism terms the emergence of a network of railway linkages to coastal towns and the use of visual art to create stylised images as posters and advertisements of these coastal destinations. The main railway companies employed 'house-artists' to depict idealised landscapes of 'everyday' tourist locations. Consistent with the observations of Chandler (2002) and the application of semiotics, arguably these posters were examples of artistic hyper-realism rather than capturing the 'everyday reality' of these destinations. Seaside resorts that were the mainstay of industrial working-class communities were at times depicted as seeking to be viewed as playgrounds of aspirational 'high society' (see Walton, 2005). In a contemporary sense, the artist's studios in the Cultural Quarter in the city of Sheffield, and the Ropewalk Arts Centre in Barton-upon-Humber in Lincolnshire, are modern incarnations of the artists' communities described above and are also a focus for tourists.

The celebrated and highly popular artist David Hockney, synonymous for much of his career with a prolific creative output in North America and in particular the visualisation of Californian culture, has become in recent years, within a UK context, a tourist standard bearer for Yorkshire and East Yorkshire landscapes. He has popularised these through different stages of his career but in recent years they have been communicated to an international audience, in the process transforming a landscape previously viewed as unremarkable (Joyce, 1999). Arguably, the visual arts have become the central means for the Regional Tourism Organisation

'Welcome to Yorkshire' to promote East Yorkshire as a 'must-see' landscape. Consistent with the view of David Hockney, paintings are able to convey images of the landscape which are beyond the capacity of the camera and photographic representations to capture. As creative focus for tourism, 'Welcome to Yorkshire' has created a David Hockney Tourist Trail and also sponsored Hockney's 'block-buster' 2013 exhibition at London's Royal Academy of Arts (see www.yorkshire. com/join-in/magazine/the-davidhockneytrail). Furthermore, the productive output of his work has been to an extent due to his spending part of the year based in a family home in the coastal town of Bridlington. Like Turner, and Tracey Emin with her association with Margate and Banksy through his Dismaland installation in Weston-super-Mare, Hockney has provided a spur for tourist visitation to a seaside town through the medium of the visual arts and his celebrity status.

Writing in 1996, Long highlighted the linkages between tourism and the visual arts through the 'Year of Visual Arts', a creative initiative in Northern England in which partnership arrangements between arts organisations and regional tourist boards were established. This was part of a wider national initiative, *Visual Arts UK*, which was instigated by the Arts Council of Great Britain in 1991, linked to a national *Arts 2000* programme which involved themed arts 'years' in the early 2000s with the aim of boosting the cultural life of UK regions and promoting tourism. More recently, in 2013, an Art Everywhere campaign was launched, with Higgins (2013) writing in the *Guardian* that 'Art Every-where promises to turn the UK into the world's biggest art gallery'. This visual arts initiative was funded by the UK entrepreneur Richard Reed (the co-founder of Innocent Drinks), the Art Fund and Tate Britain. It had 57 famous artworks voted for by 90,000 members of the public and positioned on posters and bill-boards across the UK (Higgins, 2013: 5). Thousands of multiple images of these artworks were positioned in bus stop shelters, shopping malls and other public spaces, in this instance replacing the semiotics of signs normally used to adver-tise commercial products with art images for art's sake.

The year 1996, as well as being the Year of the Visual Arts, saw the emer-gence of the Young British Artists (YBA) and their exhibition Sensation at the Royal Academy of Arts (Rosenthal, 1997). This was an iconic moment for 'Cool Britannia' and the emergence of the creative industries in the UK. The exhibition highlighted the capacity of a group of artists to express a paradigm shift, in the main a return to conceptual art as a means of expressing creative ideas. They fol-lowed in the tradition of artists such as Marcel Duchamp and Joseph Beuys who wanted to create more than 'decorative embellishment and saleable art' (Grae-venitz, 2007: 36), though ironically and arguably this is what much of the work of the YBAs became. A member of the YBA 'movement' was Tracey Emin, whose work was prominent in the opening of the Turner Gallery in her home-town of Margate in May 2012 which also demonstrated the capacity of a celeb-rated artist's work to create a draw for tourists.

Likewise, the siting of the Banksy-curated 2.5 acre Dismaland temporary 'theme park' in the seaside resort of Weston-super-Mare in Somerset, South West England, in the summer of 2015 is a significant example of the visual arts as an attractor for tourists, while also critiquing tourism as a social phenomenon. The name Dismaland is a pastiche and evokes Disneyland, perhaps the key exemplar of a visitor attraction par excellence, with the equally playful notion of the 'bemusement park' and a subversive take on the notion of amusement. Banksy chose the site of a disused lido formerly known as Tropical World and a place anecdotally that he visited as a child on holiday. The creative use of words parallels his craft as a street graffiti artist, which led on to a highly successful recent career as a gallery artist with global acclaim not least within the lucrative US art market. It would appear that Dismaland has not only highlighted Weston-super-Mare as an unlikely destination to experience a significant visual arts event but also was presented in a context other than a traditional gallery space in a city location well established for hosting art exhibitions. It also provided an opportunity for the wider promotion of a seaside destination that would benefit from additional tourist visits, albeit fleetingly. Dismaland, to use the phraseology of Plotz (2000), showed a capacity 'to draw a crowd' and, in the absence of securing an internet-generated ticket, one of the authors of this chapter observed people in long queues prepared to wait for a number of hours to see if tickets became available. The political judgement employed by the local council in approving this temporary attraction was no doubt buoyed by the knowledge that a Banksy exhibition in Bristol in 2011 had generated large crowds who had queued for hours to get access to the exhibition. Furthermore, his success in Los Angeles and New York and his political impact in Palestine suggested an enormous popularity for his curated exhibition and in the process boosted tourist receipts for the town (Brown, 2015a).

Regeneration, tourist destinations and the visual arts

Jencks noted that within post-modern society there has been a merger between architecture, the visual arts and how people interact with both the artistic content and exhibiting buildings, the architecture in some cases becoming the prime attraction. In this respect he emphasised that a new type of architecture had emerged, driven by social rather than aesthetic forces and demands for instant fame and economic growth (2005: 7). Redolent of this is North American architect Frank Gehry's Guggenheim Museum in Bilbao, which Richards (2001: 52) describes as 'a futuristic titanium-coated spacecraft which appears to have crashed into the centre of Spain's largest port, cost almost €150 million to build, and was stocked with Guggenheim artwork for a further €25 million'. This type of cultural facility was viewed as more significant as an image-making device than as an authentic must-see facility for the visual arts and, as Richards observed, the building rather than the contents becomes the crucial aspect for the tourist gaze (Urry, 1992).

Baniotopoulou (2001) highlighted how the opening of the Guggenheim in Bilbao in 1998 also heralded a time of celebrity artists operating within a materialistic and populist social climate (rather than as fluxus or activist artists), the prime example being US artist Jeff Koons's work *Puppy* sited at the Guggenheim through the sponsorship of the fashion company Hugo Boss. In this sense the museum was viewed as a marketing venue for an international fashion brand wanting to make an impact in a national fashion market. The irony of this commercial marriage of convenience would not be lost on Koons, a former marketing executive. Baniotopoulou (2001) made the observation that with the decline of traditional industries, modern art museums, most notably the Guggenheim in Bilbao, have become emblematic of what she characterises as arts-led urban regeneration and the role of so-called 'super-museums' which have the capacity for urban renewal. She cites the work of Giovanni (1997) to highlight how cities are in their ascendancy in relation to nation-states. She argues that this cultural equation should not be viewed uncritically as these so-called flagship developments can be viewed as a vehicle for marketing to reinvent the image of cities. The intangibility of this equation is the extent to which this arts-led regeneration leads to civic pride or becomes an emblem for international visitation.

Additionally, the initial plan, according to Baniotopoulou (2001), was for the conversion of Alhondiga, a derelict wine warehouse in Bilbao, into a laboratory of avant-garde artistic experimentation (she argues that this could be a model employed in the UK with artist 'colonies' inhabiting derelict warehouses in the pre-regenerated Docklands in London). Instead, it was decided that the Peggy Guggenheim brand, apparent in cities such as New York and Venice, would be housed in a specially commissioned Frank Gehry building, ironically one that would become more important as a tourist attraction than the art housed in the museum. She argues that in the third year of its operation, 2001, it had provided a substantial contribution to employment in Bilbao and more generally to the Basque economy but it was more difficult to quantify cultural and quality of life improvements. Furthermore, she highlighted how the museum failed to represent local creative and artistic production and in her view impeded it (except for artists of celebrity status). These observations are not new and have been well rehearsed, particularly through the work of Bianchini and Parkinson (1993) who highlight this strategic approach to city economic and cultural policy and planning, reimaging cities across Europe. In a UK context, for example, the town of Gateshead shares the banks of the River Tyne with the city of Newcastle and has created an infrastructure for both the performing and the visual arts through the building of the Sage performance arena and the conversion of the derelict Baltic Flour Mill into a visual arts space. This is mirrored in London in the conversion of the former Bankside power station into Tate Modern. Both have served as popular places for arts tourism. Also on the edge of Gateshead is the well-established public art installation the *Angel of the North*, which is an example of a post-1980s push to create public art as a method of attracting visitors to unlikely tourist destinations.

Public art and tourism

The term 'public art' is used widely and has many different connotations. For example, the eclectic first 'Open Air Exhibition of Sculpture' was organised by the London County Council in Battersea Park immediately after the Second World War. For Biggs (1984), this was a traditional approach to siting both decorative and commemorative sculpture in a parkland setting. Marshall emphasised how 'New British Sculpture' emerged post-1945, and focused on the detritus of urban society. For Marshall, the sculptor was 'bent on looking at ordinary things as if he had no idea of their conventional use' (1997: 17). For example, he identifies how the 1997 Hayward Gallery exhibition Material Culture concentrated on 'independent objects, occupying the space of actual things' and in his view the interpretation of sculpture expanded to become almost meaningless (1997: 27). Jarratt (2011: 8) suggests that 'during a century of sculptural innovation in Britain the dialogue with the public has shifted from gallery to plinth, then into architecture and now into public spaces'. Usherwood *et al.* emphasised that since the start of the new millennium, 'more public sculpture is now being commissioned than at any time in the last seventy-five years' (2000: v).

Mesch (2007: 198), in evaluating the work of Beuys, suggested that he viewed public art in a complex manner and talked of the importance of understanding the broader dialectic of the classical public sphere, particularly within the context of late capitalist mass culture society. Mesch argued that Beuys's work encapsulated both material art objects and what he viewed as a parallel process of action performances and of public debate, which attempted to meld the political life of society with public art and 'social sculpture'. He emphasised that art should be in the public sphere, with the mantra 'art into society, society into art' advocating an alternative social model. In the debate about the limitations of gallery space to provide accessible art post-war there was a movement within sculpture which heralded the shift towards public art and art that could be accessed outdoors. In a contemporary sense Banksy argues that an external 'wall has always been the best place to publish your work' (2006: 8). In a UK context once again, characterising another set of interpretations of public art and in particular public sculpture, Matthew Jarratt of the Arts Council England identified the challenges of public art, suggesting that 'as well as aspiring to make "Great Art for Everyone,' big public sculpture has become a prerequisite for the most ambitious public and private sector developments and regeneration schemes in the last two decades' (2011: 8).

The case of the North East of England and public art

Usherwood *et al.* noted how even with the decline of manufacturing in the North East, the region's identity remains bound up with iron, coal, muscularity and masculinity (2000: xix). In the decade preceding publication of their book containing images of 180 sculptures they voiced concern about 'sculpture fatigue', with local authorities and urban development corporations using public art as a tool of regeneration and renewal. They suggested that while sculptors living in a locality and working with support groups to produce work which expresses the feeling for localities through sculpture, the *genius loci* had become eclipsed by a multiplicity of roles that a sculpture may need to perform, from aesthetic improvement to place-making, and creating latent and invested meaning. Furthermore, Jarratt (2011: 9) contends that: public art objects commissioned over a two-decade period in the North East of England

> generated a wave of interest from developers, Health Trusts, planners and public realm designers and a growing appetite for the visual arts in public spaces which enabled hundreds of commissioning opportunities for artists within an intense period of regeneration and public building.

This questioning of public sculpture in the urban environment is extended to the role and decision-making of the artist in the location and relocation of sculpture. Usherwood *et al.* argue that work will change in meaning and that multiple and shifting audiences as well as the commissioners, designers and sculptors can all be viewed as the 'makers' and 'producers' of the work in the sense that 'they help to endow the piece with meaning' (2000: xv). Whiting and Hannam's chapter in this volume on the city of Newcastle and 'bohemias' confirms the capacity of communities to be makers, producers and consumers of the visual arts for both community and tourist consumption. The American sociologist Dean MacCannell (1976) argued that there is a process whereby such 'attractions' become accepted by local communities in a series of stages or, as he suggested, through 'social reproduction'. Gormley's 1996 *Angel of the North* is a case in point, The initial community hostility to the sculpture was replaced by community acceptance when a giant nine-metre (Alan Shearer) Newcastle United football shirt was fitted to the sculpture by a group of football fans. There was a symbolic relocation of emotion from antagonism to acceptance and affection (at least among Newcastle United supporters) which has been latched onto by marketers and 'imagineers' of urban environments and place-makers, with the *Angel of the North*, being dubbed as the 'iconic' gateway to the North East of England by the local authority, Gateshead Borough Council.

Temenos, a large public sculpture created by the artist Anish Kapoor and the architect Cecil Balmond and unveiled in 2010, was viewed by Jarratt as representative of how 'the visual arts have changed the way Middlesbrough talks about itself, and the stories others talk about us' (2011: 9). Brindley, director of the Middlesbrough Institute of Modern Art (mima), more boldly claimed that *Temenos*, positioned in a new Middlehaven development of the town as part of a masterplan by architect Will Alsop, 'since being launched to the world's media one year ago Temenos has helped generate almost £10m-worth of positive coverage for the area' (2011: 5). Both of these statements suggest that public art has many different utilities for a variety of audiences while at the same time providing a challenge as to how these claims can be validated, beyond the realm of marketing and economic 'impact' hype. This marketing process or reimagineering has a historical precedent in the UK, with marketing campaigns such as Glasgow's Miles Better and Brighter Belfast (Rose, 1993: 100). Rose also highlighted the role of the London Docklands Development Corporation (LDDC) in selling an image and establishing a sense of place, a place sold as a completely empty location or 'a new frontier awaiting settlement' (1993: 102). She argued that alternative interpretations of East End places and identities were obscured (see Sinclair, 2004). In London Docklands, Rose argued that 'the structural power of capital dominates the sense of place' (Rose, 1993: 102) and, in parallel with Docklands, the role of public sculpture is viewed as a significant part of the economic restructuring of Middlehaven rather than as being vital to community identity.

Expansive claims made by Jarratt (2011: 9) suggest how

> Middlehaven is now reinventing itself as an area in which to live and study. It is inhabited by football supporters, students, digital innovators and office workers who will experience Temenos as an unexpected and even cinematic artwork which is totally at home by the [river] Tees.

Ritchie (2011: 6) highlighted that

> Temenos is a world-class landmark, a tourist attraction and an internationally acclaimed public artwork, but in the context of Middlesbrough's regeneration, it is much more than that. As a symbol of renewal, Temenos is a bold statement of intent, signalling the transformation of derelict docks into a place of aspiration: a flagship development with a business quarter, eco-homes and a modern college to strengthen Middlesbrough's position as the Tees Valley's economic capital.

Confrontational art and tourism – the case of *House*

In relation to the East End of London it is important to note the impact of the visual artist Rachel Whiteread's work *House*, which was sited in Bow between October 1993 and 11 January 1994 and was described by the art critic Andrew Graham-Dixon as one of the most extraordinary British sculptures of the twentieth century (Warde-Aldam, 2013). This sculpture is the internal concrete mould of a house which was due to be demolished to create a green corridor around Canary Wharf. It symbolised the power of sculpture to challenge a form of regeneration which removed through large-scale demolition all trace of a traditional East End community to create a zone of gentrification. Warde-Adam noted how 'House, along with Damien Hirst's *The Impossibility of Death in the Mind of Someone Living*, was among the most important works of the era, the ones that crossed the threshold from a rather closed scene to an international phenomenon' (2013: 4).

Townsend (2004: 8) observed of Whiteread that 'repeatedly the work asks us how do we live in this world, in this particular space?' She argues that *House* is concerned with the ideology of space and is reminiscent of the readymade work and Duchamp's *art sec* – casting a space around the object. In a literal sense it provoked debates about an ageing housing stock and the process of gentrification in the East End of London; as *House* was only due to stand for three months, it was part of project within urban renewal. Townsend argues that '*House* embodied conformity to a certain conception of public art-as sanctioned cultural placebo of a site of alienation' (2004: 19). In doing so she challenged what public art was meant to symbolise, particularly in view of the hostile reaction of the local authority and some of its residents, although according to Warde-Aldam it also received widespread public support. *House* was, on a prosaic level, the cast of the space inside the house and challenged the viewer to make sense of the sight of the interior, with the exterior rendered invisible. This playing with the inside-outside of structures, objects and attractions is something which has been latched onto by image makers wishing to enhance the image of so-called non-tourist destinations.

Discussion and conclusion

Politically, socially, economically and aesthetically the visual arts have retained an important status and, as this chapter has demonstrated, they hold a powerful attraction for tourists. The previous section highlights the polarity of the use of public art as both a symbol of regeneration for Bilbao and Middlesbrough and in the case of Bow in East London a challenge to regeneration through gentrification. Rachel Whiteread exercised a form of creativity which had re-emerged particularly through the work of the Young British Artists in the UK in the early 1990s. A polarity emerged within this group, with Emin and Hirst in particular becoming celebrity artists in contrast to other artists who operated on a more community level. Therefore for all the talk of celebrated artists and the reification of the visual arts as a conduit for the marketing of big business and as an undeniable draw for tourists, there is grassroots organisation of artists within tourist destinations who remain invisible to both domestic and international visitors and who are reliant on uncertain funding regimes for studio space. They are part of networks of creative industries who are susceptible to the uncertainty of funding regimes in a time of national and international austerity. These artists are an important part of what can be termed community arts organisations where the creative outputs of artists have aesthetic utility rather than symbolising the commercial aspirations to use the visual arts to promote a destination to international visitors.

In 2015 the DCMS produced a statistical release of the economic estimates of the creative industries within the UK and in their focus on the visual arts emphasised that they are part of a larger category of the creative industries which includes the performing arts and music. Therefore perhaps inevitably it is difficult to ascribe specific statistical information to the visual arts. However, for this larger category in 2013 it was estimated that there were 300,000 people in employment. Likewise in the category of museums, galleries and libraries which also has implications for the visual arts, there were 110,000 employed in 2013. In terms of the economic value of these sectors of the creative industries, it was estimated that music and the performing and visual arts generated £5,453 million in 2013 but there was no economic estimate for museums, galleries and libraries. The reason for this was that from 2001 Chris Smith, the then Culture Secretary under the New Labour administration was responsible for removing entry charges from museums and galleries in the UK. The belief was that the visual arts had a crucial role in enriching the cultural life of the nation. Talking in 2011 on the tenth anniversary of free entry, he highlighted how

> It took me four years to achieve that: convincing reluctant colleagues; secur-
> ing additional funding; persuading some museum directors; achieving the
> removal of VAT. It was worth it, though; and the surge in visitor numbers –
> up by 150% over the last decade – has proved it.
>
> (Abbott and Needham, 2011)

Four years on and in an age of the austerity for the public sector in the UK, this ideal has been eroded with the ending of free entry to some public art galleries. For example, since its reopening in August 2015, York City Art Gallery, which previously had free (subsidised) entry, has now a charge of £7.50 per person. This raises the issue of local authority art gallery provision in popular tourist cities such as York and Brighton being largely an attraction for tourists rather than a community resource (Brown, 2015b). This undoubtedly has implications for the funding regimes for the visual arts as part of the creative industries within the UK, with the suggestion that artistic institutions and artists which previously had their own artistic integrity are increasingly subsumed into the attractions sector and perhaps in the process made an elitist activity.

References

Abbott, K. and Needham, A. (2011) From Rabbie to Rubens: 10 Years of Free Entry to Museums, *Guardian*, www.theguardian.com/culture/2011/nov/30/10-years-free-entry-museums (accessed 8 August 2015).

Arts Council England. (2013) *Great Art and Culture for Everyone*. London: Arts Council England.

Arts Council England. (2015) *Visual Arts*, www.artscouncil.org.uk/what.we.do/supporting-artfroms/visualarts (accessed 31 August 2015).

Atkinson, C. (1981) *Picturing the System*. London: ICA.

Baniotopoulou, E. (2001) Art for Whose Sake? Modern Art Museums and their Role in Transforming Societies: The Case of the Guggenheim Bilbao. *Journal of Conservation and Museums Studies*, 7: 1–5.

Banksy (2006) *Wall and Piece*. Wemding, Germany: Frimgruppe Appl.

Berger, J. (1972) *Ways of Seeing*. London: Penguin.

Bianchini, F. and Parkinson, M. (eds) (1993) *Cultural Policy and Urban Regeneration: The West European Experience*. Manchester: Manchester University Press.

Biggs, L. (1984) Open Air Sculpture in Britain: Twentieth Century Developments, in Davies, P. and Knipe, T. (eds) *A Sense of Place: Sculpture in Landscape*. Sunderland: Ceolfrith Press, pp. 13–39.

Brindley, K. (2011) Introduction, in Brindley, K., Jarratt, M., English, L. and Landon, B. (eds) *Temenos*. London: British Library.

Brown, M. (2015a) Banksy's Dismaland: 'Amusements and Anarchism' in Artist's Biggest Project yet, *Guardian*, www.theguardian.com/artanddesign/2015/aug/20/banksy-dismaland-amusement (accessed 1 September 2015).

Brown, M. (2015b) Funding Cuts Could Spell End of Free Museums and Galleries, *Guardian*, www.theguardian.com/artanddesign/2015/jul23/york-art-gallery-reopen-ceramics (accessed 11 August 2015).

Chandler, D. (2002) *Semiotics: The Basics*. London: Routledge.

DCMS (1998) *The Creative Industries Mapping Document*. London: Department of Culture, Media and Sport.

DCMS (2015) *Creative Industries Economic Estimates: Statistical Release*. London: DCMS.

Freeland, C. (2001) *But is it Art?* Oxford: Oxford University Press.

Giovanni, J. (1997) Art into Architecture. *Guggenheim Magazine (special issue)*, Fall: 18–23.

Gombrich, E.H. (1972) *The Story of Art*. London: Book Club Associates.

Graevenitz, A. (2007) Breaking the Silence: Joseph Beuys on his 'Challenger, Marcel Duchamp', in Mesch, C. and Michely, V. (eds) *Joseph Beuys: The Reader*. London: Tauris, pp. 29–49.

Higgins, G. (2013) The Gallery on Your Street. *Guardian*, 10 August.

Jardine, L. (1997) *Modern Medicis: Art Patronage in the Twentieth Century in Britain*, in Rosenthal, N. (eds) *Sensation: Young British Artists From the Saatchi Collection*. London: Thames and Hudson. pp. 40–48.

Jarratt, M. (2011) The Challenges of Public Art, in Brindley, K., Jarratt, M., English, L. and Landon, B. (eds) *Temenos*. London: British Library, pp. 8–9

Jencks, C. (2005) *Iconic Building: The Power of Enigma*. London: Frances Lincoln.

Joyce, P. (1999) *Hockney on 'Art'*. London: Little Brown.

Long, P.E. (1996) Inter-organisational Collaboration in the Development of Tourism and the Arts 1996: The Year of Visual Arts, in Robinson, M., Evans, N. and Callaghan, P. (eds) *Culture as the Tourism Product*. Sunderland: Business Education Publishers, pp. 255–278.

MacCannell, D. (1976) *The Tourist: A New Theory of the Leisure Class*. London: Macmillan.

Mcintyre, P. (2012) *Creativity and Cultural Production: Issues for Media Practice*. Basingstoke: Palgrave.

Marshall, C. (ed.) (1997) *British Art of the 1980s and 1990s: The Weltkunst Collection*. London: Lund Humphries Publishers.

Mesch, C. (2007) Letters as Works of Art: Beuys and James Lee Byars, in Mesch, C. and Michely, V. (eds) *Joseph Beuys: The Reader*. London: Tauris, pp. 198–217.

Michely, V. (2007) Letters as Works of Art: Beuys and James Lee Byars (2000, excerpt), in Mesch, C. and Michely, V. (eds) *Joseph Beuys: The Reader*. London: Tauris, pp. 88–106.

Millard, R., (2001) *The Tastemakers: UK Art Now*. London: Thames and Hudson.

Pevsner, N. (1955) *The Englishness of English Art*. London: Penguin Books.

Pine, B.J. and Gilmore, J.H. (1997) *The Experience Economy*. Cambridge, MA: Harvard University Press.

Plotz, J. (2000) *The Crowd: British Literature and Public Politics*. Berkeley: University of California Press.

Rakic, T. and Lester, J. (2013) *Travel, Tourism and Art*. Farnham: Ashgate.

Richards, G. (ed.) (2001) *Cultural Attractions and European Tourism*. Wallingford: CABI Publishing.

Ritchie, P. (2011) *Temenos*: A Symbol of Middlehaven's Transformation, in Brindley, K., Jarratt, M., English, L. and Landon, B. (eds) *Temenos*. London: British Library, pp. 6–7.

Rose, G. (1993) *Feminism and Geography: The Limits of Geographical Knowledge.* Minneapolis: University of Minnesota Press.

Rosenthal, N. (1997) *Sensation: Young British Artists From the Saatchi Collection.* London: Thames and Hudson.

Sinclair, I. (2004) *Dining on Stone.* London: Hamish Hamilton.

Towner, J. (1985) The Grand Tour: A Key Phase in the History of Tourism. *Annals of Tourism Research*, 12 (3): 297–333.

Townsend, C. (2004) When We Collide: History and Aesthetics, Space and Signs in the Art of Rachel Whiteread, in Townsend, C. (ed.) *The Art of Rachel Whiteread.* London: Thames and Hudson.

Urry, J. (1992) *The Tourist Gaze: Leisure Travel in Contemporary Societies*, London: Sage.

Usherwood, P., Beach, J. and Morris, C. (2000) *Public Sculpture of North-East England.* Liverpool: Liverpool University Press.

Walton, J. (ed.) (2005) *Histories of Tourism: Representation, Identity and Conflict.* Clevedon: Channel View Publications.

Warde-Aldam, D. (2013) Ghost House. *Apollo Magazine*, 25 October, www.apollo-magazine.com/house/ (accessed 21 September 2015).

Welcome to Yorkshire's Hockney Country (undated). www.yorkshire.com./join-in/magazine/the-davidhockneytrail (accessed 21 September, 2015).

4   Tourism and advertising as a creative industry sector

Mark Passera

Introduction

This chapter analyses the ways in which three distinct factors are shaping contemporary post-modern advertising and marketing practice. First, design thinking, behavioural economics and digital technologies are briefly reviewed. The chapter then addresses advertising as a creative field of practice and specifically how this contributes to the image and reputation of the United Kingdom for international tourism, and arguably as a leader in this field. The chapter also considers the UK as a branded tourist destination, with an emphasis on London as a cosmopolitan/multicultural world city that is distinct and separate from the rest of the country and more appropriately comparable with other 'world cities'.

Marketing communication is shifting into new terrain: one where agility, consumer-centricity, social media and the rise of an experiential component combine to make marketing communication in the UK (and especially London) not only unique, but at the forefront of innovative and creative practice. This also involves looking at how advertising and marketing are being innovative with new technologies and new ideas. The chapter goes on to analyse how the UK (and London specifically) retains a pivotal position in advertising and marketing due to a unique blend of heritage, a 'tech start up' culture and entrepreneurial *frisson* (creative clusters). These factors contribute to London's reputation as a leader in advertising and marketing. Additional and critical factors including low pay, intern culture, working conditions, job security, cost of living and portfolio careers are also highlighted. To conclude, the chapter addresses where and how the UK is advertised and marketed as a tourist destination, and how this is connected with the creative industries.

Advertising as creative industry and practice

The root of advertising, from the Latin *Advertere*, is the process whereby a target consumer group is encouraged (or manipulated) to 'turn towards' a brand, product or service. There is a long-held view that as a persuasive tool, advertising only works when it captures our attention (Percy and Rosenbaum-Elliot, 2012). Such a narrow definition may have worked historically; but today it is clear that advertising is about much more than gaining our attention. Scholars and practitioners are agreed that the nature of advertising has been transformed by digital technology (Van Dyck, 2014). Added to this is the rise of complexity and an increased focus on customer 'journeys', empathy and user experiences (Soberman and Soman, 2012; Wang, 2012).

Modern-day advertising is generating metaphors likening it to the unpredictable nature of pinball (Hennig-Thurau, 2013) and to advocacy and electronic word of mouth models (Erdogmus, 2012). Advertising today has become an amorphous, complex entity covering everything from traditional advertising vignettes (posters and radio) to modern processes of managing conversations online and creating value through corporate social responsibility engagement (Hardey, 2011). Clearly this shift is based in changing consumer behaviour. As people start to behave differently, advertising has had to adapt, both as a creative art and as a persuasive science (Soberman and Soman, 2012). The rise of digital communication technologies (£5.5 billion according to Deloitte and IPA) and in particular online conversations and social media means that advertising has moved to new spaces – social, analytics, programmatic advertising (McConnell, 2015) and online conversations (Kozinets, 2010). The debate and argument appear to be conclusive – digital advertising is the single largest spend in its sector in the UK (www.iab.co.uk; Advertising Association, 2015). The rise of an integrated media ecosystem (programmatic advertising) is where software places messages on a user's screen as a result of a combination of factors. These can include: price, browser history, cookies, user preferences, past shopping activity and geographical place (there are many more criteria). These adverts are programmed nominally by software and based on algorithms that are price-sensitive (agreed tariffs) and visibility (opportunities to see):

> Mainly it is used to refer to automated decisioning, but sometimes it's used simply to communicate that data was somehow used to decide on an audience. Use of data has been essential to media planning for a century so it's not as though data, by itself, is some stepwise improvement. What matters is what data, and how it's used.
>
> (McConnell, 2015)

A clear indication of both the transformative nature of advertising, and also the uncertainty, is the rise of programmatic advertising. Advertising is grappling with what Sir Martin Sorrell calls the battle between 'Maths Men' and 'Mad Men' or algorithm versus creative advertising (Sorrell, 2013). Advertising in the UK today is trying to combine these two potentially conflicting approaches, to become a leading creative force in understanding and launching innovative and creative advertising campaigns based on analytics and deep consumer insight. In responding to digital disruption (and innovation), consumer psychology and new approaches (behavioural economics and design thinking), the advertising industry in the UK has responded with joint ventures and partnerships. A good example of the link between design thinking and behavioural economics is provided by consultancy #Ogilvychange and the IPA (the UK professional association for the advertising industry) which have both focused on behavioural economics in recent years (www.ipa.co.uk/be). There are also emerging networks and organisations that are fostering collaboration and facilitating new ideas and practices in the field of behavioural economics applied to advertising (www.meetup.com/London-behavioural-comms-monthly-informal-drinks/).

These loose networks reflect the logic and heuristics of networks: co-creation, collaboration and crowd funding. Advertising has now started to move away from rigid and traditional notions of how to advertise, and has started to work with designers, behavioural psychologists and software engineers (Martin and Christensen, 2013). Advertising's value within brand and communication strategy is no longer a discrete entity where the 'creative' occurs. Instead we see an increase in partnerships or a new breed of agencies. Roughly, these are T-shaped (wide breadth and deep knowledge); the current traits needed include user experience (UX), digital design (responsive design), customer journey mapping, brand touch-points and deep customer empathy (Econsultancy, 2015). T-shaped is an expression attributed to Tim Brown, the CEO of IDEO, referring to individuals with a breadth of knowledge and ability – the horizontal part of the T and an added core competency such as graphic design or ethnographic research which is the vertical part of the T (Hunter, 2012). Finally a key hallmark of a T-shaped workforce includes curiosity and collaboration.

Additional forces are contributing to this hybridisation of advertising as creative practice: constant connectivity, second screening and the emergence of ad avoidance and ad blocking software. Second screening or multi-screening refers to the process whereby consumers use a variety of devices simultaneously. Scenarios include traditional television watching while scrolling through content on a smartphone or iPad (Goode and Mortensen, 2013). For advertisers, this is a perfect storm: a squeeze on revenue (return on investment and the social media debate will not go away), new consumer trends in content consumption and content creation, and shifting viewing habits (Netflix, Amazon Prime, and streaming). It has become difficult to capture attention and to engage through technology-mediated new behaviours. In the past, the interruption model worked perfectly for advertising. Also referred to as push (interruption) versus pull (digital and engaged), the interruption model was prevalent in television and radio where content was interrupted for an advert or a word from our sponsor. Today, the challenge is becoming almost insurmountable. Content streaming, content access or renting is increasingly the norm and advertising needs to adapt and rethink its game once again. Illustrative of this trend is the high response in recent research (Econsultancy, 2015) on innovative labs, analytics and more UX capability (this refers to the user experience whereby both products and advertising can be co-created or adapted based on user feedback) in advertising agencies and departments.

As media become hyper-fragmented, so has advertising. Not only do we have traditional push-based campaigns, but also integrated, responsive and experiential/engagement campaigns which attempt to secure consistency across multiple platforms. Where the UK can be viewed as innovative and creative is in these holistic campaigns, but the industry needs to react to and adapt to new consumer behaviour and media consumption patterns. These include deliberate advertising avoidance strategies, which can include ad blocking (roughly 20 per cent in the UK: http://mediatel.co.uk/), together with emerging activities such as second screening and watch again habits.

This overview of state-of-the-art changes in the advertising industry concludes by citing examples of interdisciplinary (co-creative advertising) innovative advertising campaigns and partnerships. For example and in response to changes in consumer habits and technological potential, Mindshare has created a new lab (partnership) labelled Life+ in order to reach the customer (www.mindshareworld.com/news/mindshare-launches-global-wearable-technology-unit). This example links wearable technology and the quantified self [*sic*] in a campaign for Jaguar cars at the All England Lawn Tennis Championship, Wimbledon, 2015. Wrist cuffs captured emotive data (heart rate and pulse) while spectators were watching live tennis matches. The data were then transformed into pulses and waves, equating spikes with key moments of emotion and tension in the tennis matches. This is an innovation, allowing advertisers to link and leverage physical (raw) visceral response and sentiment (http://jaguar.wimbledon.com/en_GB/wrapper/jlr/index.html). Advertising has also had to embrace design thinking, digital innovations and behavioural economics. Examples include: Virgin (www.nesta.org.uk/v-jam/), RBS (www.nilehq.com/) and Southwark Borough (http://enginegroup.co.uk/). All three share similar hallmarks: design thinking, user experience, digital insights and ultimately campaigns that can be described as non-traditional. The RBS campaign was an app (Cannes award winner 2013), the Nesta collaboration with Virgin Atlantic was a taxi-sharing app (based on ethnographic and in-depth customer research) and finally the Southwark Borough approach revolved around communication strategy and effective reach through empathy, observation and design research methods. The use of observation and empathy enabled an effective campaign tackling economic hardship and obesity, indicating the potential social and health applications of advertising innovations.

These examples demonstrate a markedly different approach and feel from traditional advertising. This ranges from a synthesis of different specialisms (digital development and user experience), to new practice and habits (wearable technology and the quantified self), to helping customers solve 'problems' with, for example, a taxi-sharing app. These innovative advertising campaigns are underpinned with traditional advertising (posters, television and billboards). The innovation is both in the methodology used and in the purpose which underpins them – the emergence of campaigns that solve problems (although some 'problems' may arguably have been created). In turn these become moments that are mentioned and referenced in online platforms, leading ultimately to positive endorsements and engagement with brands in online forums (social media). This leads to a key conclusion: the emergence of T-shaped people, synergistic alliances and an increased emphasis on interdisciplinary non-siloed working.

Advertising needs to be experiential, analytical, social, UX and focused on customer journeys: 'Consultancies will increasingly acquire into UX, creative and design areas. This means that there will be more consolidation on the agency side but also a big shortage of talent (data, UX) and that will continue' (Econsultancy, 2015).

London as a creative hub for advertising

Here we focus on advertising in London and the state of the industry in relation to demographic forces and changes in economic and employment practices. Employment numbers, composition, working practices, the rise of the 'gig economy', creative clusters and finally the 'precariat' are addressed.

According to UK government statistics, London remains the centre for creative advertising in the UK. This is based on a variety of factors including history, tradition and most importantly financial power. The iconography of advertising remains centred between London and New York. The pedigree of Ogilvy and Saatchi & Saatchi is a powerful force ensuring that London retains at the least an iconic role. The heritage element is not limited to nostalgia or past glory. A strong combination of multiculturalism, education and London's status as a financial centre combine to ensure that the city remains an advertising destination. An additional factor may be of relevance: higher education and professional qualifications. From IAB, to the IPA, IDM and Google Squared, London remains at the forefront of continuing professional development for the advertising industry.

The number of people employed in London on all aspects of advertising (including digital) was estimated to be 177,000 in 2015. This figure is down from 2014 (185,000). The total employed in advertising within the UK is roughly 500,000 (www.gov.uk/government/statistics/creative-industries-2015-focus-on). The number of UK-registered advertising business, is around 18,000 (of which 5,840 are London-based). Therefore roughly a third of the advertising sector is based in the capital. There is an almost even split between male and female employees in the advertising industry. However, the industry lacks female representation at senior levels; male staff roughly 80 per cent of all senior posts and no global agency has a female head of creative (www.forbes.com/sites/avidan/2011/04/14/the-glass-ceiling-in-advertising/). Advertising therefore remains a highly male-dominated business, and one where young white men tend to rule (Feldwick, 2015) and (DCMS, 2015). This lack of diversity is borne out in the IPA's own research which shows that only 20 per cent of employees are over the age of 40. According to a report in the *Guardian* a disproportionate 91 per cent of advertising industry staff are from a white background and over 87 per cent of senior roles are occupied by men (http://bit.ly/1ldp7hw). Just under 60 per cent of those employed in advertising and marketing have a degree (the average is 58 per cent) and 456,000 employees are white versus 43,000 black, Asian and minority ethnic (BAME).

A broader view of the nature and impact of advertising is achieved through an analysis of ancillary factors and knock-on benefits. According to Nesta, just under half a million people are employed in advertising and marketing in the UK, equating to 18 per cent of all jobs within creative industries, second only to IT, software and computer services. More importantly, the gross added value (GVA) is £10.2 billion. As advertising begins to enter new areas and spheres it will need to move beyond a very narrow pool of recruitment (young white men). Digital may be challenging for advertisers to grasp, and demonstrating the ROI of social media campaigns may be difficult, but it has now become the single largest sector. According to Credos, the Advertising Association Think Tank, ad spend in the UK is roughly £17.5 billion, of which digital (at £5.5 billion) is the largest segment, followed by television (£4.6 billion), then newspapers (£2.7 billion) (www.adaasco.org).

There is an important word of caution at this point. A new space has opened up; advertising has evolved and permeated all aspects of media through co-creation, crowd sourcing and user-generated content (Potts *et al.*, 2008). Through the use of denotative practices such as enterprise, lean start-up and entrepreneur-ship, certain aspects of the economy have now become creative, and not just because we are naming it as such. The Florida thesis on creative clusters asserts that like-minded cultural workers create synergistic creative alliances in proto Silicon Valley spaces (Banks, 2006). Advertising has now started to embrace the ethos of the new creative problem-solving approach through new cross-sectorial alliances. As new practices and new models emerge, advertising in London is (very arguably) benefiting from a vibrant creative class (Florida, 2012) with its own history and pedigree. Key to this are the stereotypical highly educated, mobile thinkers and workers who embrace a move away from traditional religious values, conformity and traditional views on sexuality, gender and equality. More open to new ideas, less dogmatic and willing to embrace a more activity- and idea-based experiential dimension, creative clusters become lightning rods for innovative ideas, practices and eventually policy. As advertising as an industry shifts into a multidisciplinary practice (Advertising Association, 2015; Econ-sultancy, 2015) it is not only new channels that are transforming the industry, but new customer behaviours and more importantly innovative responses by agencies and their employees.

A good example of this is the rise of the 'Millennial' and cause-related mar-keting dimensions (McGlone, 2011). This links with research by Nesta (2014) on knowledge spill-overs, networked innovation and diversity, where ideas are challenged and creative sparks generate 'solutions' to important problems. This would echo the earlier argument by Florida on the three Ts – talent, technology, tolerance (Florida, 2002). This is about not just increasing tolerance of differ-ence, but a more active and participative interest in social justice, sustainability and lifestyles that are referenced and 'liked' online and through social networks. These new spaces (physical and virtual) are enabling the emergence of flat, non-hierarchical creative clusters (Tornqvist, 2011).

A final consideration is the 'Precariat' and the cost of living and property in London (and other 'world cities'). The association with creativity and precari-ousness is not new and is a theme covered by many authors including Oakley and Florida (Florida, 2003). Linking the 2008 crash with a strong neo-liberal mantra, Bains (2013) has found that creativity is suffocating through funding restrictions and dwindling support at the grassroots. Creativity, and the creative class, do require support and collective spaces in order to collaborate and generate (potentially) innovative ideas, campaigns or insights. The danger with London becoming too expensive rests in the transfer of a creative class away from the city centres and hubs. Under such a scenario creative practitioners will become increasingly marginalised and ignored (Standing, 2012).

London, advertising, place branding and tourism

The role of place branding in London provides an interesting link between the creative industries and advertising. Given London's unique heritage and history, there will always be an echo within most creative ventures generated from London that creates a British identity found only in the capital city. These icons include fashion (Burberry, Paul Smith – who hails from Nottingham, however), music (from the Rolling Stones to Sir Simon Rattle), sport (Premier League, the 2012 London Olympics and the 2015 Rugby World Cup) and film (Pinewood Studios and London as a setting). London (and the UK more generally) is being advertised indirectly throughout these creative practices, and this relationship can be extended to literature, museums and galleries, publishing, design (broadly defined) and the performing and visual arts. This should also include the IT, software and computer services dimension of the creative industries as the largest sector (based on economic contribution) in the traditionally defined creative industries. We will review how advertising in these other creative sectors is also innovative and ground-breaking.

London as a creative place may be considered as part of an experiential brand construct [*sic*]. From Shoreditch (UK's London response to start-up culture and Silicon Valley) to the rise of innovative practices in the other creative sectors (pop-up shops, secret cinema and music venues), all act as totems for advertising London as a centre for creativity and innovation. The important point is place and brand being linked together (Klingmann, 2007). This is not limited only to traditional creative industries such as architecture, but also draws upon the experiential economy; London echoes this through a wide range of experiential connections, from shopping (Carnaby Street) to museums and galleries, through to fashion design and shows.

Advertising agencies use these relationships within London that are a result of what Florida would refer to as creative cities. This includes the role of creativity in spaces, in place and in clusters (Muratovski, 2012). London is a pluralistic (multicultural) city, where local planning, policy and design arguably reinforce its iconic role. Ultimately this leads London to become a symbolic construct, which then becomes advertising. An early example of branded cities, advertising, film and place marketing is the action film, *The Bourne Supremacy*. The protagonist, Jason Bourne, while fighting the enemy (the CIA), was doing so in a way that advertised not only London but Eurostar and the *Guardian*. Key here, in addition to the name-dropping within the shot at Waterloo station, is the advertising campaign online creating buzz (Gasser, 2007), with sponsorship by Mastercard, Google and Volkswagen. Another more recent example is the reboot of the James Bond franchise. The two newest films have set pieces in the UK (Scotland for *Skyfall* and London for *Spectre*); and overall they show a sophisticated use of place advertising through film.

Online competitions, discussions and engagement not only create hype, awareness and anticipation for cultural events (fashion shows, film music and exhibitions) but more importantly act as a revolution in place advertising (Ketter, 2012. All these events are UK, and specifically London, based. There is a well-established history of research showing the role of location in film as affecting tourism (O'Connor, 2010). Linking creative industries, London, advertising and digital (focusing deliberately on social media) clearly illustrates how London is able to retain its pole position as a creative centre globally through place advertising and branding. IT, fashion, publishing, television or music may be discussed on-line, but through audience discussions, audience distributor and message creator the 'product' being advertised remains London (Ketter, 2012). London is also seen through creative industries such as sport, museums and galleries. These are clear examples of successful place branding which then advertise London (and second the UK). The Olympics in 2012 and the 2015 Rugby World Cup are examples of successful place branding. The continued success of premiership football (through TV revenue) also helps advertise the UK/London as a tourist destination.

We also see events where there is a fusion between advertising (such as the example of Ogilvy), creative clusters and tech culture (http://digitalshoreditch. com). Powerful examples such as UX for the people exemplify the creative clusters paradigm first articulated by Florida (Ogilvylabs, 2015). These are fusions of creative practice across all disciplines whereby creative and innovative practice is first incubated within a place (London) and then flowers in museums, pop-up shops or in advertising agencies. This is less about advertising, and more about innovative practices (creativity as studied by Florida, 2003 and Chapain, 2010). Another good example is Soundscapes at the National Gallery (National Gallery, 2015). This exhibition is new creative (about old creative) and acts as an effective advertisement for London as a creative city.

Conclusion

Advertising today can be described as post-modern, embracing diverse platforms and increasingly wide sources for inspiration and creativity, for example behavioural economics (Ferrier, 2014). The historical dominance of London as an advertising centre remains, but is under threat. Through social media it seems that the brave new world of advertising will no longer rely on place or brand, but more on the imagination of the audience. This is nothing new, as Marshall McLuhan (1964: 201) argued: 'The continuous pressure is to create ads more and more in the image of audience motives and desires. The product matters less as the audience participation increases.'

Ironically, it seems that London as both an advertising centre and a destination for innovative, creative and fresh talent is itself possibly becoming the material of a good advertising campaign. There are a variety of forces underpinning this statement. First, there is the well-documented rise of the precariat (Bain, 2013) or the 'gig' economy. This is sometimes explained away as a portfolio career or a 'lifestyle' decision in choosing to work as a freelance. Linked to this is the economic crisis of 2008, eight years of austerity and a fairly slow economic recovery (for most of the population). Finally, any consideration of London must return to the cost of living. London is expensive, not only for accommodation, but also for travel, subsistence and many leisure activities. London may be starting to lose its lustre as a centre of creative excellence. A review of numerous awards across the advertising industry (WARC, Effie's, Cannes, www.effieindex.com/ranking/) shows that London agencies are conspicuous by their absence. Across all categories, in the past two years no UK-based creative agencies were successful. Power may be concentrated within London, but this power is financial.

There can be one concluding moment of optimism: the weather:

> Great weather is probably why Hollywood turns out some truly awful movies. Who wants to labour over a cliché-ridden script in an effort to turn into an Oscar-winner when you could be down by the pool at the Sunset Marquis? Sunny weather is great for shooting films but not so wonderful for writing them…. In comparison, London always ranks as one of the world's great creative centres. Why? Because the weather is shit.
>
> (Hegarty, 2014: 87)

References

Advertising Association (2015) 'Advertising Pays 3: The Value of Advertising to the UK's Culture, Media & Sport', www.adassoc.org.uk/publications/advertising-pays-3/, accessed 1 November 2015.

Bain, A. (2013) 'The Artistic Precariat', *Cambridge Journal of Regions, Economy and Society*, 6, 1: 3–21.

Banks, M. (2006) 'Moral Economy and Cultural Work', *Sociology*, 40, 3: 455–472.

Catmull, E. (2013) *Creativity, Inc.*, London: Bantam Press.

Chapain, C. (2010) *Creative Clusters and Innovation*, NESTA Research Paper, November, www.nesta.org.uk/library/documents/Creative_clusters_print_v2.pdf, accessed 10 August 2015.

DCMS (2015) 'Creative Industries: Focus on Employment', June, www.gov.uk/government/uploads/system/uploads/attachment_data/file/439714/Annex_C_-_Creative_Industries_Focus_on_Employment_2015.pdf, accessed 10 August 2015.

Econsultancy (2015) 'The Future of Agencies: The Progression of Agency Value in a Digital World', London, https://econsultancy.com/reports/the-future-of-agencies/, accessed 30 September 2015.

Erdogmus, I. (2012) 'The Impact of Social Media Marketing on Brand Loyalty', *Procedia – Social and Behavioural Sciences*, 58: 1353–1360.

Feldwick, P. (2015) *The Anatomy of Humbug: How to Think Differently about Advertising*, Kibworth: Matador.

Ferrier, A. (2014) *The Advertising Effect: How to Change Behaviour*, Oxford: Oxford University Press.

Florida, R. (2002) *The Rise of the Creative Class*, London: Basic Books.

Florida, R. (2003) 'Cities and the Creative Class', *City & Community*, 2, 1: 3–19.

Florida, R. (2009) 'Talent, Technology and Tolerance in Canadian Regional Development', Martin Prosperity Institute, http://martinprosperity.org/media/pdfs/3Ts-Canada-Florida-et-al.pdf, accessed 9 November 2015.

Florida, R. (2012) 'The Creative Class, Post-industrialism and the Happiness of Nations', *Cambridge Journal of Regions, Economy and Society*, 5, 1: 41–78.

Gasser, M. (2007) 'Major Brands Get behind "Bourne"', *Variety*, 12 July, http://variety.com/2007/film/markets-festivals/major-brands-get-behind-bourne-1117968443/, accessed 20 November 2015.

Goode, A. and Mortensen, N. (2013) 'Multi-Screen Viewing Behaviour', *Admap*, www.warc.com/admap, 14–17, accessed 12 July 2015.

Google (2012) 'The ZMOT Handbook', www.thinkwithgoogle.com/research-studies/2012-zmot-handbook.html, accessed 20 November 2015.

Hardey, M. (2011) 'Generation C: Content, Creation, Connections and Choice', *International Journal of Market Research*, 53, 6: 749–770.

Hegarty, J. (2014) *Hegarty on Creativity: There are no Rules*, London: Thames and Hudson.

Hennig-Thurau, T. (2013) 'Marketing the Pinball Way', *Journal of Interactive Marketing*, 27: 237–241

Hunter, S.T. (2012) 'Hiring an Innovative Workforce: A Necessary yet Uniquely Challenging Endeavour', *Human Resources Management Review*, 22, 4: 303–322.

Ketter, E. (2012) 'The Social Revolution of Place Marketing: The Growing Power of Users in Social Media Campaigns', *Place Branding and Public Diplomacy*, 8, 4: 285–294.

Klingmann, A. (2007) *Brandscapes: Architecture in the Experience Economy*, Cambridge, MA: MIT Press.

Kozinets, R. (2010) 'Networked Narratives: Understanding Word of Mouth Marketing in Online Communities', *Journal of Marketing*, 74: 71–89.

McConnell, T. (2015) 'The Programmatic Primer: A Marketer's Guide to the Online Advertising Ecosystem', www.warc.com, accessed 1 November 2015.

McGlone, T. (2011) 'Corporate Social Responsibility and Millennials', *Journal of Education for Business*, 86, 4: 195–200.

McLuhan, M. (1964) *Understanding Media: The Extensions of Man*, Cambridge, MA: MIT Press.

Martin, R. and Christensen, K. (2013) *Rotman on Design*, Toronto: University of Toronto Press,

Muratovski, G. (2012) 'The Role of Architecture and Integrated Design in City Branding', *Place Branding and Public Diplomacy*, 8, 3: 195–207.

National Gallery (2015) www.nationalgallery.org.uk/whats-on/soundscapes, accessed 11 November 2015.

NESTA (2014) 'Creative Citizens' Variety Pack', http://creativecitizens.co.uk, accessed 30 September 2015

O'Connor, N., Flanagan, S. and Gilbert, D. (2010) 'The Use of Film in Reimagining a Tourism Destination: A Case Study of Yorkshire', *Journal of Vacation Marketing*, 16: 61–74.

Ogilvylabs (2015) 'Digital Shoreditch: Festival Lab Report', www.ogilvylabs.co.uk/assets/Lab-Reports/Digital-Shoreditch-Lab-Report-2015.pdf, accessed 11 November 2015.

Percy, L. and Rosenbaum-Elliot, R. (2012) *Strategic Advertising Management*, Oxford: Oxford University Press.

Potts, Jason D. (2008) 'Consumer Co-creation and Situated Creativity', *Industry and Innovation*, 15, 5: 459–474.

Soberman, D. and Soman, D. (2012) *Flux*, Toronto: University of Toronto Press.

Sorrell, M. (2013) 'Creativity in the Age of the Maths Men', *The Drum*, 25 September.

Standing, G. (2012) 'The Precariat: From Denizens to Citizens?', *Polity*, 44: 588–608.

Throsby, D. (2010) *The Economics of Cultural Policy*, Cambridge: Cambridge University Press.

Tornqvist, T. (2011) *The Geography of Creativity*, Gloucester: Edward Elgar.

Van Dyck, F. (2014) *Advertising Transformed*, London: Kogan Page.

Wang, X. (2012) 'Media Peer Communication and Impacts on Purchase Intentions', *Journal of Interactive Marketing*, 26: 83–91.

5 Fashion, tourism and the creative industries

Corinna Budnarowska and Ruth Marciniak

Introduction

This chapter explores the relationship between fashion and tourism. In doing so, it re-examines current thinking regarding fashion tourism and the extent to which this may be classified as part of the creative industries. In particular, the chapter seeks to explore fashion as a component sector of the creative industries associated with tourism which, in a UK context, unlike other European Union member states such as France and Italy, is not typically considered to be so.

The outline of the chapter is, first, to define fashion tourism. Following this, adopting a UK perspective, the chapter explores the scope of fashion tourism, in particular fashion tourism based on manufacturing heritage (textourism) and consumption heritage (local and national fashion histories), and discusses the extent to which consumption heritage serves to provide consumers with opportunities for creative experiences, consumption of novel ideas and co-creation. A digital perspective on fashion tourism is also presented and discussed. Next, the extent to which fashion agencies such as the British Fashion Council have sought to promote fashion tourism alongside tourism agencies is examined. In doing so, the chapter seeks to understand how fashion may be seen as an asset to drive a city's economy and support regeneration. Finally, a conclusion is offered, which reviews the chapter and, in doing so, summarises the case that fashion tourism is indeed part of the creative industries.

Definition and scope of fashion tourism

Common to definitions of the creative industries is that a sector is defined in terms of a Standard Industrial Classification (SIC) of what it does, what it produces, and how it does so (Potts *et al.*, 2008). In accordance with this, for the Department of Culture, Media and Sport (DCMS) in the UK, design and designer fashion are classified as belonging to the creative industries. Potts *et al.* (2008) consider that the environment of businesses within the creative industries consists of complex social networks that rely on word of mouth, taste, cultures and popularity and, as such, consumers make decisions not solely on any price signals or inherent preferences. To this end, a definition of the creative industries offered is: 'The set of agents in a market characterized by adoption of novel ideas within social networks for production and consumption' (Potts *et al.*, 2008: 171).

This definition indicates that unique to the creative industries is that consumption is taste-driven and therefore the products and services derived from these industries are subjective to each individual. In addition, the products and services are novel in that creative products and services can take on a variety of different forms (Friedman and Jones, 2011). At the centre of why products are different is that they have their origin in 'individual creativity, skill and talent' (Department for Culture, Media and Sport, 2015). An example of what is deemed by 'taste-makers' to be such creativity, skill and talent can be found in the work of Alexander McQueen, which was shown in 2011 at New York's Metropolitan Museum of Art exhibition *Savage Beauty*, and most recently, in 2015 at London's Victoria and Albert Museum (V&A). McQueen's work provides evidence of the extent to which the fashion sector relies on a strong creative input. Accordingly, the exhibition served to reflect McQueen's rich imagination, which he poured into his work and, according to *Creative Review* (2015) 'inspire[s] new generations with the thought that creativity and fashion need not be limited by function'.

It is appropriate that the design activities associated with the fashion designer industry are classified as part of the creative industries. However, other definitions, such as that offered by the British Council (2011), indicate that what unifies creative industry activities is that they all trade with creative assets in the form of intellectual property and it is intellectual property that offers economic value. Yet Pouillard (2011) points out that different national approaches exist wherein, for example, the traditional French view is that fashion design belongs to high art and therefore designs are protected by law. In contrast, in the US fashion design is not copyright protected. The fashion design industry is therefore subjectively and culturally defined within national boundaries. For the purposes of this chapter, fashion design is defined in the UK context, this being the category of 'specialised design activities' (Department for Culture, Media and Sport, 2015). Nevertheless, the fashion industry itself views the industry as going beyond the design element to embrace retail activities including the sales of designer fashion (British Fashion Council, 2010).

Like fashion itself, fashion tourism has a very high potential to be socially pervasive, and through the media, information is frequently disseminated on fashion festivals, events, visits and exhibitions. In all, the sector is very much a part of the creative industries. To this end, what Chanel famously stated is very true: 'Fashion is not something that exists in dresses only. Fashion is in the sky, in the street. Fashion has to do with ideas, the way we live, what is happening' (ThinkExist, 2015).

Chanel's quote is very much embedded in definitions of fashion tourism wherein it can be seen as the phenomenon of people travelling to and staying in places outside their usual environment to enjoy, experiment and possibly consume fashion (Bada, 2013).

Tourism, as a business activity, in turn, contributes to the economy. Leiper (1979) focuses on tourism as involving the provision of accommodation, services and entertainment when people visit a location. As such, fashion tourism serves to provide accommodation in the form of fashion designer hotels, services such as retail services, and entertainment, for example fashion festivals. Drawing upon UK examples, the scope of fashion tourism is offered in Table 5.1. As can be seen from the list, the examples relate to creative, cultural and commercial experiences.

Table 5.1 Scope of fashion tourism

Activity	UK examples
Accommodation	Missoni Hotel, Edinburgh; Bulgari Hotel and Residences, London; Claridges, London (Diane Furstenberg suite)
Food	Thomas's at Burberry, Vigo Street, London; Hackett, Regent Street, London; China Tang at the Dorchester, Park Lane, London (Shanghai Tang brand); The Berkeley, London, designer afternoon tea, Prêt-à-Porte, a inspired by the themes and colours of the fashion world
Museums	Victoria and Albert Museum (V&A), London; Fashion and Textile Museum, Bermondsey, London; V&A Museum of Design, Dundee, Scotland; Blandford Fashion Museum, Dorset; Fashion Museum, Bath, Somerset; Silk Museum, Macclesfield, Cheshire; National Wool Museum, Carmarthenshire, Wales; Helmshore Mills Textile Museum, Lancashire; Ruddington Framework Knitters Museum, Nottinghamshire; Shetland Textile Museum, Scotland; Bradford Industrial Museum, Yorkshire
Designer outlet shopping	Bicester Village, Oxfordshire; Cheshire Oaks Deisgner Outlet, Cheshire; York Designer Outlet, Yorshire; Clarks Village, Somerset
Shopping quarters	Northern Quarter, Manchester; Carnaby Street, London; Victoria Quarter, Leeds; Metquarter, Liverpool; London Luxury Quarter, London; Hackney Hub, London
Fashion weeks	London Fashion Weekend; London Fashion Week; London Design Festival; 100% Design; Future Fabrics Expo; Brighton Fashion Week; London Collections Men; Textile Forum, London; Belfast Fashion Week; Glasgow Fashion Week; Birmingham International Fashion Week; Liverpool Fashion Week; London Alternative Fashion Week; Asian Fashion Week, London; African Fashion Week, London; Cheltenham Fashion Week
Fashion festivals	Vintage by the Sea, Morecambe, Lancashire; Curve Fashion Festival, Manchester; London Fashion Film Festival; Edinburgh International Fashion Festival; Clothes Show Live, Birmingham; Festival of Thrift, Darlington, County Durham

Consumption experiences and fashion tourism

Miller (2015) distinguishes creative and cultural tourism from fashion tourism. She indicates that fashion tourism has emerged out of creative industries tourism, shopping tourism and cultural tourism. However, it is shopping tourism that has probably received most media and academic attention (Lee, 2013; Zaiden, 2015). In the UK, shopping tourism is evident in malls and shopping villages, for example Bicester in Oxfordshire where aggressive marketing campaigns are employed to attract tourists and tour groups. A recent innovation is the Hackney Fashion Hub, which consists of new high-end destination outlet stores in the East End of London and is an example of urban districts being badged as 'fashion quarters'. Beyond the UK, Quadrilatero, Milan, Italy, and The Garment District, Toronto, Canada, provide other examples of this phenomenon.

The money generated from shopping tourism in the UK is substantial. For example, the *Guardian* (2013) states that the average foreign visitor on a shopping trip spends £680. Quoting a Visit Britain survey, it estimates that 18 million foreign tourists spent £4.5 billion, with half of this figure spent on fashion. Further afield, Miller (2015) indicates that 95 per cent of Chinese visitors to the Louis Vuitton shops in Paris come through organised tours and approximately 50 per cent of sales of luxury goods in Western Europe are generated by those living beyond the continent. It is evident that fashion designer retailers are well prepared for foreigner visitors. For example, Burberry reported in its 2013/14 Annual Report that it employs over 150 Mandarin-speaking sales associates across top Chinese tourist destinations outside Asia.

Shopping fashion destinations typically create 'characteristic experiences' for tourists (Richards and Raymond, 2000). This has been exploited recently by luxury fashion retailers and their designers, who expect to take on the role of cultural ambassadors by creating a 'third space', a non-selling area of the store, in their flagship stores, to showcase the story or 'heritage' of the brand through vehicles such as brand exhibitions or brand museums. As Martínez (2007: 2462) indicates, designer stores are now referred to as 'landmarks on the tourist route'. Another trend in fashion tourism appears to be that of seeking to modify private space into public space for tourist consumption (Evans 2003). Atelier visits are an example of this.

Creative tourism relies on the visit being experience-based, as stated by Boswijk *et al.* (2007) who claim that tourists are no longer seeking first-generation, producer-orientated experiences, but look for second- or third-generation experiences, where the distinction between the communities of producers and consumers effectively disappears. This chimed with Richards's (2011: 1246) claim that 'tourists not only visit places, they also make them'. Fashion brands and leading department stores such as Harrods, Harvey Nichols and Selfridges are under increasing pressure to make their stores into an experience, given the rise in tourist leisure shopping, where it is less about the actual purchase and more about the event and experience.

It must be noted that there is a difference between a distinct 'fashion destination' and just a place to buy fashion (Budnarowska, 2012). Fashion products can largely be bought anywhere both offline and online where many designer goods are available globally. There is, though, a more dedicated fashion tourist who seeks to buy from a distinct location, either a distinct retail store, for example Burberry's flagship store in Regent Street, London, or a distinct 'fashion capital', for example Paris. Each type of 'place' serve to offer a distinct experience, which is both desirable and memorable. So how does a place distinguish itself based on its reputation for designer fashion? This is further explored below.

Solomon and Rabolt (2009) suggest that the more affluent and 'super rich' seek out fashion destinations to visit for more than just the shopping itself and desire to be immersed in the experience of the place, especially where the goods sold are not unique to that destination. This could be said to be even truer of so-called 'high-net-worth' [*sic*] individuals (HNWI), including more or less corrupt individuals from China, Russia and the Islamic states who have accumulated obscene wealth. This 'elite' group has the resources to consume what are seen to be 'the best of everything' such as vulgar designer hotels, events, food, leisure activities and general travel. This is seen in events such as 'Ramadan Rush', the annual week of shopping in the UK after Ramadan is finished: in 2014 as much as 69 per cent of the Middle Eastern spending in that period was said to be in the UK, primarily on designer fashion (*Daily Telegraph*, 2014). UK tourism seeks to capitalise on this desire to shop by also providing the complete tourist package of accommodation, food and beverages, and event activities suitable to this market.

Through the provision of a 'fashion hotel' fashion designers have found ways of incorporating themselves into the tourist experience, thereby allowing the fashion tourist to directly experience and 'sample' the fashion designer brand (Miller, 2015). Examples of fashion designer hotels are offered in Table 5.2.

Table 5.2 Fashion designer hotel collaborations

Designer	Location
Karl Lagerfeld	Odyssey, Hotel Metropole, Monaco, France
Versace	Palazzo Versace, Australia's Gold Coast
Missoni	Missoni Hotel, Edinburgh, Scotland
Diane Von Furstenberg	The Grand Piano Suite, Claridges, London
Moschino	Maison Moschino, Milan, Italy
Christian Dior	The Dior Suite, St Regis Hotel, New York, US
Armarni	The Armani Hotel, Dubai and Milan
Bottega	The Bottega Suite, St Regis Hotel, Rome, Italy
Alice Temperley	Alice Temperley Tipi, Mauritius
Ralph Lauren	Round Hill Hotel and Villas resort, Jamaica
Bathing Ape	The Real Bape Suite, Hotel Éclat, Beijing, China
Vivienne Tam	Vivienne Tam Designer Suite, Hotel Icon, Kowloon, Hong Kong
Christian Lacroix	Hotel du Petit Moulin, Paris, France
Wilbert Das (Diesel)	UXUA Casa Hotel and Spa, Bahia, Brazil
Salvatore Ferragamo	Hotel Lungarno, Florence, Italy
Ted Baker	Hilton Hotel, Bournemouth, UK

The above offers evidence of the breakdown of traditional sectorial industries, wherein designer fashion, with a reputation founded on technical capacity to produce high-quality garments, is now an image-based industry providing high-quality consumption experiences (Jansson and Power, 2010). Indeed, Table 5.2 offers evidence of the rising trend not only towards the consumption of physical products, but also towards unique experiences. Solomon and Rabolt (2009: 316) cite Postrel (2004) as claiming that 'people prefer additional experiences over additional possessions as their incomes rise'.

The designer fashion industry has been effective in exploiting the desire for experiences via a number of tourism spectacles. One example is the 'block-buster' exhibition phenomenon (Miller, 2015) wherein a trend has surfaced for fashion designer brands to become the subject of major exhibitions in museums. In addition to McQueen's Savage Beauty exhibition, examples include Vivienne Westwood – 30 years in Fashion at the V&A in 2004 and David Bowie Is in 2013, also at the V&A, London, which featured many of his costumes and footwear. Like McQueen's exhibition, these exhibitions linked fashion, music and popular culture together as heritage, all serving to stimulate fashion tourism. The 'blockbuster' is so called because of the large amount of media attention and income generated from it. It is estimated that the Savage Beauty exhibition at the Metropolitan Museum of Art attracted over 650,000 visitors (Miller, 2015). To date, the same exhibition at the V&A has attracted 11,113 reviews on Tripadvisor. The success of Savage Beauty at London's V&A Museum was such that in order to accommodate unprecedented demand, the decision was made to keep the exhibition open throughout the night for the final two weekends of its run. When the exhibition closed at the beginning of August 2015, a total of 493,043 visitors had seen it, making it the V&A's most visited exhibit to date (V&A, 2015). Further to this, a V&A press release stated:

> Visitors have attended from 87 countries internationally, drawn primarily from the US and Europe but also including Afghanistan, Cambodia, Cayman Islands, East Timor, Ecuador, El Salvador, Kazakhstan, Mauritius, Namibia, Senegal, Suriname and Uzbekistan. Within the UK, people have travelled from Orkney in Scotland, Helston in Cornwall, the Isle of Man and the Channel Islands to see it.
>
> (V&A, 2015)

Table 5.3 illustrates the scope of the fashion exhibition phenomenon through identification of a number of fashion designers whose brand either has embarked on various tours or who, have a museum dedicated to it.

While this may be described as both creative and cultural tourism, the commercial aspect cannot be ignored and fashion designer companies are seeing the potential of museum exhibitions as important marketing tools. Consequently it is not unusual for the companies themselves to contribute to covering installation costs and sponsoring museum venues (Gamerman, 2014). This was evident in Chanel's brand-related exhibitions, Culture Chanel, where growing luxury

Table 5.3 Fashion designer museums and exhibitions

Fashion designer	Exhibition/Location
Patek Philippe	Patek Philippe Museum, dedicated designer-owned museum, Geneva
Van Cleef and Arpels	A Quest for Beauty: The Art of Van Cleef and Arpels, Santa Ana, California, US
Christian Dior	Christian Dior Museum and Garden, Granville, Normandy, France
Bulgari	The Art of Bulgari: La Dolce Vita and Beyond, 1950–1990, temporary exhibition, various locations
Cartier	Cartier: Le Style et l'Histoire, Grand Palais, Paris
Louis Vuitton	Voyages exhibition, National Museum of China, China
Hermès	Hermès Leather Forever, world tour including Tokyo and London
Chanel	'Little Black Jacket', World tour including UK, US, Canada and Asia; 'Culture Chanel', World tour including Russia and China
Alexander McQueen	Savage Beauty, New York and London

markets, for example Russia and China, have been targeted as locations (Gamerman, 2014).

In all, it is evident that a highly commercial culture is embedded within fashion tourism. As with the hotel and museum fashion consumption experiences offered above, which both serve to provide income for the fashion designer brand, 'living museums' also function to bring income to fashion companies. Traditionally the concept of living museums involves recreated historical settings that people can visit to experience themed historical periods and immerse themselves in what they could have been like. As far as the concept of 'living museums' goes for the UK fashion industry, there is a tension between maintaining the 'heritage' of a brand and of UK fashion in general, and being at the so-called cutting edge. 'Living museums' could be said to be an appropriate way of describing the traditional aspects of a department store such as Libertys or Harrods in the UK, which trade to an extent on their historical setting and quintessential British image (in spite of foreign ownership). Brands that could be said to have successfully managed to modernise and digitalise this 'living museum' experience in a contemporary setting are Selfridges in Oxford Street, London, and also Burberry's flagship Regent Street store. Popular with tourists, these brands trade on both their British heritage alongside their ability to add events and present theatre and technology to many aspects of the shopping experience. To illustrate this point, examples of creative and novel initiatives in the form of events at stores, use of technologies and retail are identified in Table 5.4.

Further examples of digital consumption experiences include the London Fashion Week's (LFW) engagement with digital content throughout London Fashion Week in February 2015. Examples are offered in Table 5.5.

Table 5.4 Fashion designers as living museums

Fashion designer	Event
Burberry	The London Regent Street store has been designed as a physical manifestation of the Burberry website, known as Burberry World Live. One example is information available for consumers to access digitally while in the store's fitting rooms.
Michael Kors	'What's in your Kors' digital media campaign, which packs an imaginary handbag for trips to various locations, e.g. Paris, Rome, Milan.
Liberty of London	The British Design Open Call event wherein designers and creative talents are given an opportunity to present their designs to an expert panel.
Selfridges	Hot Air, the retailer's own broadcasting channel, contains both video and audio content.

Table 5.5 Digital consumption experiences: London Fashion Week, February 2015

329,800 mentions of #LFW on Twitter during London Fashion Week SS15
120,000 images tagged #LFW on Instagram during LFW SS15
94% of Twitter users are aware of London Fashion Week and 74% have an interest in LFW
Nine large-scale digital outdoor screens livestreaming the Hunter Original show in cities
    such as London, Manchester, Birmingham and Glasgow

Source: www.britishfashioncouncil.co.uk/pressreleases/London-Fashion-Week–British-Fashion-Industry-Facts–Figures-AW15. accessed 29 August 2015.

While a fashion consumption experience can be obtained via place, the retail space that functions as a tourist destination, a whole city can serve to offer a fashion tourism experience. Jansson and Power's (2010) study of Milan offers a clear example of this, indicating that the city functions as a *brand platform for cultural industries*, which acts as an attraction to both visitors and investors.

The Global Language Monitor annually announces the top global fashion cities. The list below is the top 10 for 2014.

1 New York
2 Paris
3 London
4 Los Angeles
5 Barcelona
6 Rome
7 Berlin
8 Sydney
9 Antwerp
10 Shanghai

It could be said that the most successful fashion cities are those that are intrinsically linked to the creation and production of fashion, termed 'textourism', which is tourism associated with the textile industry (Crippin, 2000: 271), and these destinations form what are commonly termed the original 'fashion capitals' of the world. For example, Paris, the home of *haute couture*, and Milan since the Middle Ages have manufactured luxury goods. In fact, some theorists such as Moore and Doyle (2010) believe that luxury fashion only truly comes from places that have authentic heritage through the manufacturing of their own products, so it is less about the designer and more about the place and the craftsmanship associated with that place that command the status and attention from consumers and tourists. An example of this is organised visits to Chanel's couture atelier in Paris, which serve to augment brand bonding with both the product and the city in which it is produced (Mitchell and Orwig, 2002). This view is reinforced by Martinez (2007) who claims that designer brands with this heritage are able to be 'mythologised and historicised'.

Fashion capitals are distinguished by both their history in apparel creation and production, and their 'distinctive metropolitan cultures of consumption': their fashion consumers (Gilbert, 2006: 6). Richards (2011) proposes the notion that where tangible or authentic heritage is lacking, intangible heritage should be created by the creative industries of the destination such as fashion, in order to ensure brand distinctiveness and attract the 'creative class' tourist (Campbell, 2011).

It is evident from the above that fashion drives tourism culturally, historically and imminently (i.e. the next best place to see fashion). Tourists will visit a place with fashion as the primary motivation either to immerse themselves in the creative culture that has historically been driven by the designer fashion industry linked to the place or to experience fashion at the cutting edge through fashion shows, exhibitions or merely shopping at a fashion destination. Quoting from John Agnew, a political geographer, Breward and Gilbert (2006) indicate that fashion is now seen to play an active role in 'spatialising the world'. While once considered a secondary reason for travel (Jansen-Verbeke, 1986), fashion and fashion consumption have recently been elevated to become a primary tourist activity that determines (or strongly influences) both the travel destination and the travel itinerary (Swarbrooke and Horner, 2006). The fashion city is now an established marker of global competition between cities and forms part of the broader strategy to promote what have become known as the 'creative' or 'cultural' industries (Gilbert, 2006). This rise in 'urban tourism' stems from a desire to experience places in a different way, alongside our global knowledge of the fashions and trends associated with the destination. Some destinations are attractive for their historic and cultural fashions, some for their newly found fashion status, and others for their 'exotic' and 'traditional' fashion as intangible cultural heritage. Often this is linked to the luxury brands associated with a destination, and whether those brands are deemed to offer authentic 'heritage', 'culture' or a specific 'design signature', as described by Fionda and Moore (2009) in their 'Components of a luxury fashion brand' model.

Promotion of fashion tourism

In addition to enhancing a city's cultural heritage, it is also acknowledged that designer fashion has a positive effect on the economy of a city, attracting tourism and direct foreign investment (Pratt, 2014). This concept is not new. As Gilbert (2006) points out, cities from as early as the late nineteenth century have promoted themselves as centres for luxury shopping and, together with both fashion magazines and tourist guides, have contributed to engendering an understanding of the relationship between design, fashion and tourism.

Due to the complexity and scale of the fashion industry and its close relationships to other industries, the British Fashion Council is cautious in providing any definitive data on the direct economic impact of the fashion industry on the UK economy, states: 'Fashion directly contributes nearly £21 billion to the UK economy. It also has an indirect economic impact, in encouraging spending in other industries' (British Fashion Council, 2010).

Fashion's contribution to other industries include: events and hotel industries (e.g. London Fashion Week), museums (e.g. Victoria and Albert Museum, London, and The Fashion Museum, Bath), advertising and marketing (e.g. PUSH PR and label PR) among others, all of which contribute to the overall marketing and economic strategy of 'Brand Britain' (a brand equity vehicle established by the UK in 2007). With regard to tourism and culture, the British Fashion Council's *The Value of Fashion Report* (2010) considers the direct and indirect impact that the fashion industry has upon the wider economy and, under the banner f 'Wider and Catalytic Impacts', states (p. 21):

> **Tourism** – the UK fashion industry indirectly enhances the UK tourism industry by encouraging more international tourists to visit the UK, and their spending supports a number of jobs in the UK.
> **Culture** – The UK fashion industry contributes to what we might more widely consider to be the UK's cultural landscape.

It is arguable whether the British Fashion Council and the tourism industry bodies are doing enough to ensure that design and designer fashion are at the forefront of the 'Brand Britain' strategy. In comparison with other world fashion cities such as the established Paris, Milan and New York, and the emerging destinations of Dubai, Tokyo, Sydney, Los Angeles, Barcelona, Madrid and Amsterdam, design, fashion and tourism are not typically promoted together in London and the UK within one cohesive cultural and creative industries strategy. For example, reports produced by the British Fashion Council such as *The Value of Fashion Report* make no mention of the contribution of fashion tourism as adding value to the UK fashion industry.

In the UK, fashion events and shopping are often seen as a secondary tourist activity, whereas other countries and cities have recognised the value of promoting dedicated fashion tourism, and the UK seems to be somewhat behind on this to date, only recently fully connecting to the significance of globally recognised events such as LFW, which began in 1984 (New York Fashion Week started in

1943, Milan in 1958 and Paris in 1973 although its precursor was 1914). However, efforts are being made to change this. LFW has done much to assist in developing London as a tourist destination offering a sense of modern identity to a place that can also have the perception of being passé (think London Pearly King and Queen, Beefeaters and stereotypical use of the Union Jack and London Underground signage). The fashion tourist can often be split between wanting the quintessential British fashion experience and that of the cutting-edge fashion now associated with UK designers (Ashworth, 2003). In fact, fashion designer brands that seem most popular with international tourists appear to be those that reflect some elements of the British culture and heritage that are promoted to foreign markets. Brands that fall into this category include Burberry, Mulberry and designers like McQueen, Vivienne Westwood, Paul Smith, Lulu Guinness and Anya Hindmarch, all of whom reference UK culture and have drawn upon the Union Jack in either or both the design or the marketing of their goods. Perhaps the best example of this was McQueen's Union Jack coat designed in collaboration with David Bowie and worn by Bowie on his *Earthling* album cover. Bowie also wore it for the press coverage of the David Bowie Is exhibition at the V&A. As the *Daily Telegraph* (2012) stated: 'This coat combines elements of classic British design, represented by the Union Jack and expert tailoring learnt by McQueen on Savile Row, with an iconoclastic and subversive punk aesthetic' (*Telegraph*, 2012).

While British fashion designers themselves and the British Fashion Council's LFW have done much to promote Britain, other agencies are also engaging in promoting fashion tourism, for example Visit Britain's initiative in 2014 when it commissioned a series of short fashion films showcasing the designers and fashion icons that the UK is famous for globally. These films were used as a marketing initiative via the Visit Britain TV channel in order to promote fashion as an established cultural and creative industry in the UK. The films were released in the lead-up to LFW. While the success of these films must be acknowledged, with 4.8 million views as of 1 November 2014 (Visit Britain, 2014), this campaign could be seen as a one-off in terms of an on-going strategy to link design, fashion and tourism together within the UK. At the same time, Visit Britain has focused on other promotion activities albeit mainly outside the UK itself. Since 2011 it has been involved in a collaboration with Bloomingdales in New York termed 'All things British'. Bloomingdales created quintessential British-themed window displays in order to promote travel packages to New York, but the overall benefit to the UK inbound travel industry is difficult to determine from this type of strategy.

A further observation of Visit Britain's promotion of UK fashion tourism is that it is too London-centric. This is often the case for countries where a clear fashion capital has been determined, but given that designer fashion is steeped in heritage and authenticity, the history of UK fashion goes well beyond London, from the manufacture of clothing in the North of England, to the design and manufacture of authentic wool garments and iconic fashion textiles such as Harris Tweed and tartan in Scotland. While Visit Scotland pays some attention to the tartan heritage, it is not apparently a primary focus for it either, with far more attention paid to food and beverages than to textiles and fashion. These cultural symbols of heritage-led fashion seem largely forgotten in the recent tourism strategies of the UK through the respective fashion and tourism councils. This is a consequence of tourism not being formally recognised as a component sector of the creative industries in the UK and its weak structural links with the fashion sector.

According to the cultural policy of the British Council (2010):

> 'For many creative businesspeople the cultural value of their work is at least as important as its economic value. In a globalized, connected world many places are wrestling with the question of how to maintain their cultural identity without becoming 'living museums'.

Taking into account the above quote, it may be the case that agencies including the British Fashion Council and Visit Britain are more focused on the commercial value of fashion tourism than the cultural value.

Theory underpinning fashion tourism consumption

Tourist destinations are often determined by factors such as escapism and a sense of aspiration, which lends itself to experiencing designer fashion through visiting fashion destinations for leisure activities related to design and fashion. The media stimuli responsible for driving this were traditionally elitist fashion magazines and catwalk shows, but Khamis and Munt (2010) argue that the influence and reach of fashion are no longer constrained to these media. More recently, the diffusion of fashion has sped up through digital communications and now fashion and travel blogs promote instant trends in fashion and fashion travel, and consumers are taking more ownership of their knowledge of these sectors through engaging with blogs and vlogs (Pham, 2011). This in turn has led to consumer desire to design their own bespoke travel packages and itineraries, sparking the rise in online travel agents (OTAs) and websites where consumers 'mix and match' traditional holiday packages with more modern ways to experience a place, such as fashion tourism events and excursions. One example of such an agency is Exclusive Fashion Tours, which caters specifically for fashion tourists interested in the Made in Italy label.

In terms of the experience drivers, it could be said that media stimuli drive the interest in visiting fashion destinations. This is discussed by Goossens (2000: 305) who cites Schofield's (1996) take on Baudrillard's 'hyperreal society', claiming 'one no longer consumes products, but signs and images'. Fashion plays a key role in determining what is on trend for consumption across a number of the service industries. In all, tourists now view places as needing to be experienced, immersing themselves in the perceived culture of a destination and looking to creative spectacles, spaces and tourism (Campbell, 2011) to provide these 'experience environments'. This links to the 'experience economy' first proposed by Pine and Gilmore (1999). Tourists now seek to experience environments through their tourist experiences in order to 'create a "cultural" space connecting tourism, consumption and style of life' (Richards, 2011, citing Zukin, 1995: 83). In a digital world, where people often feel disconnected even though they are seemingly more connected, consumers use tourist experiences to lose themselves in a different culture. Places are capitalising on this by creating 'consumptional identities' through the manipulation of the culture and creative resources of a destination (Richards, 2011). The symbolic nature of this type of tourism has seen designer fashion become intrinsically entwined in this experience in recent years. Using Hofstede's (1991) 'cultural onion' model, the consumer practice of tourism includes seeking out symbols, heroes and rituals. The symbols often now sought can be the need to connect with a place through design and fashion, with the heroes being fashion designers and the rituals including shopping, fashion events and exhibitions, and experiencing fashion production first hand. Application of Hofstede's (1991) cultural onion for a UK fashion tourist experience is offered in Table 5.6.

Fashion has been incorporated into the creative industries in a post-modern society where people seek to distinguish themselves by their consumption patterns, particularly seeking symbolic values through their consumption practices (Richards, 2011, citing Bourdieu, 1984, and Wynne and O'Connor, 1998). Places have become brands in their own right, based upon the portfolio of brands and brand activity that exists within these destinations under the banner of the cultural and creative industries. Consumers relate to fashion brands for the purpose of status signalling (Tynan *et al.*, 2010) and the associations of luxury and 'authenticity' that a designer fashion brand can signify (Moore and Doyle, 2010). Friedman (2011) discusses the notion of a new wave of 'accessories tourism' that has emerged from the need (of some people) to portray status through luxury fashion consumption. Accessories represent accessible fashion for some and as such has democratised designer fashion for the global mass market. As Hickman (2006) indicates, people may not be willing to pay hundreds of pounds for a designer outfit they may wear only a few times. However, they may be more inclined to pay hundreds of pounds for a handbag they can use every day.

Han *et al.* (2010) define four types of fashion consumer in terms of purchase behaviour for the purposes of status signalling: *patricians* ('old money' who seek inconspicuous branding and do not seek status from consumption);

Table 5.6 Application of Hofstede's cultural onion to a UK fashion tourist experience

Practices	
Symbols	Mulberry Bayswater Bag; McQueen skull print scarf; Paul Smith stripe cuff links
Heroes	Vivienne Westwood, Alexander McQueen, Sarah Burton, Paul Smith
Rituals	Socially and individually: visits to Selfridges, Dover Street Market
Values	Sustainable fashion, designer fashion

parvenus (social climbers who crave status and seek conspicuous brands that convey wealth); *poseurs* (who crave status but lack the financial means, so will often seek out imitations); and *proletarians* (resistant to status signalling and not trying to stand out or fit in). In terms of capitalising on the consumer who craves status, *parvenus* and *poseurs* are the main groups susceptible to strong brand marketing that conveys symbolic consumption and status signalling. These consumers are often active co-creators (Shirky, 2010) and convey their status not only through the way that they dress, but through all aspects of consumption, from gadgets and lifestyle accessories to food and travel, and they also often feel the need to disseminate their consumption to others through such media as blogs, which then in turn encourage others to want a similar consumption experience. It is these consumers who will stay in the fashion designer hotels, and visit the latest fashion exhibitions, events and retail stores, ensuring that they immerse themselves in the full fashion tourism experience. Alternatively, the kinds of tourism experiences that *patricians* would potentially be interested in would be, for example, visiting Brora's flagship store off Sloane Square, London, to make a cashmere purchase or making a visit to the Isle of Harris, Scotland, to see Outer Hebrides weavers at work via a Harris Tweed tour. Alternatively, *proletarians* may be interested in visiting 430 Kings Road, London, to see the site where Vivienne Westwood and Malcolm McLaren's first 'punk' clothes shop, Sex, was located.

Campbell (2011) postulates that public sector intervention in creative development involves three approaches: creative industries (e.g. fashion), creative cities (e.g. tourism) and creative class (e.g. the tourist). The creative class tourist, according to Campbell, either works in the creative field or craves creativity in his or her life. This conceptualisation relates clearly to Richard Florida's much-criticised notion of the 'creative class', as discussed in the Introduction and conclusions in this volume. These days, digital media have heightened a 'tendency toward seeking leisure experiences that stretch one's limits and provide novel stimuli' (Goossens, 2000: 303), which fashion tourism could be said to do by combining a desirable lifestyle activity with a unique way of experiencing a place.

Swarbrooke and Horner (2006), quoting from Frommer and Frommer (1996), claim that tourists crave new ways to visit old destinations for status consumption and this is why fashion has become more of a primary motivator, and is responsible for the rebranding and regeneration of several places as fashion destinations or fashion world cities. An example of this is Antwerp, Belgium, which has rebranded itself as a fashion destination (Martínez, 2007). Kaat Debo, director of the Fashion Museum in Antwerp, suggests that this has become the case due to the fashion 'creatives' who live in and are associated with the city. She points out the importance of having a fashion museum in such cities in that tourists often are not able to visit ateliers as these are busy working. Therefore the museum serves to provide them with the direct fashion experience they desire (Beljanski, 2010).

Fashion destinations

Fashion destinations need to be relevant and contemporary, and will need to continuously reinvent the experience in order for tourists to keep visiting. For example, Richards (2011, citing Crewe and Beverstock, 1998) asserts that places that seek to distinguish themselves through 'consumptional identities' need to reconstruct the place as a centre of consumption by manipulating its culture and creative resources. Antwerp has successfully done this through the establishment of its fashion museum. Successful regeneration looks at the 'fashion mix' and mixes expected brands with the avant-garde (Martínez, 2007). This appears to be at odds with the DCMS (2015) definition of fashion, which is placed in the creative industries group 'Design: product, graphic and fashion design'.

Richards and Wilson (2006) believe that the success of a creative destination relies upon the use of *creative spectacles*, *creative spaces* and *creative tourism*. Creative spectacles can take the form of events such as fashion weeks, wherein creative spaces require the creation of what are termed cultural districts (for example, London's Hackney Fashion Hub), creative 'hot spots' (Richards, 2011), creative clusters (Evans, 2009) or creative precincts (Hee *et al.*, 2008).

As indicated earlier in the chapter, fashion has a wider remit, for example in regard to retailers that are not linked exclusively with designer fashion but still attract consumers and tourists for their creative and cultural associations. Examples include the vintage retailers clustered in and around Portobello Road, London; Brick Lane, London; Edinburgh's Grassmarket; and the Northern Quarter, Manchester. Visit Britain has a web page dedicated to vintage fashion shopping. Likewise, the website Creativetourist.com, which prides itself on uncovering 'the best art and cultural events, and publishes insider guides to some of the UK's most creative destinations' (Creativetourist.com, 2015), also has web pages dedicated to vintage fashion shopping. Beyond vintage, examples of destination fashion retailers which are successful in attracting consumers to travel distances to visit them and serve to provide innovation, offer differentiation and a lasting memory include Cricket, Liverpool, Cruise, Glasgow and Flannels, Manchester. The Cricket menswear store in Liverpool is described on the tourist website, Visit Liverpool, as a 'legendary' boutique. Flannels features on the Visit Manchester website. These examples, again serve to identify flaws in the DCMS definition of what is considered to be a creative industry and shows that the lines are blurred.

Conclusion

> Fashion is an impulse that leads the trends of the times, a banner of the cultural image of an International metropolis. In the world today, the vanguard of fashion is a city's symbol of dynamism.
>
> (Zhang, 2005: 87, cited by Gilbert, 2006: 3)

Since the emergence of the DCMS creative industries framework in the UK and its 'export' as a model, as discussed in the Introduction to this volume, it can be acknowledged that the world has changed significantly, largely in terms of the digital shift towards consumer mobility, connectivity and the desire to co-create, meaning that the prominence of cultural and creative industries has increased immensely in economic terms. Market economies are now more reliant upon the service economy for growth (Potts *et al.*, 2008), and as such the cultural and creative industries are now widely recognised as contributors to a country's economic growth. The digital economy has opened up the creative industries to global audiences that are now more creatively educated (or indoctrinated by global brands) and want first-hand cultural and creative experiences based on what they have seen online and in offline media. Designer fashion plays a key role in this economic growth, largely through exports and fashion commerce, but also through the cultural heritage and status that the UK's and other countries' fashion industries hold worldwide. This in turn promotes fashion tourism for the UK, both domestic and international.

The chapter illustrates the complexity that exists between fashion, tourism, the creative industries and commerce. Further to this, the chapter establishes that the fashion designer industry is defined within national boundaries. In addition, the fashion industry itself touches a number of other industries. As outlined by the OECD (2009), the main drivers for developing creative and tourism policies are preserving heritage; economic development; regeneration; and developing a cultural understanding. This chapter has served to illustrate that fashion tourism contributes to fulfilling all of these. Second, through the examination of the novel initiatives and creativity of fashion designers themselves and the retailers and marketers working in the fashion designer sector, the chapter functions to illustrate that fashion tourism is very much embedded in the creative industries. This may be best summed up by Ed Vaizey, Minister for the Creative Industries in 2010, who stated in reference to the British Fashion Council's *Value of Fashion Report* (2010):

> British Fashion has the talent, creativity and skills to rival anywhere in the world … fashion makes a significant contribution to the UK economy and confirms British fashion's status as one of our most important creative industries.

References

Ashworth, G.J. (2003) Heritage, Identity and Places for Tourists and Host Communities. In Singh, S., Timothy, D.J. and Dowling, R.K. (eds) *Tourism in Destination Communities*, Oxford and Cambridge, MA: CABI Publishing, pp. 79–97

Bada, O. (2013) *The Emerging Role of Fashion Tourism*, unpublished thesis, http://publications.theseus.fi/bitstream/handle/10024/63259/Olubukola%20Bada%20%20Final%20Thesis.pdf, accessed 20 September 2015

Beljanski, T. (2010) Interview with Kaat Debo, *UGLED Magazine*, 10 September 2010, http://ugledmagazine.blogspot.co.uk/2010/09/interview-with-kaat-debo-director-of.html, accessed 30 August 2015

Boswijk, A., Thijsson, T. and Peelen, E. (2007) *The Experience Economy: A New Perspective*, London: Pearson

Bourdieu, P. (1984) *Distinction: A Social Critique of the Judgment of Taste*, translated by R. Nice, Cambridge, MA: Harvard University Press

Breward, C. and Gilbert, D. (2006) *Fashion World Cities*, Oxford: Berg

British Council (2010) *Mapping the Creative Industries: A Toolkit*, London: British Council, Creative Economy Unit

British Council (2011) *What are Creative Industries and Creative Economy, Creative Cities?*, http://creativecities.britishcouncil.org/creative-industries/what_are_creative_industries_and_creative_economy, accessed 28 August 2015

British Fashion Council (2010) *The Value of Fashion Report*, London: BFC

Budnarowska, C. (2012) Fashion Retail Formats as Tourist Retail Destinations and Attractions. In McIntyre, C. (ed.) *Tourism and Retail: The Psychogeography of Liminal Consumption*, London: Routledge, pp. 169–186

Campbell, P. (2011) You Say 'Creative', and I Say 'Creative', *Journal of Policy Research in Tourism, Leisure and Events* 3: 18–30

Creative Review (2015) *Alexander McQueen: Savage Beauty at the V&A*, www.creative review.co.uk/cr-blog/2015/march/alexander-mcqueen-savage-beauty, accessed 29 August 2015

Creativetourist.com (2015) *About Us*, www.creativetourist.com/about, accessed 18 September 2015

Crewe, L. and Beverstock, J. (1998) Fashioning the City: Cultures of Consumption in Contemporary Urban Spaces, *Geoforum* 29(3): 287–308

Crippin, K. (2000) The Threads that Tie Textiles to Tourism. In Hitchcock, M. and Nuryanti, W. (eds) *Building on Batik: The Globalization of the Craft Community*, Aldershot: Ashgate, pp. 271–284

Daily Telegraph (2012) David Bowie Is Retrospective at the V&A: What to Expect, *Daily Telegraph*, 12 September 2012

Daily Telegraph (2014) The Ramadan Rush Brings Arab Shoppers to UK Stores, *Daily Telegraph*, 28 July 2014

Department of Culture, Media and Sport (DCMS) (2015) *Creative Industries Economic Estimates*, London: DCMS

Evans, G. (2003) Urban Planning in East London. In Kirkham, N. and Miles, M. (eds) *Cultures and Settlement: Advances in Urban Futures*, Volume 3, Bristol: Intellect Books, pp. 15–30

Evans, G. (2009) From Cultural Quarters to Creative Clusters – Creative Spaces in the New City Economy, *Urban Studies* 46: 1003–1040

Fionda, A.M. and Moore, C.M. (2009) The Anatomy of the Luxury Fashion Brand, *Journal of Brand Management* 16(5–6): 347–363

Friedman, V. (2011) The Rise of Accessories Tourism, *Financial Times*, 13 October

Friedman, W.A. and Jones, G. (2011) Creative Industries in History, *Business History Review* 85(2): 237–244

Frommer, A. and Frommer, P. (1996) *Arthur Frommer's New World of Travel*, New York: Macmillan

Gamerman, E. (2014) Are Museums Selling Out?, *Wall Street Journal*, www.wsj.com/articles/are-museums-selling-out-1402617631, accessed 28 August 2015

Gilbert, D. (2006) From Paris to Shanghai: The Changing Geographies of Fashion World Cities. In Breward, C. and Gilbert, D. (eds) *Fashion's World Cities*, Oxford: Berg, pp. 3–32

Goossens, C. (2000) Tourism Information and Pleasure Motivation, *Annals of Tourism Research* 27(2): 301–321

Guardian (2013) Tourists Splurge 4.5bn in Shops, *Guardian*, 27 February

Han, Y.J., Nunes, J.C. and Drèze, X. (2010) Signaling Status with Luxury Goods: The Role of Brand Prominence, *Journal of Marketing* 74: 15–30

Hee, Limin, Schroepfer, Thomas, Nanxi, Su and Ze, Li (2008) From Post-industrial Land-scape to Creative Precincts: Emergent Spaces in Chinese Cities, *International Development Planning Review* 30(3): 249–266

Hickman, M. (2006) How Accessories Have Saved the Fashion Industry, *The Independent*, 9 March 2006

Hofstede, G.H. (1991) *Cultures and Organizations: Software of the Mind*, London and New York: McGraw-Hill

Jansen-Verbeke, M. (1986) Inner-city Tourism: Resources, Tourists and Promoters, *Annals of Tourism Research*, 13(1): 79–100

Jansson, J. and Power, D. (2010) Fashioning a Global City: Global City Brand Channels in the Fashion and Design Industries, *Regional Studies* 44(7): 889–904

Khamis, S. and Munt, A. (2010) The Three Cs of Fashion Media Today: Convergence, Creativity and Control, *Journal of Media Arts Culture Collection* 8(2): 1–15

Lee, Y. (2013) Effect on the Tourism Motivation and Tourism Destination Image Affected to Shopping Tourism Destination Choice, *International Journal of Digital Content Technology and its Applications* 7(11): 416–421

Leiper, N. (1979) The Framework of Tourism, *Annals of Tourism Research*, October/December: 390–407

Martínez, J.G. (2007) Selling Avant-garde: How Antwerp Became a Fashion Capital (1990–2002), *Urban Studies* 44(12): 2449–2464

Miller, J. (2015) The Emergence of Fashion Tourism as a Valuable City Asset, Bilbao Fashion Forum, May, www.youtube.com/watch?v=WhwjBi2q0EI, accessed 29 August 2015

Mitchell, M.A. and Orwig, R.A. (2002) Consumer Experience Tourism and Brand Bonding, *Journal of Product and Brand Management* 11(1): 30–39

Moore, C. and Doyle, S. (2010) The Evolution of the Luxury Fashion Retailing Business Model, conference presentation at the 17th Recent Advances in Retailing and Services Science Conference (EIRASS), 2–5 July, Istanbul, Turkey

OECD (2009) *Tourism and the Creative Economy*, Geneva: OECD Studies in Tourism

Pham, M. (2011) Blog Ambition: Fashion, Feelings and the Political Economy of the Digital Raced Body, *Camera Obscura* 26(76): 1–37

Pine, B.J. and Gilmore, J.H. (1999) *The Experience Economy*, Cambridge, MA: Harvard Business School Press

Postrel, V. (2003) *The Substance of Style: How the Rise of Aesthetic Value Is Remaking Commerce, Culture and Consciousness*, New York: Harper Perennial

Potts, J., Cunningham, S., Hartley, J. and Ormerod, P. (2008) Social Network Markets: A New Definition of the Creative Industries, *Journal of Cultural Economics* 32: 167–185

Pouillard, V. (2011) Design Piracy in the Fashion Industries of Paris and New York in the Interwar Years, *Business History Review* 85(2): 319–344

Pratt, A. (2014) *Cities, the Cultural Dimension. Future of Cities Working Paper*. Canberra: Australian Government Office for Science

Richards, G. (2011) Creativity and Tourism: The State of the Art, *Annals of Tourism Research* 38(4): 1225–1253

Richards, G. and Raymond C. (2000) Creative Tourism, *ATLAS News* 23: 16–20

Richards, G. and Wilson, J. (2006) Developing Creativity in Tourist Experiences: A Solution to the Serial Reproduction of Culture?, *Tourism Management* 27(6): 1209–1223

Schofield, P. (1996) Cinematographic Images of a City – Alternative Heritage Tourism in Manchester, *Tourism Management* 17(5): 333–340

Shirky, C. (2010) *Cognitive Surplus: Creativity & Generosity in a Connected Age*, London: Penguin Books

Solomon, M.R. and Rabolt, N.J. (2009) *Consumer Behavior in Fashion*, Upper Saddle River, NJ: Pearson/Prentice Hall

Swarbrooke, J. and Horner, S. (2006) *Consumer Behaviour in Tourism*, Oxford: Butterworth Heinemann

ThinkExist.com (2015) http://thinkexist.com/quotes/coco_chanel, accessed 28 August 2015

Tynan, C., McKechnie, S. and Chhuon, C. (2010) Co-creating Value for Luxury Brands, *Journal of Business Research* 63(11): 1156–1163

V&A (2015) Around-the-clock Opening Announced for Final Weekends of Alexander McQueen: Savage Beauty, News Release, www.vam.ac.uk/__data/assets/pdf_file/0004/256918/Savage-Beauty-Press-Release-Late-openings.pdf, accessed 28 August 2015

Visit Britain (2014) www.1185films.com/assets/visit-britain-case-study.pdf, accessed 1 September 2015

Wynne, D. and O'Connor, J. (1998) Consumption and the Postmodern City, *Urban Studies* 35(5–6): 841-864

Zaiden, E.A. (2015) Tourism Shopping and new Urban Entertainment: A Case Study of Dubai, *Journal of Vacation Marketing* 7: 1–13

Zhang, R. (2005) Greetings the World with our Smiles. Interview with Chu Yunmao, Director of the City Image Institute of Donghua University, *Shanghai Expo 2010 Magazine*, February: 87–88

Zukin, S. (1995) *The Cultures of Cities*, Cambridge, MA: Blackwell

6 Urban planning, architecture and the making of creative spaces

Ian Strange

Introduction

This chapter explores a reconfiguring relationship between planning, architecture and the creative industries. Through its discussion, it addresses the ways in which planning for the built environment of the creative industries contributes to establishing tourist and/or creative spaces. The chapter traces the development of policy in this area as it attempts to provide a framework in which the development and construction of creative spaces of quality design are promoted and established. The chapter offers a narrative that reveals the tensions and conflicts inherent in the management and regulation of urban planning and architecture and their relationship with tourism and the creative economy. First, it discusses the process of how the cultural industries are mapped in the UK in relation to architecture as a creative occupation. This offers a largely descriptive account of the mapping exercises undertaken and what they reveal about the economic geography of the UK's creative sector. Second, it considers some of the literature related to the development of creative cities and the creative economy, exploring its urban focus and the way urban planning is associated with developing creative spaces. Third, the chapter examines some of the issues related to the interrelationships between architecture and the planning of creative spaces in the context of urban tourism and place promotion. Although it uses examples related to the experience of England and the rest of the UK, the chapter also considers the relationships between the development of architecture, urban planning and the creative economy internationally.

The mapping of creative industries

The creative industries were defined initially in the UK in the government's *Creative Industries Mapping Document* (DCMS, 2001). Here they were defined as 'those industries which have their origin in individual creativity, skill and talent and which have a potential for wealth and job creation through the generation and exploitation of intellectual property' (DCMS, 2011, p. 6). This definition resulted in a classification into 13 sub-groups that was essentially a 'best judgement' of what constituted the creative industries (Creative Skillset, 2013, p. 6).

This conceptualisation has not gone uncriticised, as the definition, classification and methodology for assessing what the creative contribution to economic growth might have been highly contested (Bakhshi *et al.*, 2013, 2015; Creative Skillset, 2013). While not wishing to enter into a full discussion of this debate, it is worth noting that the approaches to mapping and assessing the contribution of the creative industries (let alone what counts as a creative industry) have moved to using what has come to be known as the 'dynamic mapping methodology'.[1] Bakhshi *et al.*'s study *A Dynamic Mapping of the UK's Creative Industries*,[2] introduced the notion of creative intensity as a measure for establishing a new classification of the creative industries as it sought to work its way through what it argued was a less than rigorous approach to understanding what the creative industries are and what the creative economy comprises. Here, what determines whether or not an industry is defined as 'creative' is the extent to which it 'employs a significant proportion of creative people, as identified by those being employed in a creative occupation' (Creative Skillset, 2013, p. 11). As a method, creative intensity, Bakhshi *et al.* argued, could help distinguish

> 'creative industries' from other industries which also employ creative talent … [because] … although large numbers of individuals are employed in creative occupations in many industries, only a small number of these – the 'creative industries' – have exceptionally high levels of creative intensity.
>
> (pp. 6–7)

In January 2014 the dynamic mapping methodology and creative intensity approach were adopted by DCMS as its official measure for developing economic estimates of the creative industries. The outcome of this was the identification of nine creative sectors with 30 individual occupations and 31 specific industries (DCMS, 2014). Based on this methodology, the most recent national data on the creative industries (Bakhshi *et al.*, 2013; DCMS, 2015) suggest that total employment in the creative economy in the UK stands at approximately 2.8 million jobs and that the number of jobs in the creative industries (including creative and support jobs) is 1.8 million.[3]

The UK geography of this creative economy is very uneven, with a high concentration of the workforce in London and the South East of England (Bakhshi *et al.*, 2015, p. 5). For example, 16.4 per cent of jobs are located in London compared to 5.4 per cent the North East of England. In the creative industries specifically this unevenness continues. For example, one in 17 of all jobs was in the creative industries sector (5.8 per cent) in 2014. However, this ranged from one in 30 jobs in Northern Ireland to one in eight jobs in London. Overall, nearly one-third of all creative industry jobs (31.8 per cent) are based in London (DCMS, 2015, p. 6). Clearly, the creative economy is significant for London, accounting for 15.5 per cent of all jobs, compared with 8.3 per cent for the total UK workforce (Bakhshi *et al.*, 2015, p. 26). However, the geography of current growth in the sector reveals a slightly more complex picture. Bakhshi *et al.*'s, latest research (2015, p. 27) suggests that the fastest growing parts of the UK's creative economy over this period have been the East of England, the West Midlands and the North East of England. With the exception of Scotland, which has experienced a negative growth rate on average in its creative economy over this period, London has been the slowest growing region.

Both the creative economy and creative industries employ fewer women than the UK economy as a whole. In 2014, 36.1 per cent of jobs in the creative economy and 36.7 per cent of jobs in the creative industries were filled by women. For the UK economy as a whole, 47.2 per cent of jobs were filled by women (DCMS, 2015, p. 7). In terms of ethnicity, in 2014 11 per cent of jobs in the creative economy were filled by people from black, Asian and minority ethnic (BAME) communities. Similarly, 11 per cent of jobs in the creative industries were filled by BAME workers. Between 2013 and 2014, there was an 8 per cent increase in BAME workers in the creative industries compared with a 5.1 per cent increase for white workers (DCMS, 2015, p. 7).

Mapping architecture as a creative occupation

One of the sectors included in the original DCMS classification was architecture. Despite some changes in the way the mapping of this broad sector has been undertaken, architecture as a sector within the classification of the creative industries, remains. As a creative industry group, architecture has four creative occupations associated with it using the Standard Occupational Classification (SOC) codes 2010 (see Table 6.1).

This grouping accounts for 7 per cent of creative industry employment (Creative Skillset, 2013), with a creative intensity of 64 per cent (Bakhshi *et al.*, 2015). In terms of economic impact, the architecture sector produced £3.6 billion of gross value added in 2013, a rise of 2.7 per cent from 2012 (£3.5 billion). Between 2008 and 2013, architecture's GVA increased by an average of 0.2 per cent per year. The most recent data on employment in architecture are equally revealing. For example, there are some 136,000 architecture-related UK jobs in the creative economy. The geography of this employment reflects the unevenness of the creative economy and creative industries more generally, with the largest concentrations of architects in the UK to be found in London (27.2 per cent), the South East (12.3 per cent), East of England (11.2 per cent) and Scotland (9.4 per cent) (DCMS, 2015). Having outlined the economic geography of the UK's creative sector and architecture as a creative occupation, the chapter

Table 6.1 Architecture as a creative occupation – SOC 2010 codes

2,431	Architects
2,432	Town planners
2,435	Chartered architectural technologists
3,121	Architectural technologists and town planning technicians

now moves on to more discursive consideration of the relationship between the idea of the creative city and urban planning.

Creative cities and urban planning

There is a large volume of literature that seeks to examine the growth of culture and creative practices as they manifest themselves itself in particular places. This literature focuses on a range of scales from analyses of cultural production in global cities to explorations of the very localised and concentrated creative practices of individual sectors and/or groups of creative people. Despite differences in the scale of analysis and focus of study, what tends to connect this literature is its predominantly urban gaze addressing such issues as how the cultural economy of cities operates, what the cultural industries are, or what constitutes a creative city. For some commentators the term creative city itself reflects 'the urbanistic context and infrastructure within which creative industry innovation and growth take place' (O'Connor and Kong, 2009, p. 1). It is also a term that has come to be normatively associated with the development of positive economic and (sometimes social) outcomes for cities flowing from the growth of a local cultural and creative economy. Highly influential in the development of this approach has been the work of Landry (2000) and Florida (2002). Through such works (and others) culture and creativity came to be seen as offering significant ways in which cities can refashion their economies and boost economic development in the early decades of the twenty-first century. In the UK for example, creative strategy development at national level has tended to promote clusters for the local economic development of places, and less often for their social renewal. Documents such as *Creative Britain* (DCMS, 2008) or *Digital Britain* (DCMS, 2009) exemplify this prioritisation of the economic over social forms of development.

While terms such as the creative economy and the creative industries have been much debated and contested in the academic literature – with some writers arguing that there is still a very weak conceptualisation of the relationship between, for example, the creative economy and the city (Pratt and Hutton, 2013) – this has not prevented attempts to measure and assess the contribution of the creative economy to individual cities and nations (Pratt and Hutton, 2013; Lee, 2014).[4] There is also no shortage of literature and guidance on how to *do* culture and creativity for cities, both at a national level and more locally. Yet as Pratt (2010) make clear 'the notion of a creative city stands as much for political and social mantra as an urban, social or economic policy' (p. 14). This conceptual and policy slipperiness surrounding the idea of the creative city highlights its performative nature and the extent to which it can be used and moulded to suit the development aspirations of city planners, politicians and developers, providing them comfort in their pursuit of renewed city spaces and urban identities (Watson and Taylor, 2014, p. 2430).

Kunzmann (2004) has described this turn to creativity and culture in the planning of cities as 'a friendly virus' infecting planners and the planning profession across Europe, and coming into spatial planning through debates on the future of the European city (p. 384). Kunzmann's paper was a call to the planning profession to take culture and creativity to its heart, based on a set of seven assumptions about the relationship of culture to cities and planning (culture sharpens the image of a city; culture strengthens urban identity; culture enhances the value of locations; culture entertains; culture educates; culture boosts creativity; and culture contributes to local economic development and job creation) (p. 384). Without going into an extensive discussion of each of these, it is clear that these assumptions have come to be played out across many European cities in their search for urban renewal. From some of the early research on culture and urban renewal such as those by Bianchini and Parkinson (1993), Landry (2000), Scott (2000) and Evans (2001) to more recent analyses, a cultural approach to urban planning is advocated. What many of these works seek to do (through both theoretical and empirical analysis) is make a case for developing policies to tackle the uneven economic and social impacts of both 'globally consumed elements of culture and more localised community culture in city development' (Kunzmann, 2004, p. 397).

It is interesting to examine how some of these ideas around the relationship between culture and planning have been (and are being) played out at different spatial scales of planning. Kunzmann's 2004 paper offered some important pointers for planners here, with its articulation of how EU-wide research programmes related to territorial development (such as INTERREG and ESPON) should be refocused to include culture as a key aspect of their programme objectives. Kunzmann makes a similar case for the national level with the argument that national spatial objectives should be more clearly integrated with debates about national culture and identity, and national cultural assets, and how these national debates might engage with those around the growing multiplicity of heritage(s) and identities of communities in towns and cities. It is no coincidence that this call for planning to take more account of culture and creativity arrives at the same time in the UK as a re-evaluation of what it means to do planning: shifting from being about land use towards being characterised by spatial planning (Davoudi and Strange, 2009). Spatial planning is hard to define; there was no single definition of what it meant to do spatial planning. Rather, there was a broad set of themes and ideas related to planning as being a collaborative, participative, integrative and visionary process. This has led to a rather vague understanding of what spatial planning is within the planning profession (Davoudi and Strange, 2009; Tewdwr-Jones *et al.*, 2010). However, the arrival of 'spatial planning' in the UK in the mid-2000s, with its focus on planning beyond traditional land use, certainly offered the opportunity for 'culture' to become part of what planning did and what planners planned for. While not explicitly linked to spatial planning, initiatives such as the EU's Capital of Culture programme became bound up with the language of spatial planning in those UK cities bidding for Capital of Culture status as their bidding processes and discussions became connected to local planning and development agendas. Similarly, the turn to heritage and a concern with conserving the historic environment evident throughout UK cities in the last 20 years has led many to develop programmes of reuse and adaptation of their (often Victorian industrial) historic assets, turning them to uses designed for creative occupations, creative workspaces and cultural and leisure activity. Urban waterfront and canal-side developments are the obvious examples here, but others such as urban warehouse and mill redevelopments illustrate the movement to use older urban infrastructure for new creative or cultural spaces.

However, within a UK context the formal acknowledgement of spatial planning as *the* approach to planning was short-lived.[5] Following the arrival of the Coalition government in 2010, the planning system came under scrutiny as part of the government's localism agenda, a process characterised by attempts to remove and/or reduce central government control. Here, the planning system was conceptualised as being cumbersome, bureaucratic, inefficient and slow, as well as being insensitive to the needs and development aspirations of local neighbourhoods, communities and developers. The result was the introduction of the National Planning Policy Framework (NPPF) in 2012. The NPPF was designed to rectify these criticisms, with an intention to 'simplify' the planning system by making it less complex and more accessible to the public and developers. The NPPF brought with it a number of changes to the way the planning system was to operate and function in England (not least the arrival of neighbourhood planning), reducing thousands of pages of extant guidance and planning documentation into 52 pages, subsequently added to with further planning guidance.

Overall, a close inspection of the framework document and the subsequent guidance reveals little mention of how to plan for creative sectors of the economy, or the creative industries specifically, other than stating that planning authorities should 'plan positively for the location, promotion and expansion of clusters or networks of knowledge driven, creative or high technology industries' (DGLC, 2012, p. 7). Whether local planning authorities will, or indeed can, plan 'positively' waits to be seen, but it is undoubtedly the case that many cities are beginning to engage in serious work around the development of creative and high-technology space (Bakhshi *et al.*, 2015). What will be interesting to see is the extent to which any development mirrors earlier attempts at planning for creative space. Certainly previous examples of planning for culture in cities have tended to prioritise large-scale infrastructure development, for example where cities have sought arenas and events venues with their higher urban branding value in contrast to smaller-scale, more local or neighbourhood-level developments perceived not to have the same promotional or branding purchase (Long and Strange, 2009). However, such smaller, more localised concentrations of creative spaces have often been those that have led the cultural renewal process for those parts of cities left behind by the onset of urban deindustrialisation (Pratt, 2009; Chapain and Comunian, 2010; Pappalepore *et al.*, 2014). Some of these spaces have fallen away as they have become subject to the broader gentrification of their neighbourhoods and the growth of more commercialised forms of cultural production and consumption. Others, however, have remained and continue to offer alternatives spaces and examples of urban culture and creative hotspots (Richards, 2014, p. 127; Cooke, 2015). Additionally, we are increasingly seeing a rise in what have come to be identified as 'pop-up' or temporary cultural spaces (Bishop and Williams, 2012; Colomb, 2012) such as the 'ruin bars' in derelict buildings in Budapest (Richards, 2014, p. 127) where what is often seen as being important is the experience of 'the audience' in their encounter with the space (Richards, 2014, p. 127). In the UK, research on neighbourhood planning is still in its infancy (Parker and Street, 2015; Parker *et al.*, 2015) but what is clear is that within this emerging literature it is difficult to see anything that would suggest significant local debate about planning for the cultural life of neighbourhoods or, more specifically, a concern with the planning of localised creative spaces.

Creativity, architecture and urban planning

What the above discussion shows is that creativity is important to cities and that 'culture' has become an integral part of 'doing' urban development and renewal. This appears to be the case both in relation to the development of cultural policy and in relation to the development of cultural infrastructure as part of the growth of a city's symbolic economy (Zukin, 1995). Key in the rise of both policy and infrastructure has been the uses of creativity or culture to attract people to places – to work as tourism. However, the relationship between tourism and creativity is a complex one (Richards, 2011) where creative tourist environments comprise many different interpretations and meanings of creativity. As Richards (2014, p. 121) makes clear:

> In the context of tourism … creative people can be attracted as 'creative tourists', creative products such as theatre, films or architecture function as tourist attractions, people visit cities to sample the atmosphere developed through the creative process and 'scenes' and cities themselves can form creative environments that attract visitors as well as residents.

One outcome of the policies and practices that might lead cities to use creativity in search of tourists is the argument that the arrival of the events and iconic structures and buildings that have been deployed in the search for this creative tourism has produced places that are similar to each other. This repetition of what are essentially consumer experiences has led many critics to see such processes as resulting in the creation of cloned spaces or placeless landscapes (see the reviews in Richards, 2014). Paradoxically, the reaction of many cities to this critical response has been to use the creation of the 'iconic structure' to search for local specificity and distinctiveness in the reformation of their urban identities. Klingmann's (2007) research on blandscapes and architecture as part of the experience economy highlights how architecture can be used to create brand identity for cities. This work demonstrates that cities such as New York and Bilbao 'have used architecture to enhance their images, generate economic growth and elevate their positions in the global village' (Richards, 2014, p. 122). Here the functionality of the architecture is less important than its role in the marketing of the city. Others have also shown how a city's identity and branding through a created iconic set of buildings and infrastructure is not just the preserve of cities in the deindustrialising West, and that the possibility of urban 'sameness' is, for example, a real challenge for Middle Eastern cities if they are to avoid what has been termed the 'Dubaisation' of their urban imaginaries and identities (Al Rabadya, 2012). As Ponzini and Nastasi (2011) in their discussion of iconic developments in Abu Dhabi argue, the outcome of such architectural creativity appears to be becoming 'a high culture theme park in a Western-style luxury suburbia' (p. 59).

Many of the 'iconic' developments which have come to be identified with particular cities have been designed by a cadre of superstar architects or 'starchitects' (Ponzini and Nastasi, 2011) regularly called upon and commissioned to produce 'signature buildings' for cities in their competition to attract visitors and investment. Focusing on case studies of such starchitecture in Abu Dhabi, Paris and New York, Ponzini and Nastasi chart how, in the search for distinctive forms of architecture (and despite variation in the socio-political context of each commission), the result has been a replicated and formulaic sameness of design where the architect is often seen to be more important or better known than the building. In Abu Dhabi, the development of its cultural cluster is seen largely by Ponzini and Nastasi as the outcome of the ruling elite's desire to accumulate a 'theme park' of Western cultural institutions unrelated to any broader plans for the development of the Emirate. In Paris, successive waves of large-scale development projects from the 1980s are seen as being driven primarily by national and municipal politicians attempting to legitimise their desire to transform the Parisian metropolis. In contrast, in New York, Ponzini and Nastasi argue that large-scale architectural projects have progressed almost outside, or at a distance from, elected political intervention. Here the public sector has played a much smaller role in pursuing architectural mega-projects. Rather, the key players have been developers keen to use new developments and buildings that might act as their own marketing materials. In all these cases, it is the cachet that the 'starchitect' brings to the architectural product that connects and binds these geographically distinct examples together. What the case studies in Ponzini and Nastasi's book reveal is that quite different socio-political circumstances of development (which result in locally specific forms of project decision-making and delivery) are mixed with recurring motives for architectural production – the creation of iconic urban infrastructure and/or the political desire to transform the city.

Much of this has happened in what Sklair and Gherardi (2012) see as a period of transition from monumentality to iconicity in architecture. Their thesis is that iconicity in architecture is fundamentally a resource in the struggle for meaning and power in urban development by a transnational capitalist class in the global era:

> the production and representation of architectural icons in the pre-global era (roughly before the 1960s) were mainly driven by those who controlled state

and/or religious institutions, whereas the dominant forms of architectural iconicity for the global era are increasingly driven by those who own and control the corporate sector and the central institutions of capitalist globalization.

(p. 59)

Comprising those who own and control transnational corporations, globalising politicians and bureaucrats, globalising professionals and global marketing and media organisations, the transnational capitalist class (TCC) operates in various combinations to produce and represent iconic architecture in cities. For Sklair and Gherardi, it is not so much the starchitects who should be the focus of study, but rather the interactions between these elements of the TCC that need exploration. What is interesting in their study is how iconicity is referred to within cities and how the significance of structure and style is transmitted through the way such structures are described. Their discussion of the promotional web-based texts used to describe a range of iconic structures (the Wembley Stadium Arch, the Tabira-cho Town Hall, the Glasgow Science Centre, the Gas Science building, Toyosu, and the Al Sharq and Iris Crystal Towers in Dubai, for example) illustrates how specific architectural or technical elements of a building are used to highlight creativity in design, innovative use and/or the application of new construction materials. Moreover, the analysis highlights how such structures are used to establish their paramount place in the urban skyline and the way they seek to establish a solidity or fixity on the urban imagination (Sklair and Gherardi, 2012, pp. 61–64). This imagination is one that is both locally rooted but also (and perhaps more significantly) directed 'elsewhere where it is promoted by circulating its images over the media and by the narratives that surround its design and construction' (p. 64). This notion of a duality of imaginations has often been seen as making the building result in a rather alienated or disconnected structure from its particular local context. However, as Sklair and Gherardi show, architectural practices have responded to such criticism by establishing a discourse or 'rhetoric of context', where buildings are often said to be 'created for the city that hosts them and fitting 'to the time, place and culture in which they are located' (p. 65). Here, localised objectives, such as creating greater community attachment, improving local quality of life and delivering better environmental conditions, are often invoked as the beneficial outcomes of such forms of development. Yet these localised rationales for development also coexist alongside market demands for development that enable the production of icons at the point of the delivery of structures – in this sense buildings can be iconic before they are produced. Sklair and Gherardi describe this as the paradox of the timelessness of architectural icons. Quoting David Chipperfield and his criticism of the term iconic:

> The sort of new icon architecture … has a certain danger that everything has to look spectacular, everything has to look like it's changing the world, even if it's really not doing that much. I'm not purposely avoiding making an

icon. An icon just happens.... Clients now say that they are looking for an icon, and I know that means it has got to look blobby, actually.... Now we have to have an instant icon. It has to say it's an icon at the very point of delivery.

(2012, p. 66)

Historically, some of the most important landmarks (and iconic structures) in cities have been hotels, those developments designed to cater for a growing mobile upper and middle class since the early nineteenth century. The grand hotels of London, Paris and New York, for example, came to be seen as symbolic of the vitality of those growing urban metropolises over the nineteenth and early twentieth centuries, while the grand hotels in, for example, the colonial cities of Singapore, Hong Kong and Bombay (now Mumbai) came to represent the power of the colonial economy (McNeill, 2008). However, as McNeill makes clear, such grandeur and iconic status in this form of development coexisted with less luxurious forms of hotel. One of the significant aspects of these grand hotels was that they were often world-renowned for their exterior architecture yet, as McNeill posits, one clear characteristics of contemporary hotel design is 'the focusing of aesthetic detail on the interior rather than the exterior of buildings... part of a universal retraction from the nature of hotels as civic landmarks' (p. 385). In this instance hotel lobbies and bars become destinations for urban residents, as much as for urban tourists or business visitors. It is well known that many cities have used hotel development as a way to boost their local economies through tapping into tourism and the business convention trade. Despite the growth of the middle and budget hotel sector to accommodate this market, a striking feature associated with this process has been a revival in the grand hotel (Beaverstock *et al.*, 2004; McNeill, 2008, p. 386) through the form of skyscraper development – the Burj al Arab in Dubai being perhaps the most celebrated example, or the JW Marriott Marquis Dubai which is currently the world's tallest (single-use) hotel. However, what is more interesting is that such skyscraper hotels are often in mixed-use developments where the hotel occupies a building's uppermost floors, with the highest hotel currently being the Ritz-Carlton, Hong Kong. Here, the cityscape becomes yet another commodity sold to visitors in their consumption of the iconography of the hotel (McNeill, 2008, p. 387).

Conclusion

This chapter has attempted to outline a reconfiguring and evolving relationship between planning, tourism and the creative industries, exploring the ways in which urban planning and architecture contribute to establishing tourist and/or creative spaces. Overall, the chapter has navigated through the development of policy in this area as cities seek to establish frameworks in which the evolution and construction of creative spaces of quality design are promoted and established. It reveals a narrative of tensions and conflicts inherent in the management and regulation of urban planning and architecture and their relationship with tourism and the creative economy. The literature related to the development of creative cities and the creative economy, with its largely urban focus, suggests that at both a conceptual and a policy level there is a slipperiness and performativity associated with it that allow city planners, politicians and developers to shape their aspirations in pro-growth-oriented ways in the pursuit of urban renewal and urban identities.

The chapter has also discussed how the cultural industries are mapped, specifically in the UK, and how architecture is defined as a creative occupation. What this demonstrates is that while architecture makes an important economic contribution to the UK economy, its spatial distribution is highly uneven, heavily concentrating its practices and employment opportunities in London and the South East of England. In its exploration of the interrelationships between architecture and the planning of creative spaces, the chapter has highlighted how architectural pieces (often in the form of iconic structures) are a major component of the urban planners' toolkit for tourism and place promotion. What the discussion shows is that architecture is read as a symbol both of the creativity of the individual architect (and sometimes architectural team or practice) and of the place in which the building or structure is situated and has become an integral part of urban development and renewal. As the creative economy literature makes clear, this seems to be the case both in relation to the development of a wider pursuit of architecture as part of cultural policy and in relation to the development of cultural infrastructure produced by architecture as part of the growth of a city's symbolic economy (Zukin, 1995).

Notes

1 The dynamic mapping methodology involves a three-stage process.

> First, a set of occupations are identified as creative. Second, the workforce intensity of these occupations is calculated for each industry in the economy. Third, based on the distribution of creative intensity across industries, a threshold intensity is identified, above which all industries are determined to be creative for measurement purposes and all those below are not.
>
> (Bakhshi *et al.*, 2015, p. 12)

2 Creative intensity is defined thus:

> for every industry – as defined by a set of Standard Industrial Classification (SICs) codes – the intensity i.e. the proportion of the industry's workforce employed in the selected occupations in the first stage is calculated. For example, SIC code 5912, the 'Motion Picture, video and television programme post-production activities' industry employed 12,000 people in 2012 (rounded to the nearest 1,000), of whom 8,000 were working in creative occupations. Accordingly, its creative intensity calculated from these rounded figures, is $8,000/12,000=67$ per cent in that year.
>
> (Bakhshi *et al.*, 2015, p. 12)

3 The creative economy includes those people who are in creative occupations outside the creative industries as well as those employed in the creative industries.

4 A recent study by Lee (2014) has sought to examine the effectiveness of creative industry policies to stimulate urban economies. The research suggests that the creative

industries do lead to wage and employment growth in the local economy, and that this is related to how the creative industries drive growth in other sectors 'through spill-overs or as part of production processes', and their 'integration into production chains, or by increasing local demand' (p. 467). This might suggest therefore that the policy concentration on these industries has not been without some success.

5 Academic criticism of spatial planning as both a practice and a political project of the New Labour government is well developed in the planning literature, with many arguing that in practice the turn to spatial planning made little difference to shaping how development and planning operated (Haughton *et al.*, 2010; Allmend-inger, 2011).

References

Al Rabadya, R. (2012) 'Creative cities through local heritage revival: a perspective from Jordan/Madaba', *International Journal of Heritage Studies*, 18, pp. 1–16.

Allmendinger, P. (2011) *New Labour and Planning. From New Right to New Left*, London, Routledge.

Allmendinger, P. and Haughton, G. (2012) 'Post-political spatial planning in England: a crisis of consensus?', *Transactions of the Institute of British Geographers*, 37(1), pp. 89–103.

Bakhshi, H., Davies, J., Freeman, A. and Higgs, P. (2015) *The Geography of the UK's Creative and High-Tech Economies*, London, NESTA.

Bakhshi, H., Freeman, A. and Higgs, P. (2013) *A Dynamic Mapping of the UK's Creative Industries*, London, NESTA.

Beaverstock, J.V., Hubbard, P.J. and Short, J.R. (2004) 'Getting away with it? The chang-ing geographies of the super-rich', *Geoforum*, 35, pp. 401–407.

Binachini, F. and Parkinson, M. (eds) (1993) *Cultural Policy and Urban Regeneration: The West European Experience*, Manchester, Manchester University Press.

Bishop, P. and Williams, L. (2012) The Temporary City, London, Routledge.

Chapain, C. and Comunian, R. (2010) 'Enabling and inhibiting the creative economy: the role of the local and regional dimensions in England', *Regional Studies*, 44(6), pp. 717–734.

Colomb, C. (2012) 'Pushing the urban frontier: temporary uses of space, city marketing and the creative city discourse in 2000s Berlin', *Journal of Urban Affairs*, 34(2), pp. 131–152.

Cooke, P. (2015) 'The resilience of sustainability, creativity and social justice from the arts and crafts movement to modern day "eco-painting"', *City, Culture and Society*, 6, pp. 51–60.

Cowell, R. (2013) 'The greenest government ever? Planning and sustainability in England after the May 2010 elections', *Planning Practice & Research*, 28(1), pp. 27–44.

Creative Skillset (2013) *Classifying and Measuring the Creative Industries*, London, Cre-ative Skillset.

Davoudi, S. and Strange, I. (2009) *Conceptions of Space and Place in Strategic Spatial Planning*, London, Routledge.

DCMS (2001) *The Creative Industries Mapping Document*, London, Department of Culture, Media and Sport.

DCMS (2008) *Creative Britain. New Talents for a New Economy*, London, Department of Culture, Media and Sport.

DCMS (2009) *Digital Britain*, London, Department of Culture, Media and Sport/BIS.

DCMS (2014) *Creative Industries Economic Estimates*, January, London, Department of Culture, Media and Sport.

DCMS (2015) *Creative Industries Economic Estimates*, January, London, Department of Culture, Media and Sport.

Department for Government and Local Communities (2012) *National Planning Policy Framework*, London, DCLG.

Eugen Ratiu, D. (2013) 'Creative cities and/or sustainable cities: Discourses and practices', *City, Culture and Society*, 4, pp. 125–135.

Evans, G. (2009) 'Creative cities, creative spaces and urban policy', *Urban Studies*, 46(5&6), pp. 1003–1040.

Evans, G.L. (2001) *Cultural Planning: An Urban Renaissance?*, London, Routledge.

Florida, R. (2002) *The Rise of the Creative Class – and How It's Transforming Work, Leisure, Community and Everyday Life*, New York, Basic Books.

Florida, R. (2004) *Cities and the Creative Class*, London, Routledge.

Foord, J. (2008) 'Strategies for creative industries: an international review', *Creative Industries Journal*, 1(2), pp. 91–113.

Grodach, C. (2013) 'Cultural economy planning in creative cities: discourse and practice', *International Journal of Urban and Regional Research*, 35(5), pp. 1747–1765.

Haughton, G., Allmendinger, A., Counsell, D. and Vigar, G. (2010) *The New Spatial Planning: Territorial Management with Soft Spaces and Fuzzy Boundaries*, London, Routledge.

Klingmann, A. (2007) *Brandscapes: Architecture in the Experience Economy*, Cambridge, MA, MIT Press.

Kostopoulou, K. (2013) 'On the revitalized waterfront: creative milieu for creative tourism', *Sustainability*, 5, pp. 4578–4593.

Külliki Tafel-Viia, Viia, Andres, Terk, Erik and Lassur, Silja (2014) 'Urban policies for the creative industries: a European comparison', *European Planning Studies*, 22(4), pp. 796–815.

Kunzmann, K.R. (2004) 'Culture, creativity and spatial planning', *Town Planning Review*, 75(4), pp. 83–404.

Landry, C. (2000) *The Creative City: A Toolkit for Urban Innovators*, London, Comedia and Earthscan.

Lee, N. (2014) 'The creative industries and urban economic growth in the UK', *Environment and Planning A*, 46, pp. 455–470.

Long, J. and Strange, I. (2009) 'Mission or pragmatism: cultural policy in Leeds since 2000', in Bramham, P. and Wragg, S. (eds) *Sport, Leisure and Culture in the Postmodern City*, Farnham, Ashgate, pp. 63–82.

McNeill, D. (2008) 'The hotel and the city', *Progress in Human Geography*, 3(3), pp. 383–398.

O'Connor, J. and Kong, L. (2009) 'Introduction', in Kong, L. and O'Connor, J. (eds) *Creative Economies, Creative Cities: Asian–European Perspectives*, Dordrecht, Springer Press, pp. 1–8.

O'Connor, J. and Shaw, K. (2014) 'What next for the creative city?', *City, Culture and Society*, 5, pp. 165–170.

O'Connor, J. and Xin Gu (2010) 'Developing a creative cluster in a postindustrial city: CIDS and Manchester', *The Information Society*, 26, pp. 124–136.

Pappalepore, I., Maitland, R. and Smith, A. (2014) 'Presuming creative urban areas. Evidence from East London', *Annals of Tourism Research*, 44, pp. 227–240.

Parker, G. and Street, E. (2015) 'Planning at the neighbourhood scale: localism, dialogic politics and the modulation of community action', *Environment and Planning 'C': Government and Policy*, 33(4), pp. 794–810.

Parker, G., Lynn, T. and Wargent, M. (2015) 'Sticking to the script? The co-production of neighbourhood planning in England', *Town Planning Review*, 86(5), pp. 519–536.

Ponzini, D. and Nastasi, M. (2011) *Starchitecture: Scenes, Actors and Spectacles in Contemporary Cities*, Turin, Umberto Allemandi.

Pratt, A.C. (2009) 'Urban regeneration: from the arts 'feel good' factor to the cultural economy: a case study of Hoxton, London', *Urban Studies*, 46(5–6), pp. 1041–1061.

Pratt, A.C. (2010) 'Creative cities: tensions within and between social, cultural and economic development', *City, Culture and Society*, 1(1), pp. 13–20.

Pratt, A.C. (2015) 'Resilience, locality and the cultural economy', *City, Culture and Society*, 6, pp. 61–67.

Pratt, A. and Hutton, T. (2013) 'Reconceptualising the relationship between the creative economy and the city: learning from the financial crisis', *Cities*, 33, pp. 86–95.

Richards, G. (2011) 'Creativity and tourism. The state of the art', *Annals of Tourism Research*, 38(4), pp. 1225–1253.

Richards, G. (2014) 'Creativity and tourism in the city', *Current Issues in Tourism*, 17(2), pp. 119–144.

Scott, A.J. (2000) *The Cultural Economy of Cities*, London, Sage.

Shaw, K. (2014) 'Melbourne's creative spaces program: reclaiming the "creative city" (if not quite the rest of it)', *City, Culture and Society*, 5, pp. 139–147.

Sklair, L. and Gherardi, L. (2012) 'Iconic architecture as a hegemonic project of the transnational capitalist class', *City*, 16(1–2), pp. 57–73.

Tewdwr-Jones, M. (2012) *Spatial Planning and Governance: Understanding UK Planning (Planning, Environment, Cities)*, London, Palgrave.

Tewdwr-Jones, M., Gallent, N. and Morphet, J. (2010) 'An anatomy of spatial planning: coming to terms with the spatial element in UK planning', *European Planning Studies*, 18(2), pp. 239–257.

Thomas, N.J., Harvey, D.C. and Hawkins, H. (2013) 'Crafting the region: creative industries and practices of regional space', *Regional Studies*, 47(1), pp. 75–88.

Vivant, E. (2013) 'Creatives in the city: urban contradictions of the creative city', *City Culture and Society*, 4, pp. 57–63.

Watson, A. and Taylor, C. (2014) 'Invisible agents and hidden protagonists: rethinking creative cities policy', *European Planning Studies*, 22(12), pp. 2429–2435.

Zukin, S. (1995) *The Culture of Cities*, Oxford, Blackwell.

7 Opportunities and challenges for South Korean tourism and creative industries

Sangkyun Kim and Chanwoo Nam

Introduction

Governments at all levels play a crucial role in planning and developing systemic frameworks for tourism products and infrastructure (Nyaupane and Timothy, 2010; Ruhanen, 2013) Their involvement and direction through policy to establish more comprehensive development and overall competitiveness for tourist destinations are well documented (Dodds, 2006; Hall, 2007; Liu, 2003). Governments ideally are impartial and without private interests, so are able to design coherent long-term strategies and policies in accordance with the public interest and implement them through legislation (Bramwell, 2011; Dodds, 2006). In the context of tourism, Goeldner *et al.* (2000, p. 1) define tourism policy as: 'A set of regulations, rules, guidelines, directives and development/promotion objectives and strategies that provide a framework within which the collective and individual decisions directly affecting tourism development and the daily activities within a destination [are addressed]'.

Despite the importance of the governmental role and policy in tourism development, the current literature on 'tourism and the creative industries' or 'tourism and creativity' has focused mainly on the welcome growth of creative tourism as an alternative to mass forms of cultural tourism. It is particularly evident in North American, continental European and UK cities where the development of creative practices in tourism and the significance of creative tourism as a distinct field of tourism development have been noted (Long and Morpeth, 2012; Richards, 2011; Richards and Wilson, 2007). However, relatively little attention has been paid in tourism policy and regulation to the symbiotic relationships between tourism and the creative industries and their impacts on tourism growth from the government perspective.

This field of tourism policy and research into regulation seems to be marginal in Asian contexts where the notion of creativity in connection with tourism is recent and still at its infancy, with the exception of studies on: (1) the *Hallyu* phenomenon and its impacts on tourism growth and new tourism patterns in South Korea (Kim, S. *et al.*, 2009); (2) the Japanese contents tourism and popular culture related to Japanese animation or *manga* (Beeton *et al.*, 2013; Ng, 2008); and (3) the Thai government's national support and master plans and policies for the development of the creative economy in the tourism sector (Wattanacharoensil and Schuckert, 2014). It is worth mentioning that Hong Kong, Singapore and Taiwan have also positioned themselves as leading nations for cultural and creative industries (hereafter CCIs), and have formulated and implemented supportive government policies promoting the development of CCIs in conjunction with the tourism industry as a vehicle for creative development (Chang and Lee, 2014; Hui, 2006; Ooi, 2007). For instance, the Taiwanese government announced its development of CCIs in 2002 and introduced the Law for the Development of Cultural and Creative Industries in 2010 (Chang and Lee, 2014).

This chapter addresses the relative lack of attention to the symbiotic relationships between tourism and the creative industries in non-European and non-English-language settings. It aims to discuss how the Korean government has been evolving in response to the opportunities and challenges generated by the *Hallyu* phenomenon in order to support and promote more sustainable growth of the nation's tourism and creative industries as well as to maximise the spin-off effect of the *Hallyu* phenomenon in the Korean tourism industry. Kim S. *et al.* (2009, p. 312) define the *Hallyu* phenomenon or the Korean Wave as 'a new wave of Korean-generated popular cultural products (music, computer games, food and traditional and contemporary fashion) that extends throughout South and East Asia'.

This chapter further attempts to synthetically review and evaluate existing academic research papers, government reports and documents on Korean tourism strategies and policies in relation to the *Hallyu* phenomenon during the period 2005–2014. Examples and discussions are therefore contextualised within the identified *Hallyu*-related tourism plans, strategies and policies implemented by the Korean government. The following sections will include a review of Korean inbound tourism patterns and the *Hallyu* phenomenon, the Korean government's administration of tourism and creative industries, and identification and discussion of current opportunities and challenges facing Korean tourism and creative industries from the government perspective. Some remarks will be presented in the conclusion.

Korean inbound tourism patterns and the *Hallyu* phenomenon

Following the Korean War (1950–1953) and its aftermath, the first inbound tourism figures of any significance were produced in 1962, when 15,184 tourists were recorded (MCT, 2005). The Korean government's export-oriented policies have primarily encouraged manufacturing industry, giving lower priority to the culture and tourism sectors. This emphasis on an export-driven economic policy initially resulted in business travellers being seen as the major inbound tourist market. Leisure travellers became increasingly significant from the early 1970s and by 2000–2004 they comprised more than 70 per cent of arrivals, while business visitors only accounted for 5 per cent (compared to 60 per cent and 16 per cent respectively in 1986–1989) (MCT, 2002, 2004, 2005). The successful hosting of the 1988 Seoul Olympics and the 2002 FIFA World Cup marked a turning point in the development of tourism in South Korea (hereafter Korea), conveying the attractiveness of the country to a global audience (Kim and Morrison, 2005; Lee *et al.*, 2005; Lee and Taylor, 2005).

Thus Korea has not traditionally been a leading exporter of popular culture or a major tourist destination in Asia. However, the tourism industry in Korea has undergone unprecedented growth and faced multiple changes since 2000, thanks to the recent emergence and continuing popularity and influence of the *Hallyu* phenomenon that broadly encapsulates a variety of popular cultural activities and expressions, including TV dramas, movies, TV variety shows, Korean pop music (K-pop), computer games, fashion and food (Kim, S. *et al.*, 2009; Shim, 2006; Yang, 2012). To a greater extent, the growth of the Korean tourism industry is often related to and generated by the creative industries, which in Korea broadly comprise the following sectors: (1) cartoon; (2) animation; (3) arts (e.g. creative arts and performances); (4) media and broadcasting (e.g. TV and radio); (5) music; (6) design and fashion; and (7) (computer) games (KOCCA, 2012). This is loosely aligned with the definition of the Department for Culture, Media and Sport (DCMS) in the UK that is broadly used in the same context of tourism and creative industries. It encompasses advertising, architecture, art and antiques, computer games, crafts, design and fashion, film and video, music, performing arts, publishing, software and TV and radio (DCMS, 2001).

According to the *Hallyu* Future Strategy Forum (2012), *Hallyu* is worth US$5.6 billion in economic value and US$95 billion in asset value. The positive effects of *Hallyu* can be summed up in four points: (1) the annual growth of cultural and creative industries revenues; (2) growing interest in Korean popular culture; (3) increasing sales of Korean products; and (4) increasing number of tourists visiting Korea for a variety of reasons. As such, the *Hallyu* phenomenon is the nexus of the creative and tourism industries in Korea. This social and cultural phenomenon has attracted significant interest from industry practitioners and academic researchers in a variety of ways, and has been studied by international scholars across multiple disciplines, including media and communication studies (e.g. Hanaki *et al.*, 2007; Kim, D.K. *et al.*, 2009; Oh, 2009; Ryoo, 2009; Shim, 2006), cultural studies (e.g. Cho, 2011; Huang, 2011; Joo, 2011), and fandom studies (Kim, 2015; Madrid-Morales and Lovric, 2015). Tourism studies associated with the *Hallyu* phenomenon and its broader impact on the Korean tourism industry are another important subject area (for example, Kim, 2012a, 2012b; Kim *et al.*, 2007; Kim, S. *et al.*, 2009; Kim *et al.*, 2015; Lee and Yoo, 2011; Su *et al.*, 2011).

The Korean administration of tourism and creative (culture) industries

The development of tourism (and culture) has progressed a great deal due to the export-orientated policies of previous Korean governments, which primarily encouraged the growth of manufacturing sectors, even after the Tourism Promotion Act (TPA) was passed in 1961 and the Korean National Tourism Organisation (hereafter KNTO) was established in 1962 (Shim, 2012). A crucial turning point for the Korean tourism and creative industries was in 1994 when sole responsibility for tourism and culture policies was transferred to the Ministry of Culture and Tourism from the Ministry of Construction and Transportation. Creative industries in Korea were formally labelled 'cultural industries' until the early 2000s. The Ministry of Culture and Tourism (hereafter MCT) since then has played a crucial role in implementing a comprehensive and ongoing Korean government policy towards the tourism and creative industries. The independence of the Korean tourism and cultural or creative industries administration reflects the strong will of the Korean government to recognise the potential of and stimulate the development of tourism and creative industries for its national economy.

From the early 1990s the Korean government's response to cultural globalisation (predominantly influenced by the American and Japanese creative industries) was to promote media and popular culture rooted in the creative industries as national strategic industries (Ryoo, 2009; Shim, 2006). This was based on an awareness of the importance of culture and its industrial development as well as Korea's resistance to a serious Western challenge to political sovereignty and cultural integrity, in part through media liberalisation (Ryoo, 2009; Shim, 2006). Korea's brutal past experience of Japanese colonisation was a further consideration in the formulation of the Korean government's policies to develop and promote indigenous Korean popular culture and media (Ryoo, 2009; Shim, 2006).

In 2006, the MCT was renamed the Ministry of Culture, Sports and Tourism (MCST) to stimulate further development of the sport sector along with tourism and culture, aiming to promote and support gifted individuals in sport as well as to become one of the global leaders in the sector. Since then, the MCST has become the central government organisation responsible for the cultural and creative industries, pursuing policies in such fields as culture, arts (e.g. creative arts and performances), sports, tourism, religion (e.g. religious affairs), media and broadcasting and (promotional) advertising including new media (MCST, 2012). It is interesting to note the inclusion of sports and religion for the first time in the context of creative industries from the Korean government perspective.

Along with the MCST, the Korean central government's tourism and cultural policies are carried out by the KNTO, the Korea Culture and Tourism Institute (KCTI) and Korea Creative Content Agency (KOCCA) (MCST, 2012). The task faced by the MCST is supported and delegated to the above three national agencies which were established as government-invested corporations under the MCST. The KNTO is a policy-implementing agency with 27 overseas branches tasked with promoting the country's tourism industry (MCST, 2012). It is commissioned to play a key role in enhancing the competitiveness of the Korean tourism industry. The KCTI is a national research institute set up to support the MCST in evaluating current tourism policies and implementing more effective and efficient tourism strategies, policies and regulations in the area of culture and tourism. It is sponsored by the MCST as a representative think-tank that leads the development of creative and tourism industries policy (MCST, 2012).

The KOCCA is the latest government agency established in 2009 to efficiently support the growth of the cultural and creative industries by combining the following existing agencies – Korea Broadcasting Institute, Korea Culture and Content Agency, Korea Game Industry Agency, Cultural Contents Centre, and Digital Contents Business Group of Korea IT Industry Promotion Agency (KOCCA, 2012). It aims to promote human resource development projects to acquire capacities which may lead to forming the basis of creativity and developing policies for the promotion of the creative industries. It also supports the development of specialised culture technologies, the commercialisation of creative content, and the promotion of various overseas expansion projects to develop the creative industries into an export industry (KOCCA, 2012).

Opportunities for Korean tourism and creative industries

Approximately 60 per cent of international inbound tourists state that the *Hallyu* phenomenon influenced their decision to visit Korea, and it is estimated that over 3.3 million enthusiastic *Hallyu* fans from around the world, many of whom come from Asia, Europe and North and South America, visit Korea and spend an average of US$2,100 per person during their stay (KNTO, 2014). Accordingly, the MCST and the tourism- and creative industries-related government agencies such as the KNTO focused on the development of the creative products and spaces as tourism attractions. Also, a variety of tourism programmes for international *Hallyu* fans was developed to create more inbound tourism benefits to Korea and to enhance their visit experiences. In total, 41 *Hallyu*-related tourism programmes were developed by the Korean government agencies between 2007 and 2011 (Lee, 2011; MCST, 2012, 2013b, 2014). They include K-pop concerts, fan meetings with the *Hallyu* stars, and sightseeing tours at major film tourism locations, and TV station tours in partnership with the major Korean entertainment agencies (e.g. S.M. Entertainment and JYP Entertainment) that manage Korean celebrity profiles.

In particular, there has been a growing demand to organise K-pop concerts and fan meetings with K-pop groups such as SS501, ZE:A, and Girls' Generation due to the unprecedentedly growing popularity of K-pop around the world (Joo, 2011; Madrid-Morales and Lovric, 2015). The KNTO invites more than 5,000 overseas K-pop fans every year to K-pop concerts including the Asia Song Festival in autumn and the Dream Concert in summer (Chae, 2011). In addition, tourists can attend several music programmes run by two of the biggest Korean TV networks such as MBC's (Munhwa Broadcasting Corporation) weekly music programme *Show! Music Core* and KBS's (Korean Broadcasting System) *Immortal Song*, which feature K-pop groups and singers, with the financial and administrative support of the KNTO.

Since 2004, the KNTO has also been promoting more than 60 film tourism locations from famous Korean TV dramas and films that have been well received by international audiences (KNTO, 2014). As various thematic sets from TV dramas and films lure millions of *Hallyu* tourists, government agencies including the KNTO have been designing and developing film tourism in partnership with media production companies and travel agencies for the purpose of tourism marketing and promotion since the year 2000 (Lee, 2011). The growth and popularity of film tourism associated with the *Hallyu* phenomenon has been well documented in tourism studies (Kim, S. *et al.*, 2009; Kim *et al.*, 2007; Kim, 2010, 2012a, 2012b; Yoon *et al.*, 2015). According to Lee (2011), 26 local governments in Korea invested more than US$510 million in the development of film tourism destinations between 2000 and 2012, as Korean TV dramas and films became popular throughout Asia and beyond.

Furthermore, the Korean government noted the magnitude of planning and developing frameworks for tourism and creative industries' infrastructure to encourage the synergistic and sustainable growth of tourism and creative industries directly related to the *Hallyu* phenomenon. In this regard, the Korean government focused on the development of creative physical spaces where *Hallyu* fans as consumers and tourists meet and validate the *Hallyu* phenomenon, given that symbolic production for the development of 'themed and staged experience' (MacCannell, 1973) and the role of creative spaces as a major source of symbolic production and consumption for contemporary tourism have become more prominent (Lash and Urry, 1994; Zukin, 1995). Four key areas were identified.

First, the MCST has adapted the model of Hollywood Boulevard in the US and the Avenue of Stars in Hong Kong to adorn one of its streets with monuments, a plaza and sculptures related to Korean TV dramas, films and K-pop music (Lee, 2011). This *Hallyu* Star Street will be located on a 1.08 km section in Chungmuro, the mecca of the Korean film industry in Seoul (which is socially and culturally symbolic for both domestic and international tourists), adjacent to the Korea National Theatre Namsan tower, the Namsan Korea traditional village and traditional palaces which are already popular tourist attractions in Seoul (MCST, 2012). *Hallyu* Star Street is under construction and its construction proclamation ceremony and event were held in March 2014.

Second, a K-pop concert hall, long desired by the K-pop music industry in particular, will be completed in late 2016. The venue, tentatively dubbed K-pop Arena, will have a main concert hall accommodating approximately 18,000 attendees and a second venue with around 2,000 seats (MCST, 2012). This decision was made after the KCTI proposed the concept, and a group of Korean music and performing arts experts reviewed the proposal in terms of its size, accessibility, economic feasibility and environment (Lee, 2011). Industry insiders had long called for such a concert hall to be built to cater for and encourage the long-lasting growth of K-pop and the *Hallyu* phenomenon. Since K-pop is a booming creative industry with an enormous fan following from all over the world flying to Korea to watch K-pop concerts, the MCST expects an increased number of tourists arriving for K-pop concerts leading to the sustainable popularity of K-pop thanks to the above project (MCST, 2012).

Third, the *Hallyu* Complex Centre, the largest cultural and creative industries complex in Korea, will be constructed in Goyang, Gyeonggi province, located north of Seoul. The gross area is 995,000 m², and the centre includes media and broadcasting production and editing facilities including various-sized studios, a *Hallyu* theme park and a *Hallyu* MICE (meetings, incentives, conventions and exhibitions) complex including hotels and other facilities. Approximately US$1 billion from both the public and the private sectors will be budgeted for the project which is due for completion in 2018 (KOCCA, 2012). Also, it will play an important role in conducting research on the *Hallyu* phenomenon and the operation of cultural exchange programmes with other countries' private sectors. The plan is for this complex to be a hub for international cultural exchange that also promotes joint international developments, exemplifying the globalisation of the creative industries. The development of a *Hallyu* Cultural Tourism Belt has been under consideration in conjunction with the *Hallyu* Complex Centre to maximise synergy of the Korean tourism and creative industries' sector (MCST, 2013a). Last but not least, the MCST plans to create *Hallyu* Experience Facilities in Seoul, Daegeon and Muju in order to provide *Hallyu* tourists with opportunities to experience in depth Korean cultural products such as films, TV dramas, K-pop and computer games, to participate in fan meetings and the filmmaking process, and to learn the Korean language and its broader culture (Lee, 2011).

Along with the above development of infrastructure and tourism programmes, the MCST and KNTO have concentrated on overseas marketing in an effort to make *Hallyu* a long-lasting phenomenon and to attract more inbound tourists. They jointly make TV advertisements for overseas TV stations and promotional video clips for online marketing campaigns that feature *Hallyu* stars. In fact, the *Hallyu* phenomenon is widely used as a marketing tool among government agencies, in particular the KNTO, and Korean companies due to the worldwide popularity of Korean culture (Yang, 2012).

More recently, the MCST and KNTO have launched aggressive marketing campaigns in China, Singapore and other Asian countries, taking advantage of the TV dramas *My Love from the Star* and *The Heirs*, which have been immensely popular across Asia since they were first aired in 2013 (MCST, 2014). According to MCST (2014), a TV commercial featuring the K-pop group Big Bang will be aired in China, Japan, Russia and other parts of the world to publicise the latest slogan 'Imagine your Korea', in order to boost interest in Korea among foreign audiences. According to the participants in this study, it is assumed that these marketing policies of the Korean government have been effective in appealing to potential tourists to Korea.

Challenges and barriers to effective implementation of *Hallyu*-related tourism and creative industries policy

The recent remarkable growth and popularity of Korean tourism and creative industries sectors (including films, TV dramas, online computer games, K-pop music and other types of popular cultural products) are closely associated with the *Hallyu* phenomenon, and cannot be fully understood without the Korean government's promotion of and support for the creative industries over the past 20 years. This must be viewed in conjunction with its wider investments in other relevant industries, in particular information and communications technology (Chae, 2011; Kwon and Kim, 2014; Nam, 2008; Shim, 2012). Despite the above opportunities being welcome, the major challenges or barriers facing the Korean government in its search for more effective and sustained responses to the *Hallyu* phenomenon and its relationships with the tourism and creative industries can be summarised in four parts.

First, the *Hallyu* phenomenon has become an instrument for Korean national economic growth and development, and tourism is in turn one of the major carriers of economic growth in the field of culture and the creative industries and vice versa. Tourism has become more important for the Korean national economy than ever before: the tourism industry accounted for 2.2 per cent of Korean Gross Domestic Product (GDP) and tourism receipts amounted to US$12.3 billion in 2011 (MCST, 2011). The Korean tourism industry achieved an average annual growth rate of around 10 per cent in terms of inbound tourist arrivals for the period 2009–2013. Accordingly, as illustrated above, the MCST in general and the KNTO in particular have made a great effort to develop a series of tourism strategies and campaigns to reformulate the image of Korea and promote the country as a competitive tourism destination.

However, the latest Korean tourism policy and its three objectives still remain mainly focused on economic growth. These are, by 2018: (1) to host 17 million foreign tourists each year; (2) to create 300,000 new tourism industry jobs; and (3) to achieve annually 230 million domestic tourists across Korea (MCST, 2013b). These economy-driven objectives do not seem different from the country's first five-year tourism development plan launched in 1996 under an export-driven economic policy (Kwon and Kim, 2014; Shim, 2012). At that time, the government provided financial and institutional assistance to the private sector for tourism development projects such as hotels, tourist complexes and other infrastructure development related to tourism. In comparison, the current trends and patterns of the Korean tourism industry have been transformed in terms of the scope and focus that underlie the interwoven nature of culture, creativity and tourism because of the *Hallyu* phenomenon. It is hard to believe that broader social, cultural and environmental contexts and outcomes for its much wider contribution to, for example, quality of life, ideas, aesthetics, societies and identities that go beyond economic values have seldom been included in government policy, given that the importance of their inclusion in the tourism and creative industries-related policy framework has been highlighted (Long and Morpeth, 2012; Richards, 2011).

Second, the MCST has sub-national tourism policies within the national tourism policy framework. They include 'medical tourism development policy', 'MICE ... tourism promotion initiatives' and 'the policy of tourist accommodation' (MCST, 2013b). However, it is a large oversight that there were no specific visions and goals linked to *Hallyu*-related tourism until 2011 when a new five-year *Hallyu*-related tourism plan was launched (including the above four major projects, namely *Hallyu* Star Street, the K-pop concert hall, the *Hallyu* Complex Centre and *Hallyu* experience facilities) (Lee, 2011; MCST, 2012). This means that comprehensive mid- and long-term tourism policies and/or strategies emphasising the direct and indirect values of *Hallyu*-related tourism have not been formulated (Lee, 2011). Again, it is difficult to understand this lack of a comprehensive plan and policy, given that the Korean government has viewed *Hallyu* as a key factor behind the dramatic increase in international tourist arrivals to the country for at least the last 10 years. It is only evident that the Korean government has developed substantial tourism programmes or products and infrastructure for the growth of the tourism and creative industries (Kwon and Kim, 2014). Rather, these are considered as immediate, one-off or occasional attempts to implement improvised responses to the *Hallyu* phenomenon for immediate economic gain as opposed to a more strategic, long-term approach.

Third, a lack of systematic integration and coordination between the MCST and key national agencies of the tourism and creative industries sector such as the KNTO, KCTI and KOCCA may be noted. As mentioned earlier, the Korean government has recognised the longstanding connections between tourism and the creative industries since the initiative of the Ministry of Culture and Tourism in 1996. The *Hallyu* phenomenon is one of the key factors in the Korean government's recent policy for both tourism and the creative industries. Nonetheless, insufficient systematic communication among those government agencies and the MCST was evident, given that each agency works independently rather than all collectively. Even worse, there is little evidence that the MCST operates as overseer of *Hallyu*-related tourism policy implementation in order to create a synergy between the KNTO, KCTI and KOCCA.

Last but not least, as mentioned previously, the Korean government has been implementing various development and marketing strategies to capitalise on the spin-off effect of the *Hallyu* phenomenon on tourism and the creative industries. However, there has been little investigation into the long-term feasibility and sustainability of the *Hallyu*-related projects which have been implemented, with little or no follow-up assessments and evaluations from the central government body, the MCST. As such, the practical effectiveness and economic influence of *Hallyu* tourism policies must be more accurately examined for *Hallyu*-related policies to be more effective and sustainable. This is because the effectiveness of *Hallyu* tourism policies has never been evaluated in practice, despite the fact that the government budget related to *Hallyu* increased by 27.3 per cent, equivalent to US$68.7 million, between 2012 and 2013 bringing the total budget to US$319.9 million across 40 business areas, mainly tourism and the creative industries (MCST, 2013c).

Examples of lack of government coordination include the indiscriminate and uncontrolled promotion, support and approval of the construction of new TV drama and film settings as potential film tourism destinations. Since one of the major *Hallyu*-related tourism products is visits to the locations of popular Korean TV dramas and films (Kim *et al.*, 2007; Kim, S. *et al.*, 2009), the Korean central and regional governments have recognised the potential and significance of film tourism and have attempted to develop and promote its destinations. As of 2013, 34 TV drama and film production towns had been developed in Korea (Kim *et al.*, 2015; Yoon *et al.*, 2015). Most of these towns were constructed by local governments to stimulate economic development, enhance the image and awareness of the regions, and fulfil the political desires of local government officials (Kim *et al.*, 2015). For the above reasons, local governments in Korea were willing to subsidise their construction with no clear or feasible long-term plan. Large amounts of government money have been wasted on such indiscriminate and uncontrolled development of these film tourism locations (Kim *et al.*, 2015; Yoon *et al.*, 2015). Although a number of production towns have successfully managed to attract other TV dramas or films, the majority of these locations have experienced deteriorating profitability and even closure and demise (Kim *et al.*, 2015).

Conclusion

The relationships between tourism and the creative industries within the context of the current Korean tourism industry's growth and trends have been noted in this chapter, and the *Hallyu* phenomenon is indeed a metaphor for the interwoven nature of tourism and the creative industries. With this in mind, the Korean government, and in particular the MCST and the key governmental agencies including the KNTO, KCTI and KOCCA, have played a crucial role in generating and implementing a series of strategies, marketing campaigns, tourism programmes and *Hallyu*-related infrastructure to maximise the opportunities for the Korean tourism and creative industries sectors. Despite the ongoing efforts of the Korean government, it has clearly been faced with various challenges or barriers to implementing a more effective policy for tourism and the creative industries in response to the *Hallyu* phenomenon. They include: (1) an economic growth-driven one-off or inconsistent government policy and regulations which disregard broader social, cultural and environmental contexts and outcomes for the sustainability and longevity of the *Hallyu* phenomenon and its wider contribution to tourism and the creative industries; (2) a lack of systematic mid- and long-term strategies, policies and regulations for *Hallyu*-related tourism; (3) a lack of integration and coordination between the MCST and key national tourism-related agencies such as the KNTO, KCTI and KOCCA; and (4) a scarcity of longitudinal approaches to market research and long-term trend analyses, and little or no follow-up assessments and evaluations of the implemented *Hallyu*-related projects funded by the Korean government.

Therefore, it is essential for the Korean government to establish a strategy and goals comprising a comprehensive plan for *Hallyu*-related tourism in order to create a more effective and efficient administrative process and achieve the objectives of its national tourism policy in conjunction with the creative industries. The Korean government should also design a long-term development strategy for tourism and the creative industries, rather than implementing improvised or one-off responses to market changes, since it plays a crucial role in controlling and monitoring the sustainability of these industries (Hall, 2007; Liu, 2003). It is equally important for the Korean government to monitor and respond to the diversity of *Hallyu*-related tourism products and the constantly changing tourist profiles including needs and wants associated with the *Hallyu* phenomenon. This necessitates developing a systematic communication channel to facilitate effective collaboration and cooperation between relevant government organisations (e.g. MCST, KNTO, KCTI and KOCCA) so that they share information in the planning, implementation and evaluation stages. Last, the Korean government needs to become more concerned with the socio-cultural and environmental impacts of developing and promoting tourism and the creative industries, as policy-makers should know how to manage the potential benefits and costs of a destination's development. This chapter offers important implications for other countries that may have an interest in developing tourism and the creative industries as key and strongly related strategic industries.

References

Beeton, S., Yamamura, T. and Seaton, P. (2013). The mediatisation of culture: Japanese contents tourism and popular culture. In J. Lester and C. Scarles (eds) *Mediating the tourist experience: from brochures and virtual encounters* (pp. 139–154). Farnham: Ashgate.

Bramwell, B. (2011). Governance, the state and sustainable tourism: a political economy approach. *Journal of Sustainable Tourism*, 19(4), 459–477.

Chae, J.Y. (2011). *A study on policy alternatives for the development of new Korean waves.* Seoul: Korea Culture and Tourism Institute (KCTI).

Chang, W.S. and Lee, Y. (2014). Policy momentum for the development of Taiwan's cultural creative industries. *Current Issues in Tourism*, 18(11), 1088–1098.

Cho, Y. (2011). Desperately seeking East Asia amidst the popularity of South Korean top culture in Asia. *Cultural Studies*, 25(3), 383–404.

DCMS (Department for Culture, Media and Sport) (2001). *Culture and creativity.* London: DCMS.

Dodds, R. (2006). Sustainable tourism and policy implementation: lessons from the case of Calviá, Spain. *Current Issues in Tourism*, 10(1), 46–66.

Goeldner, C.R., McIntosh, R.W. and Ritchie, J.R.B. (2000). *Tourism: principles, practices, philosophies* (8th edn). New York: John Wiley & Sons.

Hall, C.M. (2007). *Tourism planning: policies, processes and relationship* (2nd edn). Harlow: Prentice Hall.

Hallyu Future Strategy Forum (2012). *Hallyu seeks sustainability.* Seoul: Hallyu Future Strategy Forum.

Hanaki, T., Singhal, A., Han, M., Kim, D. and Chitnis, K. (2007). Hanryu sweeps East Asia: how Winter Sonata is gripping Japan. *The International Communication Gazette*, 69(3), 281–294.

Huang, S. (2011). Nation-branding and transnational consumption: Japan-mania and the Korean wave in Taiwan. *Media, Culture & Society*, 33(1), 3–18.

Hui, D. (2006). *Study on the relationship between Hong Kong's cultural and creative industries and the Pearl River Delta.* Hong Kong: Centre for Cultural Policy Research, The University of Hong Kong.

Joo, J. (2011). Transnationalization of Korean popular culture and the rise of 'Pop nationalism' in Korea. *The Journal of Popular Culture,* 44(3), 489–504.

Kim, D.K., Singhal, A., Hanaki, T., Dunn, J., Chitnis, K. and Han, M.W. (2009). Television drama, narrative engagement and audience buying behaviour. *The International Communication Gazette,* 71(7), 595–611.

Kim, J.O. (2015). Reshaped, reconnected and refined: media portrayals of Korean pop idol fandom in Korea. *Journal of Fandom Studies,* 3(1), 79–93.

Kim, S. (2010). Extraordinary experience: re-enacting and photographing at screen tourism destination. *Tourism Planning and Development,* 7(1), 59–75.

Kim, S. (2012a). Audience involvement and film tourism experiences: emotional places, emotional experiences. *Tourism Management,* 33(2), 387–396.

Kim, S. (2012b). A cross-cultural study of on-site film-tourism experiences among Chinese, Japanese, Taiwanese and Thai visitors to the Daejanggeum Theme Park, South Korea. *Current Issues in Tourism,* 15(8), 759–776.

Kim, S., Long, P. and Robinson, M. (2009). Small screen, big tourism: the role of popular Korean television dramas in South Korean tourism. *Tourism Geographies,* 11(3), 308–333.

Kim, S.S. and Morrison, A.M. (2005). Change of images of South Korea among foreign tourists after the 2002 FIFA World Cup. *Tourism Management,* 26(2), 233–247.

Kim, S.S., Kim, S. and Heo, C. (2015). Assessment of TV drama/film production town as a rural tourism growth engine. *Asian Pacific Journal of Tourism Research,* 20(7), 730–760.

Kim, S.S., Argusa, J., Lee, H. and Chon, K. (2007). Effects of Korean television dramas on the flow of Japanese tourists. *Tourism Management,* 28(5), 1340–1353.

KNTO (Korean National Tourism Organisation) (2014). *An investigation on Hallyu tourism market.* Seoul: KNTO.

KOCCA (Korean Cultural Content Agency) (2012). *Creative society and strong cultural nation: future contents vision and policy task.* Seoul: KOCCA.

Kwon, S.H. and Kim, J. (2014). The cultural industry policies of the Korean government and the Korean Wave. *International Journal of Cultural Policy,* 20(4), 422–439.

Lash, S. and Urry, J. (1994). *Economies of signs and space.* London: Sage.

Lee, C. and Taylor, T. (2005). Critical reflections on the economic impact assessment of a mega-event: the case of 2002 FIFA World Cup. *Tourism Management,* 26(4), 593–603.

Lee, C., Lee, Y. and Lee, B. (2005). Korea's destination image formed by the 2002 World Cup. *Annals of Tourism Research,* 32(4), 839–858.

Lee, T.H. and Yoo, J.K. (2011). A study on flow experience structures: enhancement or death, prospects for the Korean wave. *Journal of Travel & Tourism Marketing,* 28(4), 423–431.

Lee, W.H. (2011). *Inbound tourism policy using the Korean wave.* Seoul: Korea Culture and Tourism Institute (KCTI).

Liu, Z. (2003). Sustainable tourism development: a critique. *Journal of Sustainable Tourism,* 11(6), 459–475.

Long, P.E. and Morpeth, N. (2012). Critiquing creativity in tourism. In M. Smith and G. Richards (eds), *Routledge handbook of cultural tourism* (pp. 304–310). London: Routledge.

114   *Sangkyun Kim and Chanwoo Nam*

MacCannell, D. (1973). Staged authenticity: arrangements of social space in tourist settings. *American Journal of Sociology*, 79(3), 589–603.

Madrid-Morales, D. and Lovric, B. (2015). Transatlantic connection: K-pop and K-drama fandom in Spain and Latin America. *Journal of Fandom Studies*, 3(1), 23–41.

MCST (Ministry of Culture, Sports and Tourism Republic of Korea) (2011). *Korean tourism industry 2011 annual report*. Seoul: MCST.

MCST (Ministry of Culture, Sports and Tourism Republic of Korea) (2012). *Cultural policy 2011 annual report*. Seoul: MCST.

MCST (Ministry of Culture, Sports and Tourism Republic of Korea) (2013a). *2013 action plan*. Seoul: MCST.

MCST (Ministry of Culture, Sports and Tourism Republic of Korea) (2013b). *Korean tourism industry 2012 annual report*. Seoul: MCST.

MCST (Ministry of Culture, Sports and Tourism Republic of Korea) (2013c). *Hallyu white paper*. Seoul: MCST.

MCST (Ministry of Culture, Sports and Tourism Republic of Korea) (2014). *Korean tourism industry 2013 annual report*. Seoul: MCST.

MCT (Ministry of Culture and Tourism Republic of Korea) (2002). *Korean tourism 2002 annual report*. Seoul: MCT.

MCT (Ministry of Culture and Tourism Republic of Korea) (2004). *Korean tourism 2004 annual report*. Seoul: MCT.

MCT (Ministry of Culture and Tourism Republic of Korea) (2005a). *Korean tourism 2005 annual report*. Seoul: MCT.

Nam, S. (2008). The politics of 'compressed development' in new media: a history of Korean cable television, 1992–2005. *Media, Culture and Society*, 30(5), 641–661.

Ng, B.W. (2008). Hong Kong young people and cultural pilgrimage to Japan: the role of Japanese popular culture in Asian tourism. In J. Cochrane (ed.), *Asian tourism: growth and change* (pp. 183–192). Oxford: Elsevier.

Nyaupane, G. and Timothy, D. (2010). Power, regionalism and tourism policy in Bhutan. *Annals of Tourism Research*, 37(4), 969–988.

Oh, I. (2009). Hallyu: the rise of transnational cultural consumers in China and Japan. *Korea Observer*, 40(3), 425–459.

Ooi, C.S. (2007). Creative industries and tourism in Singapore. In G. Richards and J. Wilson (eds), *Tourism, creativity and development* (pp. 240–251). London: Routledge.

Richards, G. (2011). Creativity and tourism: the state of the art. *Annals of Tourism Research*, 38(4), 1225–1253.

Richards, G. and Wilson, J. (2007). *Tourism, creativity and development*. London: Routledge

Ruhanen, L. (2013). Local government: facilitator or inhibitor of sustainable tourism development? *Journal of Sustainable Tourism*, 21(1), 80–98.

Ryoo, W. (2009). Globalization, or the logic of cultural hybridization: the case of the Korean wave. *Asian Journal of Communication*, 19(2), 137–151.

Shim, D. (2006). Hybridity and the rise of Korean popular culture in Asia. *Media, Culture & Society*, 28(1), 25–44.

Shim, W.S. (2012). *Change of situational conditions of tourism in the future and directions for new tourism policy*. Seoul: Korea Culture and Tourism Institute (KCTI).

Su, H.J., Huang, Y., Brodowsky, G. and Kim, H.J. (2011). The impact of product placement on TV-induced tourism: Korean TV dramas and Taiwanese viewers. *Tourism Management*, 32(4), 805–814.

Wattanacharoensil, W. and Schuckert, M. (2014). Reviewing Thailand's master plans and policies: implications for creative tourism? *Current Issues in Tourism*, online first, 1–26, accessed 21 June 2015.

Yang, J. (2012). The Korean wave (Hallyu) in East Asia: a comparison of Chinese, Japanese, and Taiwanese audiences who watch Korean TV dramas. *Development and Society*, 41(1), 103–147.

Yoon, Y., Kim, S. and Kim, S.S. (2015). Successful and unsuccessful film tourism destinations: from the perspective of Korean local residents' perceptions of film tourism impacts. *Tourism Analysis*, 20(3), 297–311.

Zukin, S. (1995). *The cultures of cities*. Malden, MA: Blackwell.

8 *Genius loci* reloaded

The creative renaissance of Nantes and
Saint-Etienne

*Charles Ambrosino, Vincent Guillon and
Dominique Sagot-Duvauroux*

Since the middle of the 2000s, the creative city concept (Landry, 2000; Florida, 2002, 2005) has gradually informed debates related to the governance and development of urban areas in France. This has occurred through a discourse which seeks to praise the territorial virtues of culture and creativity. This concept emerged in Anglo-Saxon countries and has since seduced many local decision-makers in France. However, unlike in countries such as the United Kingdom or Australia, the creative economy has never led to the development of a clearly identified and specific French national policy. It is true that the creation of the Direction Générale des Médias et des Industries Culturelles within the Ministère de la Culture in 2009 demonstrates that the traditional remit of cultural industries (cinema, publishing, music) has been extended to a number of activities related to the production of creative content (a pluralist approach to media, the inclusion of the advertising and videogame industries, etc.). In similar vein, a major study carried out by INSEE[1] (2009) with regard to the composition of France's creative class and one commissioned by the state and carried out by EY[2] (2013), which prefigured the creation of the France Creative[3] digital platform, contributed to building the first comprehensive overview of the cultural and creative industries[4] at the national scale. In particular, the study highlighted the economic importance of these industries (5 per cent of jobs in France) as well as their concentration in large metropolises (Chantelot, 2010; Liefooghe, 2015; a recent analysis of the Grand Paris creative ecosystem has not challenged these findings.[5] Incidentally, these studies and the political and institutional constructs they build are based on a rather narrow definition of the creative economy when compared to other national contexts (software, fashion, luxury, advertising and heritage are not included) and have not put creativity on the agenda at the ministerial level. Generally speaking, this chapter suggests that one needs to look at the local scale to understand the ways in which the creative economy paradigm is being implemented in France.

Culture and creativity are thus central to city strategies, and are seen as resources which are mobilised and used in political, economic or touristic projects. This new trend has benefited from the increasing power of cities in terms of public policy implementation, but also from the post-industrialisation of urban economies, in which culture is part of territorial showcasing. Without a doubt,

Paris has always been considered one of the most creative cities in the world, in cultural as well as touristic terms. The city is the number one tourist spot in Europe, boasts one of the best museum districts in the world and is considered to be a creative city par excellence. However, other cities in France, such as Lyon, Lille, Nantes, Saint-Etienne, Nice or Marseille are worth exploring to illustrate the French attitude towards the creative city paradigm (see Figure 8.1). Two of these cities, Saint-Etienne and Nantes, are taken as examples in this chapter because of their earlier strategies to promote their creative soul as an urban development tool.

Figure 8.1 Location of Nantes and Saint-Etienne (in black on the map) © Jennifer Buyck, 2015.

Saint-Etienne has attempted to recover from the industrial and demographic crises which deeply affected the city through a project centred on design and on the use of local resources tailored to contemporary needs. Design is perceived as a support of shared territorial values and is deeply anchored in Saint-Etienne's industrial history. This city-scale project generated a wide mobilisation of local elites and cuts across several fields of public action: economic development, culture, tourism, education and urban design. More than just a 'flagship development projects', the Cité du Design claims to offer a wide-ranging vision of design, centred on the invention of new lifestyles through objects, images and services. It has contributed to putting Saint-Etienne on the tourist map. It also repositions the city in the creative economy, by presenting design as a tool capable of converting creativity and cognitive work into an economic activity.

Since the end of the 1980s, the city of Nantes has sought to place itself on the cultural map by means of a series of original events aimed at offering an alternative city narrative to that of a past dominated by the shipping industry. Thanks to the work carried out by a number of individuals with privileged positions in national and international networks (such as Jean Blaise, the Royal de Luxe street performing art company), Nantes is progressively developing its image as a cultural hub through a small number of targeted projects mainly based on presenting art in public areas. Art and music festivals such as the Folles Journées and the Biennale de l'Estuaire contemporary art festival are just a few of the events punctuating an impressive cultural calendar of which the reputation now extends far beyond the borders of the *pays de la Loire* region. Capitalising on this reputation and led by a strong, bold and deeply involved team employed by the local council, Nantes, as an artistic brand, is greeted each year by a growing, enthusiastic and largely local audience.

The main purpose of this chapter is to explore the way these two former industrial metropolises (Nantes and Saint-Etienne) have managed to nurture and sustain a post-industrial narrative around the creative city doxa, promoting themselves as creative industry centres and/or cultural tourist destinations. During the 1990s, following two different paths, they initiated an urban renaissance process by promoting a new form of tourism, culture-led regeneration projects and concomitantly creative industry policies. A comparison between the two cities is illustrative of the French context of the connections between tourism and creative industry sectors. Moreover, it should allow us to analyse how cities without a strongly recognised cultural capacity have derived advantages in the global competitive context of tourism by following an endogenous path by emphasising their *genius loci*.

Creative cities: the 'French touch'

Creative clusters, cultural districts, creative cities.... In recent years, these words appear not only in academic literature but also in the speeches of politicians to describe the development strategy of a territory that relies on creative industries. Examples of cities that have boosted their economy through investment in culture (Bilbao, Nantes, Liverpool, etc.) are widely reported. The UN has since 2008 been publishing regular reports on the creative economy (UN, 2008, 2010, 2013). However, the terms given above are misleading in that they refer to significantly different realities and analysis. The term 'cluster' for example, refers to industrial economics and describes a concentration of firms belonging to the same sector in a given territory. 'Creative city' emphasizes the ecosystem that a city offers to stimulate innovation and creativity. Creative clusters and creative cities are at the heart of the great changes that the world economy is currently experiencing.

Literature related to these concepts and their translation into territorial policies are heavily influenced by the national context in which they are set. Thus, an Italian school developed around the cultural district concept and built upon works related to the 'Third Italy' (Becattini, 1991), marked by the presence of a dense network of small and medium enterprises specialised in an activity belonging to the same value chain where family links and trust are a cement. The British school is strongly influenced by the performative dimension of the creative economy in the new international economic context. As early as the 1990s, urban policies were aimed at positioning the United Kingdom in the field of cultural and creative industries (DCMS, 2001). The Californian school (Scott, 2000) is based on Michael Porter's works related to industrial clusters and also on Jane Jacobs's urbanisation effects in order to analyse the creative city as a complex ecosystem.

Debates about creative cities and clusters appeared belatedly among French academics and practitioners. It was not until the mid-2000s that these concepts were used as analytical frameworks by researchers (L'Observatoire, 2009; Vivant, 2009; Chantelot, 2010; Vivant and Tremblay, 2010; Saez, 2012; Ambrosino and Guillon, 2013; Liefooghe, 2015; etc.) and as a model for development by some metropolises. France is cultural before being creative. Such resistance can be explained historically by the role of the Ministère de la Culture in the definition of cultural policy instruments and objectives. The appointment of Jack Lang as minister of culture in 1981 did indeed introduce a degree of economic concern in the field of culture, but not in ways that addressed territorial issues: supporting cultural industries, defending the *culturelle exception* and professionalising cultural management. Throughout the 1980s, even the spirit of decentralisation gave birth to spatially oriented cultural policies aiming at a better dissemination of national culture (Urfalino, 2004; Saez, 2005).

The mobilisation of artistic creation and expression gained momentum at the beginning of the 1990s in the field of urban social development (Metral, 2000; Chaudoir and Maillard, 2004; Bruston, 2005) and in the promotion of new places inspired by cultural and artistic squats and positioned at the margins of urban centres and subsidised cultural institutions (Lextrait and Kahn, 2005; Raffin, 2007). Above all, this trend reflects a demarcation rationale vis-à-vis the state-initiated policy aiming at the democratisation of an elite and decontextualised culture. At this stage, issues related to urban regeneration and local development remained secondary. Although there appears to be an economisation of culture at the local scale, it is particularly visible in prestigious cultural projects (amenity, events and hosting big names of the art sector) of which the effects are measured in terms of attractiveness, visibility and development of tourism in parts of or entire areas. Montpellier, Rennes and Grenoble are very good examples of the introduction of the economic argument in urban cultural development strategies (Le Galès, 1993; Négrier, 1993; Saez, 1995).

In this sense, national contexts influenced the heteronomy of cultural policies in the 1990s. In the Anglo-Saxon world, the idea of a creative city brought with it the temptation to dissolve culture as a sector of public policy in a vast concept of local development (Bianchini and Parkinson, 1993; Landry, 2000). In France, however, no conceptual apparatus emerged to promote such a decompartmental-isation of cultural policies. The creative city as a reference was mobilised, but was often misused when compared with the initial concept (Landry and Bianchini, 1995) and limited to a label to showcase a local yet little contextualised cultural offering. The mere performative dimension of the creative city can thus not in itself explain how a number of French cities have led integrated development strategies that have combined tourism, industrial and urban policies through the use of specific cultural resources. The examples of Saint-Etienne and Nantes are relevant in showing how the developments take place at the local scale, outside national cultural policies, and how these different concepts developed by academic literature have gradually been mobilised to justify the chosen strategies or to obtain funding. They show that these two cities have been able to overcome their constraints and lack of natural or heritage assets in order to design development strategies that are based not on existing tourism or on a new iconic building as was the case in Bilbao, but rather on an image or an ambience supported by a narrative rooted in the city's history which allows it to renew itself.

In this chapter, we adopt an evolutionist approach (Boschma and Martin, 2010) to analyse the way in which these two cities have gradually built their urban design on culture, creativity and tourism. We will attempt to shed light on the evolution of these territories by stressing three points: learning, path dependency and small historical events. Like individuals, organisations learn from the past by converting the experience gained from resolving problems (organisational learning) into decision-making procedures (routines). These procedures transfer the know-how needed to solve recurring problems from individuals to organisations. For example, over time, the city of Nantes has acquired expertise in the field of organising major events in public spaces. The second perspective related to path dependency means that history is important. Past choices condition future choices and determine a path constraint which is more or less narrow. The tourism strategy of a territory with a strong historic heritage will be heavily influenced by the enhancement of this heritage. A city with an industrial past will paradoxically benefit from a baseline in terms of innovation. The trajectories of territories can also be explained by 'small historical events', which are often unpredictable and can substantially influence opportunities for evolution. Project trajectories also bear the impression of particular figureheads. They therefore have a non-reproducible and idiosyncratic dimension.

Saint-Etienne: design is the new 'urban mantra'

Over the past 30 years, the city of Saint-Etienne has undergone deep economic, social and urban change. The major icons that shaped its industrial history (Manufrance, GIAT, the metal and bicycle industries, mining, weapon production, narrow weaving, trimmings, etc.) and part of its working-class identity have now disappeared or have considerably weakened. The city's population dropped from 220,000 inhabitants in 1975 to 173,000 in 2015. Neither the numerous financial support programmes targeted at struggling companies nor policies (encouraged by the state) aimed at acquiring and redeveloping brownfield sites were successful in reversing the decline of the local production system and the resulting demographic fall. The fact that the state played a major role in planning until the early 1990s acted as a brake on the involvement of local elites in political and cultural policies and in the design of collective strategies to solve the crisis (Béal *et al.*, 2007). These local elites prioritise vertical relations with the state, rather than an involvement in stakeholder coalitions built around development projects such as the ones that appeared at that time in many lagging industrial cities (Harding, 1997). The election of Mayor Michel Thiollière in 1994 initiated a new cycle of local strategies oriented towards residential attractiveness, quality of life and the image of the city. But the cornerstone of this change of approach was laid two years before, when Thiollière was still in charge of urban planning as an elected member of the local council. In 1992, the city commissioned the famous architect Ricardo Bofill for an urban design project aiming to make the city centre more attractive, as had been done in Montpellier, Glasgow, Bilbao and Genoa for example. In such a context, cultural policy could be based on the city's local development strategy and design became a defining element of a territorial narrative which underpins collective action (Guillon, 2011). The closer linkage between the creative economy and tourism through design is the result of this cooperative process whereby local stakeholders adjust to the conditions imposed by globalisation and the end of an industrial cycle.

The emergence of distinctiveness: Saint-Etienne and design

An arena of collective action in the field of design emerged in Saint-Etienne at the end of the 1980s under the impetus of Jacques Bonnavel, the then head of the École Régionale des Beaux-Arts. In particular, a postgraduate degree in design and research was set up in this higher education institution. This pioneering initiative led by an art school was developed in a spirit of collaboration with the local industries. Experiments conducted in this context benefited from nationwide support and advertising through *Azimuts*, the design journal published by the school. This raised awareness among local stakeholders with regard to these issues and gave Saint-Etienne the opportunity to position itself as a 'city of design' from the beginning of the 1990s. At the same time, the new modern art museum, which was supported by one of the biggest local companies, the Casino group, started a design collection which was unique in the country, taking advantage of the fact that it was still possible to acquire works at a relatively low price. This young institution was essentially interested in industrial design, in other words in objects mass-produced mechanically for the mass market. This design collection aimed at becoming a marker of local history characterised by the creation of manufactured objects. Several collaborations were initiated on this basis between the museum of modern art, the École des Beaux-Arts and the engineering school in order to train students in innovation by design.

Following the study carried out by Catalan architect Ricardo Bofill, the mayor called on town planner Jean-Pierre Charbonneau to support him in the implementation of his urban planning and regeneration policy. His desire to improve the quality of a large number of public spaces was constrained by the city's limited financial resources. It was in this unfavourable context that Jean-Pierre Charbonneau encouraged him to rely on the dynamism and reputation of the city's higher education institutions in the fields of art, architecture and design. An original tool was developed to make this possible: the Atelier espace public, in which the city council offered graduates opportunities to work on urban regeneration projects. These workshops were cross-disciplinary and brought together designers, architects and artists from Saint-Etienne who collaborated with the city council's technical, planning and public space department. The aim was to rehabilitate small sites with a high social value (squares, tram lines, footpaths, school entrances, etc.) and to enhance them through cheap and swiftly implemented designs. Interventions dealt with street furniture, signage and built or landscaped elements. This work was the basis of the linkage between urban and cultural policy in Saint-Etienne. According to Jean-Pierre Charbonneau, the objective was to 'give birth to a sort of style which would be the signature of a Saint-Etienne school of public space'. Over 130 sites were subject to the designs of the Atelier espace public. The renewal of the city (*renouveau stéphanois*[6]) was made possible by the organisation in 2005 of the major event called Transurbaines. The national daily newspaper *Libération* of 15 June 2005 referred to this as 'Saint-Etienne during moulting'. The city's physical transformation process became a spectacle magnified and aestheticised through multiple artistic and staged interventions in public space. This event attracted many visitors and was considered a springboard for the city's bid for the 2013 Capital of Culture title which was in fact won by Marseille.

From the Biennale du Design to a new territorial narrative

Under the initiative of the director of École des Beaux-Arts, the Biennale du Design de Saint-Etienne was launched in 1998. It rapidly gained support from the mayor who was keen to see the city organise an international event reflecting the territory and its repositioning. The Biennale showcased initiatives and collections which emerged around design from the early 1990s.The first edition was rather tentative but the Biennale soon became a major event: it aimed at providing an exhibition of progress in the fields of object and urban design. It also sought to integrate a wide spectrum of innovations by design centred on users (services, the public, technologies, etc.). The Biennale had several aims: to strengthen local skills in design, to support the local production system, urban marketing and promoting Saint-Etienne as a destination for tourists. It was the first step in bringing tourism and cultural industries closer and this link has strengthened ever since. The local industrial base, characterised by a high concentration of small and medium-sized enterprises and industries, was involved from the start and its awareness and profile raised. The event's popularity and the presentation of extra-territorial experiments promoted design as a good and a service that increase companies' competitiveness. Moreover, the success of the event has contributed to rooting it in several of the city-region's cultural spaces.

Design is perceived as an expression of shared territorial values that are deeply rooted in Saint-Etienne's industrial and manufacturing history and community (Varenne, 2006). Heritage institutions contribute to producing an identity narrative about the 'culture of the object and of innovation' that would reflect a sort of *genius loci* via its political interpretation. The wish to make history an operating force of the territorial strategies' development has proved to be effective. The representation of Saint-Etienne as a pioneering site in the field of design – not to say its cradle – gained momentum in the discourse of local stakeholders. This situation led to a reconciliation between the city's industrial past and its future, its potential for reimaging; and a reconciliation between the inherited expertise and the potential for a revived creative metropolis to be built. Two heritage projects are symbolic of the development of this narrative. Urban policy-makers eventually accepted them after a long period of lack of interest: the reopening of the museum of art and industry and the completion of the church of Saint Pierre designed by Le Corbusier. At the beginning of the 2000s, the renovation of the museum of art and industry, led by architect Jean-Michel Wilmotte, put this heritage institution back at centre stage. Until then it had been considered the unwanted witness of a past the city was attempting to forget. A new place therefore appeared for the heritage institution serving the new territorial strategy. Its strong networks in the local society allowed it to strengthen and promote the narrative of the 'roots of design' and the territory's legitimacy in the field of industrial innovation and the applied arts. In terms of institutional communication and branding, Saint-Etienne was reconceived as a 'land of creation and innovation'. It is in this light that one needs to envisage the completion in 2006 of the church of Saint-Pierre de Firminy-Vert, designed by Le Corbusier. The building, which had been abandoned since 1978, became the heritage symbol of the 'Saint-Etienne, métropole design' project. The development of the architect-designer's largest European urban complex was thus completed 50 years after the first *unité d'habitation*. Since then, local authorities and not-for-profit organisations have been actively campaigning for it to be listed as a UNESCO World Heritage site. During the same period, a second flagship element of Saint-Etienne's renewal appeared, inspired by the success of other European cities in terms of tourism and marketing: the 'starchitecture' of Norman Foster's Zenith.

Cité du Design: the spearhead of a creative renaissance

Saint-Etienne did not become the European Capital of Culture, but it was awarded UNESCO's Creative City status for design in 2010. This was symbolic, and it contributed to branding the territorial project of which Cité du Design was the main element. It was during a trip to Japan to prepare for the second edition of the Biennale du Design that Jacques Bonnaval, the then director of École des Beaux-Arts, discovered the International Design Centre in Nagoya. The project for a new international design centre in Saint-Etienne was inspired by the Japanese model and publicly announced during the 2002 Biennale by the minister of culture. It was decided that it would be located on the brownfield site where the old national weapon-manufacturing plant had been. This was a symbolic place that offered sufficient space to accommodate a building for production, training, research and exhibition in the field of contemporary design. This location also resulted in the redevelopment of an industrial site on one of the city's major axes which had been disused since 2003. Moreover, it gave an opportunity to design a project on a wider urban scale that covers the entire Manufacture – Plaine Achille area where the new Zenith building designed by Norman Foster is located. The architectural competition for Cité du Design was won by Finn Geipel and Giulia Andi and their project aroused much controversy (Zanetti, 2010, 2011). Local associations for the preservation of heritage fought against the destruction of administrative buildings and directors' houses required for the construction of the Cité. These organisations criticised a vision which they felt gave too much weight to technical and production innovation compared with the working-class, political and social dimensions of industrial history. This selective memory chimes perfectly with the narrative about the creativity of Saint-Etienne and with the local decision-makers' intention to 'recodify' the signification of a city which was until then perceived through its working-class and mining culture. The Cité du Design was built with financial support from state and European structural funds. It was the culmination of a process whereby a distinctive territorial resource was built over a 20-year period. It was opened in 2009 and is a platform for higher education, research, economic development, awareness raising and dissemination in the field of design. It also aims to bring together local stakeholders around this theme, including secondary schools and higher education institutions through their involvement in a design consortium, chambers of commerce and industry, businesses, actors in the cultural and tourism sectors, etc. The Biennale du Design still remains the main vector for the promotion of the territory and of its local skills. For example, the 2013 edition attracted over 140,000 visitors, including a large delegation from UNESCO's Creative Cities network.

The last element of the territorial strategy lies in the creation of a cultural district around the Cité du Design in order to encourage 'permanent linkages between technologies, design, art, culture and leisure' as well as the emergence of a creative ecosystem. Activities promoted within this 100 ha 'park city' include a wide range of creative industries. The complex includes a business incubator (in particular in the media sector), the Mixeur (a co-working space developed by Saint-Etienne Métropole), the École Nationale d'Art et de Design, the International Rhône-Alpes Médias platform (IRAM) and the Optique Vision centre but also the Fil contemporary music centre, Zenith and, as from 2016, Comédie de Saint-Etienne. The regeneration of this inner-city area was built around the Manufacture d'armes block and aims at enlarging the current city centre, perhaps even doubling its size (Mortelette, 2014). The mix of functions including industries, higher education, housing and services is central to this project which seeks to make the central areas attractive for visitors and most importantly for the creative classes (Miot, 2015) who were trained in the city and, it is hoped, will remain there. The creative district is a symbol of the renewal of Saint-Etienne and has above all been developed as a showcase, with the risk of being somewhat disconnected from the rest of the city. But this reality raises a number of issues in terms of the metropolitan urban design project's sustainability: how can the idea of a renaissance based on the culture of design be disseminated at an international scale if the inhabitants of Saint-Etienne themselves are peripheral to it?

The creative awakening of Nantes between a tourist narrative and urban cultural development

Nantes has been one of the most attractive cities of France for the past 15 years partly because of its cultural vitality reflected by a wide range of projects: some based on heritage such as the restoration of the Château des Ducs de Bretagne and the reopening of Musée des Beaux-Arts in 2016; economic and urban projects, with the Quartier de la Création cultural cluster presented as a place of artistic production and territorial revitalisation; urban artistic projects which attract artists whose role is to give meaning to the territory, for example during the Biennale de l'Estuaire, the Royal de Luxe parades and the Machines de l'Ile, as well as world-famous festivals such as the Folles Journées. These events were initially aimed at making the city visible on the national and the international scales and they have recently been connected in order to create a tourist destination which is not only aimed at businesses. The city has also established an organisation called Voyage à Nantes to create a narrative around tourism for the city and to promote the sector. A sightseeing tour is thus developed each year and materialised by a green line that meanders through the city and invite visitors and inhabitants can follow to explore its more or less famous cultural places. However, Nantes's tourist development through culture is the result of a long process during which the aims of local cultural policies underwent major changes depending on the various opportunities that arose. Three main phases can be identified in this process whereby tourism was developed in Nantes through cultural activities (Sagot-Duvauroux, 2010). In the 1990s, culture was perceived as a factor of identity and international prestige. In the 2000s, cultural policy was included in urban design and gave birth to the Quartier de la Création. As from the end of the 2000s, the various cultural attributes of the city were used to build a narrative making Nantes an attractive and distinctive destination for tourists.

Changing the image of the city through culture

Like many industrial cities, Nantes faced the closure of a large number of production plants in the 1980s. The most important event undoubtedly occurred in 1987 when the shipbuilding sites located on Ile de Nantes closed down, thus leaving a vast brownfield area available for redevelopment. Young Socialist Mayor Jean-Marc Ayrault, who was elected in 1989, decided to reinvigorate the city through culture. It is true that at that time Nantes was often referred to as a sleeping beauty which had paid little attention to the valorisation of its heritage assets, its riverside location and its creative vitality. The cultural policy which was then adopted rested on two main aspects. On the one hand, emerging artists were promoted, in particular those in the fields of music and plastic arts (Guibert, 2010); on the other hand, artists and cultural entrepreneurs whose influence was increasingly international were supported. Unlike many other similar-sized cities, Nantes did not base its cultural policy so much on a major amenity (e.g. museum, theatre, opera house) as on innovative projects.

The cultural image of the city therefore bears the impression of a few symbolic initiatives whose success related is as much to the personality of the project leaders as to the determined support of the local council (Sagot-Duvauroux, 2010). The creation of the Festival des Allumés by Jean Blaise played an important role in the identification of 'made in Nantes' art. The festival is made visible through its international programming and it has aroused keen interest from the population thanks to the exploitation of various locations in the city, in particular industrial brownfield sites. It has allowed Nantes to build links with other metropolises such as Barcelona, Saint Petersburg, Naples and Buenos Aires. The arrival of the Royal de Luxe follows the same logic. The performances of this street arts company permeates the city and involve the people as actors. International cooperation (with Africa, China, South America, etc.) opens the events up to the world. The Folles Journées, a third example, are based on the same ingredients: offering spectators an offbeat experience compared with traditional cultural events – in this case through classical music concerts held all day in a place that was for many years unique (the Congress Centre), and through various formats (short or long), with stars and not so famous artists. Here again, the international dimension of the event allows the population and the creators to collaborate with artists and producers from other countries. Through 'made in Nantes', cultural entrepreneurs (Jean Blaise, Pierre Oréfice, René Martin) who work alongside artists play a key role and are promoted as much as the artists they showcase.

During the 2000s, these initiatives evolved and were central in the strategies that aimed at turning Nantes into an original destination for tourists. The Festival des Allumés gave birth to Lieu Unique, an outstanding national theatre located in the old LU factories. In turn, Lieu Unique gave birth to their Biennale de l'Estuaire in 2007, an itinerary through contemporary sculptures along the Loire estuary. The Royal de Luxe gave rise to the Machines de l'Ile project led by Pierre Oréfice and François Delarozière. The machines, which are located at the heart of the creative quarter, are pieces from a museum, games, public transport, and elements of the townscape and are today central to the city's attractiveness for tourists. Folles Journées gave birth to other Folles Journées in cities throughout the world, whether Tokyo, Lisbon or Bilbao, thus demonstrating Nantes's know-how at the international scale, and promoting the city's prominence at the global scale. Town planner Alexandre Chemetov was commissioned with the master planning for the island. The western point was quickly identified as the correct location for these different cultural amenities (Morteau, 2015).

In 2006, Nantes joined a European network of cultural clusters, the European Creative Industries Alliance (ECIA). This generated new opportunities that were welcomed by Jean-Louis Bonnin, the then director of cultural affairs for the city (Graveleine, 2011). The project no longer solely comprised building a campus for the arts, but aimed to strengthen the position of Nantes Saint-Nazaire in the field of cultural tourism and to develop a real economy around the cultural and creative industries. International benchmarking and the choices made by local elected members led to the promotion of a metropolitan cluster on the Ile de Nantes (Santagata, 2002; Morteau, 2015), designed like an ecosystem linking social, urban, economic and cultural issues. Numerous experts were commissioned to lead the debate on the programming of the future quarter and the role that digital technologies could play in it. A project for a Quartier de la Création on the Ile de Nantes was thus in the making. This raises the question of corporate hospitality for creative enterprises, in particular in terms of their real estate needs and cooperation arrangements. Gradually, the Quartier de la Création turned into a structure of governance for the creative cluster set up in 2011. Public authorities sought to build links between universities, art schools and creative enterprises based on a cluster approach. Many events were thus planned in order to foster the inter-organisational exchanges needed for the creative ecosystem to work. The specialisation of the Quartier de la création cluster was strengthened in 2014 with more attention being given to spill-overs from cultural activities to the local economy after Nantes took part in the ECIA European project. Moreover, there was an increased specialisation in the digital sector which led to the award of the French Tech label.

'Voyage à Nantes': how to stage Nantes's tourist assets

The flexibility of Chemetov's masterplan, the emergence of the Quartier de la création, the adoption of the Nantes Saint-Nazaire (SCOT) in 2007 and the city's wish to become a tourist destination led Jean Blaise, the then director of the Lieu Unique to devise a project that would address both these issues. This project was the Biennale de l'Estuaire, a tourism itinerary between Nantes and Saint-Nazaire around works of art designed on site. Landscape and artistic creation play a reflexive role here as each o offers a perspective on the other – landscape on works of art and works of art on landscape. The first edition was in 2007, the same year as the reopening of the Château des Ducs de Bretagne. It speeded up the redevelopment of the western end of the Ile de Nantes around Hangar à

Bananes and the regeneration of Nefs de la Loire where the Machines de l'Ile are found today (the elephant is the most iconic). Their monumental character reminds us that ships used to be built in the same place in the past.

As well as being a space of production, the Ile de Nantes is also a place of consumption, leisure and recreation, these being the basis of the city's tourism strategy organised by a *société publique locale* (SPL) called Le Voyage à Nantes, the city's tourism management organisation. This agency brings together a wide range of public and private organisations and offers various amenities related to heritage and culture (Château des Ducs de Bretagne, the museum of the history of Nantes, the Hab art gallery), attractions for leisure (Galerie des Machines, Grand Eléphant and Carrousel des Mondes Marins), events (Biennale de l'Estuaire) and a tourist information centre. Today, Voyage à Nantes is the structure of governance for a cultural and tourist cluster which is developing in parallel to the Quartier de la Creation. Its activity is centred on digital technologies thanks to the Nantes Tech label.

The main task for local elites in Nantes at present is to build on the previously mentioned initiatives in order to strengthen and perpetuate the cultural image which is now associated with the city: the showcasing of key amenities (the Château, Eléphant, the works produced during the *Biennale de l'Estuaire*, the museums) is combined with the valorisation of a creative and fun atmosphere. The city's green space unit has set up stations potagères, a type of game designed by artists for public spaces. Itineraries also link shopping streets, artists' workshops, places for socialising used by the locals, places from which to admire the landscape, parks and gardens, cultural amenities and public art, etc. Over the past 25 years, stakeholders in Nantes have thus been successful in fostering the creative awakening of a provincial city which was until then visited by few tourists, by basing their approach on an original tourism-oriented narrative in which the urban atmosphere plays as important a role as heritage resources.

Conclusions

At the national scale, Nantes and Saint-Etienne today put themselves forward as creative and/or tourist cities. Such an attitude would have been unthinkable some 20 years ago: who would have imagined that these two old industrial cities, famous for their decline rather than their capacity to innovate, would be able to claim to be part of the knowledge economy or artistic avant-garde in the early 2000s? These two metropolises' recent evolutions are interesting examples of ways in which the idea of the creative city is used to link cultural, tourism and industrial policies for the benefit of urban development.

The construction of specific and idiosyncratic amenities

Whether in Nantes or in Saint-Etienne, the use of strategies of territorial distinction relies on local stakeholders' capacity to identify, valorise and convert a number of 'latent' resources (way of life, know-how, industrial memory, cultural heritage) into 'active' resources (Greffe, 2006; Gumuchian and Pecqueur, 2007). Even though neither of these two cities had sufficient 'given' resources to promote at the end of the 1980s (heritage, an iconic amenity, a concentration of cultural resources, etc.), public sector organisations embarked upon turning a number of specific and idiosyncratic amenities into 'built resources' (a pole for tourism, an agglomeration economy, a creative quarter): design for Saint-Etienne and cultural and artistic dimensions of made in 'Nantes'. In both cases, path dependency, which determined the range of future choices based on past choices, was paradoxically rather low, given the need for restructuring. The change in trajectory was facilitated by the failure of past trajectories and by the recodification of the spirit of these places.

The most striking aspect of this process is its incremental dimension. The creative renaissance of Nantes and Saint-Etienne has been led by individual pioneers and is intrinsically linked to a number of cooperations stemming from opportunities: emblematic cultural entrepreneurs such as Jean Blaise, Pierre Oréfice or René Martin (in Nantes), Jacques Bonnaval and Jean-Pierre Charbeanneau (in Saint-Etienne) met mayors who had a strong sense of entrepreneurship and experimentation. Together they evolved and built a strategic vision in which action prototyping prevails over planning. The convergence of interests allowed individuals rather than institutions to build upon initiatives. These remarkable individuals were able to convince various stakeholders, including artists, entrepreneurs, politicians and planners, of the feasibility and interest of their project. They are catalysts who generate new cooperation and learning processes that lead to a gradual reconfiguration of territorial policies. One can identify a transfer of individual know-how to organisational learning which means that local strategies are less vulnerable to the turnover of key individuals.

Telling the story of change: the territorialising force of the narrative

The innovations collective action in Nantes and Saint-Etienne are based on the development of a territorial narrative derived on a selection of memories. It has overcome a number of negative representations by generating a new imagery that disregards some aspects of the cities' heritage such as decline, deindustrialisation, loss of population, etc. This original story told to the outside world and picked up by the media, visitors, elected members and the local population gives a sense of unity in the present time and acts as a starting point for debate about the cities and their future needs and expectations. In Saint-Etienne, the promotion of design as a territorial value has consolidated the city's industrial heritage and the development of its local innovative capacity. This, however, implies some controversial decisions: conflicts arise frequently between advocates of the local technical history (know-how related to manufacture, invention of technical and commercial processes) and advocates of social history (class struggle, relationships of domination, etc.). Such conflicts reflect the lack of consensus that strategic and one-sided exploitation of local history can generate. Generally, local stakeholders' stories told to others, whether in France or abroad, appear to have performative effects on the history they build. The transformation of Ile de Nantes is one example: the Quartier de le Création would probably not have been built if the Festival des Allumés, the conversion of the old LU factory into a cultural centre and the setting up of the Machines de l'Ile had not already made local stakeholders realise that art and culture could be the driving force of this old industrial territory's regeneration.

Ambience as a resource for a new creative tourism

The recent evolution of Nantes and Saint-Etienne also shows that the implementation of contemporary territorial projects depends on the conditions in which they are staged and on the integration of more cross-cutting initiatives. The linking of policies for cultural, tourism and urban development is based on a 'weakening of the dichotomy between tourists and inhabitants for the benefit of a visitor-consumer' (Fabry *et al.*, 2015). This makes authenticity and quality of life at least as desirable as traditional infrastructure for leisure. This type of hybridisation of local public policy is in part the product of the fruitful collaboration between culture and planning. Cultural projects are thereby generated which have a real urban dimension as well as planning projects that structurally integrate cultural, leisure and recreational activities.

The convergence between the spectacle of creation (artistic, cultural and technical), leisure opportunities and liveability gives urban production a cultural value which circulates among multiple communities (visitors, residents, workers, etc.). The attention paid to fostering specific amiences reflects the wish to build links between various resources (artistic, commercial or social amenities), a wide range of fields of action (design of public space, artistic programming and transport services) and stakeholders who operate in various areas (bar tenders, bookseller, gallery owners, craftspeople, cultural entrepreneurs). The cases of Nantes and Saint-Etienne are in this sense a reflection of the ways a specific cultural ambience is valorised. It is these ambiences, rather than infrastructure, that local stakeholders aim at promoting – an approach which therefore differs from the amenity-led approach that has hitherto been the cornerstone of local cultural policies. A range of technical and creative skills (alternative management of green spaces and street lighting, public space design, installation of works of art, original street furniture, etc.) are thus mobilised in order to transform urban spaces. The logic of cultural tourism is therefore also altered to the extent that the experience of the city based on the senses and the imagination is as good a reason for people to visit it as a tour of the prestigious institution. Such a strategy, however, requires constant innovation in order to maintain the evanescent dimension of tourism based on events (Nantes) and creativity (Saint-Etienne).

Notes

1 Institut national de la statistique et des études économique.
2 Formerly Ernst and Young.
3 The *France créative* platform brings together all professional associations and unions representing the stakeholders of cultural and creative arts www.francecreative.fr.
4 The cultural and creative activities taken into account are: plastic arts and graphic design (including architecture and design), music, cinema, television, radio, live entertainment, the press, publishing and video games.
5 This study carried out in May 2015 by Institut d'Aménagement et d'Urbanisme de la Région d'Ile-de-France shows that about half of the country's cultural and creative industries are concentrated in this area www.iau-idf.fr/savoir-faire/nos-travaux/edition/lecosysteme-creatif-en-ile-de-france-1.html.
6 Title of the cover of *Télérama* magazine no. 2891, 11–17 June 2005.

References

Ambrosino C. and Guillon V. (2013), The Creative City: A French Perspective, in Kunzmann K. and Yan T. (eds), *Creative Cities in Practice*, Beijing: Tsinghua University Press, 242–248.

Béal V., Dormois R. and Pinson G. (2007), Redeveloping Saint-Étienne. The Weight of the Inherited Structure of Social and Political Relationships in a French Industrial City, in Burkner H.J. (ed.), *Urban Trajectories under Conditions of Decline. Economic Crises and Demographic Change as a Trigger for New Concepts of Regeneration*, Berlin: LIT-Verlag.

Becattini G. (1991), The Industrial District as a Creative Milieu, in Benko G. and Dunford M. (eds), *Industrial Change and Regional Development: The Transformation of New Industrial Spaces*, London and New York: Belhaven Press, 102–116.

Bianchini F. and Parkinson M. (1993) *Cultural Policies and Urban Regeneration*, Manchester: Manchester University Press.

Boschma R. and Martin R.L. (2010), *The Handbook of Evolutionary Economic Geography*, Cheltenham: Edward Elgar.

Bruston A. (2005), *Des cultures et des villes, mémoires au futur*, La Tour d'Aigues: l'Aube.

Chantelot S. (2010), Vers une mesure de la créativité: la construction de la classe créative française, *Revue d'économie régionale et urbaine*, 3, pp. 511–540.

Chaudoir J. and Maillard de J. (2004), *Culture et politique de la ville*, La Tour d'Aigues: l'Aube.

DCMS (2001), *Creative Industries Mapping Document*, London.

DCMS (2004), *Culture at the Heart of Regeneration*, London.

Devisme L. (2009), *Nantes, petite et grande fabrique urbaine*, Marseille: Parenthèses.

EY (2013), *Les Secteurs culturels et créatifs européens, générateurs de croissance*, Étude commandée par le Groupement Européen des Sociétés d'Auteurs et Compositeurs (GESAC); Paris: Ernst & Young et Associés.

Fabry N., Picon-Lefebvre V. and Pradel B. (2015), *Narrations touristiques et fabrique des territoires. Quand tourisme, loisirs et consommation réécrivent la ville*, Paris: L'Oeil d'Or.

Florida R. (2002), *The Rise of the Creative Class and How It's Transforming Work, Leisure and Everyday Life*, New York: Basic Books.

Florida R. (2005), *Cities and the Creative Class*, London: Routledge.

Graveleine de F. (2011), *La Création prend ses quartiers. Les chroniques de l'Ile de Nantes*, Nantes: Place Publique.

Greffe X. (2006), *La Mobilisation des actifs culturels de la France. De l'attractivité culturelle du territoire à la nation culturellement créative*, Paris: Ministère de la Culture et de la Communication, Délégation au développement et à l'action internationale, Département des études, de la prospective et des statistiques.

Guibert G. (2010), La scène musicale à Nantes. De la ville perçue à la ville vécue, in Grander M., Guibert G., Pajot S. and Sagot-Duvauroux D., *Nantes, la Belle Eveillée, le pari de la culture*, Toulouse: Editions de l'Attribut, 109–130.

Guillon V. (2011), Mondes de coopération et gouvernance culturelle dans les villes. Une comparaison des recompositions de l'action publique culturelle à Lille, Lyon, Saint-Étienne et Montréal, Thèse de doctorat en Science Politique, University of Grenoble.

Gumuchian H. and Pecqueur B. (2007), *La Ressource territoriale*, Paris: Economica.

Harding A. (1997), Urban Regimes in a Europe of the Cities, *European Urban and Regional Studies*, 4 (4), 291–314.

IAU (2015), L'Écosystème créatif en Île-de-France, Étude réalisée par l'Institut d'aménagement et d'urbanisme de la région d'Île de France.

INSEE (2009), La créativité, clé de l'économie fondée sur la connaissance, *Economie Lorraine*, 199–200.

Landry C. (2000), *The Creative City: A Toolkit for Urban Innovators*, London: Earthscan Publishers.

Landry C. and Bianchini F. (1995), *The Creative City*, London: Demos/Comedia.

Le Galès P. (1993), Rennes: Catholic Humanism and Urban Entrepreneurialism, in Bianchini F. and Parkinson M. (eds) *Cultural Policies and Urban Regeneration*, Manchester: Manchester University Press, 178–198.

Lextrait F. and Kahn F. (2005), *Nouveaux territoires de l'art*, Paris: Éditions Sujet/Objet.

Liefooghe C. (2010), Économie créative et développement des territoires: enjeux et perspectives de recherche, *Innovations*, 31, 181–197.

Liefooghe C. (2015), *L'économie créative et ses territoires: enjeux et débats*, Rennes: Presses Universitaires de Rennes.

Martin-Brelot H., Grossetti M., Eckert D., Gritsai O. and Kovács Z. (2010), The Spatial Mobility of the 'Creative Class': A European Perspective, *International Journal of Urban and Regional Research*, 34 (4), 854–870.

Métral J. (2000), *Cultures en ville ou de l'art et du citadin*, La Tour d'Aigues: Éditions de l'Aube.

Miot Y. (2015), De la ville industrielle à la ville créative: les cas de Roubaix et de Saint-Etienne, in Liefooghe C., *L'Économie créative et ses territoires – enjeux et débats*, Rennes: Presses Universitaires de Rennes, 99–119.

Morteau H. (2015), Gouvernance des clusters culturels pour un développement territorial: une étude comparée internationale, Thèse de doctorat en Aménagement et Urbanisme, University of Angers.

Mortelette C. (2014), La Cité du Design, un équipement culturel pour relancer le territoire stéphanois?, *Belgeo*, http://belgeo.revues.org/12606, accessed on 29 July 2015.

Négrier E. (1993), Montpellier: international Competition and Community Access, in Bianchini F. and Parkinson M. (eds), *Cultural Policies and Urban Regeneration*, Manchester: Manchester University Press, 135–154.

Nelson R. and Winter S.G. (1982), *An Evolutionary Theory of Economic Change*, Cambridge, MA: Belknap Press of Harvard University Press.

L'Observatoire (2009), *La Ville créative, concept marketing ou utopie mobilisatrice?*, Grenoble: Observatoire des politiques culturelles.

Raffin F. (2007), *Friches industrielles. Un monde culturel européen en mutation*, Paris: L'Harmattan.

Saez G. (1995), Villes et culture: un gouvernement par la coopération, *Pouvoirs*, 73, 109–123.

Saez G. (2005), L'action publique culturelle et la transition territoriale du système politique, in Douillet A.-C. and Faure A. (eds), *L'Action publique et la question territoriale*, Grenoble: Presses Universitaires de Grenoble, 229–250.

Saez G. (2012), Le tournant métropolitain des politiques culturelles, in Saez J.-P. and Saez G. (eds), *Les nouveaux enjeux des politiques culturelles. Dynamiques européennes*, Paris: La Découverte, 23–71.

Sagot-Duvauroux D. (2010), La scène artistique nantaise, levier de son développement économique, in Grander M., Guilbert G., Pajot S. and Sagot-Duvauroux D., *Nantes, la Belle Eveillée, le pari de la culture*, Toulouse: Editions de l'Attribut, 95–108.

Santagata W. (2002), Cultural Districts, Property Rights and Sustainable Economic Growth, *International Journal of Urban and Regional Research*, 26 (1), 9–23.

Scott A. (2000), *The Cultural Economy of Cities*, London: Sage Publications.

United Nations (2008), *Creative Economy Report. The Challenge of Assessing the Creative Economy Towards Informed Policy-making*, Geneva and New York: United Nations.

United Nations (2010), *Creative Economy Report, a Feasible Develoment Option*, Geneva and New York: United Nations.

United Nations (2013), *Creative Economy Report, Widening Local Develoment*, Geneva and New York: United Nations.

Urfalino P. (2004), *L'Invention de la politique culturelle*, Paris: Hachette.

Varenne P.H. (2006), Saint-Étienne métropole: le pari du design, *Pouvoirs locaux*, 71, 25–34.

Vivant E. (2009), *Qu'est-ce que la ville créative?*, Paris: Presses Universitaires de France.

Vivant E. and Tremblay D.-G. (2010), *L'Économie créative. Revue des travaux francophones, note de recherche de la chaire de recherche du Canada sur les enjeux socio-organisationnels de l'économie du savoir*, Montreal: Téluq-UQAM, University of Quebec.

Zanetti T. (2010), La Manufacture d'Armes de Saint-Etienne: un conflit mémoriel, *Norois*, 4 (117), 41–55.

Zanetti T. (2011), La Manufacture d'Armes de Saint-Etienne: un patrimoine militaire saisi par l'économie créative, *In Situ*, 16, http://insitu.revues.org/206, accessed on 29 July 2015.

9 Bohemias and the creation of a cosmopolitan tourism destination

Creative practice and consumption in the Ouseburn Valley, Newcastle upon Tyne, UK

James Whiting and Kevin Hannam

Introduction

Tourism has been described as involving a desire for a break from the everyday and a removal of the self from working life and the home environment (Urry 2002). It has also often been seen as a process of temporary 'escape' from the bounds of the tourist's home culture. Other perspectives on travel and tourism activities, however, suggest that many experiences of the 'elsewhere' include similar activities and behaviours as are found in tourists' everyday lives in the home environment (Edensor 2007). The term 'tourist bubble' or 'environmental bubble' has usually been applied to the practices of 'mass' tourists (Cohen 1972, 1979) whose mobilities are often portrayed as a desire for a 'leisure-plus' environment while holidaying.

Our discussion focuses on the mobilities of working artists in the cultural quarter of Newcastle upon Tyne – the Ouseburn Valley. We argue that the working artists in the Valley, while almost all defining themselves as 'travellers' who have a desire to 'get off the beaten track', in many ways exhibit similar behaviours to those that they display in their home lives. Desires for a dedifferentiation of leisure and work in the home environment and for living and working in the provincial bohemia of the Ouseburn Valley in everyday life are matched by a desire to experience totemic bohemias in often larger cities when travelling. Inspiration is also sought in the elsewhere and as such the *vocation* of artist is present when both home and away. Although many artists in the study therefore may denigrate the 'tourist bubble' and experiences of travel that rely upon the 'traditional' tourist infrastructure, there is a parallel 'creative-cosmopolitan' environmental bubble on display.

Creative cities and bohemias

The importance of 'creativity' to regional and national economies has been well documented in both policy and academic circles since the millennium (DCMS 2001) and two strands of creative city discourse can be found in the literature. First Charles Landry (2000) proposes the idea of 'creativity' within the sphere of governance of urban areas, in the ways in which local municipalities and their officers can become creative in their administrations and their working practices. This view of creativity is concerned with how cities can 'work better' and be better administered and governed, often through collaborative approaches and 'joined up thinking'.

The second and arguably more influential strand (see Evans 2009) of creative city thinking emanates from the work of Richard Florida (2002), and is much more concerned with facilitating economic growth in free market contexts. Recent policy directions have highlighted the continuing national importance of creative industries as an export earner for the UK (UKTI 2014), with the sector employing 1.8 million people by 2014 (DCMS 2015). At the urban level, there has been a substantial interaction between the realms of policy and practice in recent years, with the work of Florida in particular influencing economic growth agendas at the level of municipal or urban government (Evans 2009; Peck 2005). Creativity as a broad process is often argued to occur at the urban level due to the possibility of interactions between differently minded people in concentrated, often cosmopolitan, environments, who can share knowledge, generate new ideas and work on projects due to geographical proximity (Florida 2002; Hall 1998).

Ironically, the areas of cities outlined by Florida, and increasingly focused on by local authorities as growth nodes, traditionally would have been seen as 'bohemias', and spaces of marginal lifestyles that embodied romantic values (Wilson 2000), often nominally at least, opposed to the interests of capitalist production and emerging consumer culture (Kauffmann 2004; Seigel 1986). Creativity, within new divisions of global labour, as it has the possibility of generating new products, markets and services, has been looked at as a strategy to rejuvenate 'declining' cities, such as Newcastle upon Tyne, which have lost their traditional manufacturing and industrial bases due to well-documented shifts in patterns of industrial location and production.

Florida (2002) among others (Brooks 2000; Ray and Anderson 2000) deciphers a new form of 'creative worker' at once at ease with the market economy and also desirous of certain aspects of libertarian and self-expressive lifestyles associated with countercultural impulses and bohemias from the 1800s onwards. Florida himself has been criticised for being far too broad in his definition of 'creative working', with his creative class including artists and financial knowledge workers, groups of people who in many ways might have very divergent value systems and lifestyles (Markusen 2006).

As such, following the theoretical reasoning above, many cities have attempted to grow, nurture or sometimes create 'bohemias', or creative quarters that through their appeal to the values and lifestyles of young, educated and tech-savvy workers may attract enough human capital to reach a 'critical mass' of creativity and to reap economic rewards (Evans 2009; Peck 2005). The irony of a form of state-sponsored mass-produced bohemia, however (Forkert 2013), and the ability of such zones to maintain true creative impulses under pressures of regulation and gentrification is contested (Curran 2007; Long 2009; Zimmerman 2008), for, as in Florida's own research, 'generica' and mass spaces of consumption are precisely the areas of cities that his creative class is attempting to escape. This has led in some urban areas to a very 'arm's length' form of governance – a desire to govern such spaces without the appearance of governance – to allow them to retain senses of freedom and spontaneity that are seen to be important to the creative process (Krivy 2013).

Such zones have also become important leisure and tourist resources for cities, and reflect a move towards more individualised forms of tourist consumption that can be defined as creative (Richards 2011; Richards and Wilson 2007), in that consumers wish to be co-authors of their own experiences and to enjoy 'creative' ambiences and environments. The overt promotion of such districts as leisure and tourist resources may, for many cities, be a relatively new phenomenon, but bohemias, such as Paris's Montmartre, have arguably always attracted users from their broader urban areas (Seigel 1986), and the Haight-Ashbury area of San Francisco saw a huge influx of visitors in the summer of 1967 (Medeiros 2005). Following these themes, our discussion focuses on the development of the Ouseburn Valley as a leisure and tourist resource, and also on the Valley as a tourist-generating area for other bohemias.

The Ouseburn Valley as a creative leisure and tourism destination

The Ouseburn Valley, Newcastle upon Tyne, lying on the line of Hadrian's Wall, has developed from being a centre of the Industrial Revolution in the North East of England to being a centre for the creative and digital industries, with facilities for the Valley's workers and for leisure and tourism use (see Figure 9.1). The Valley, originally home to an array of early industrial endeavours including flax milling, tanning, lead mining, coal extraction and transport, and glassmaking from the sixteenth century onwards, suffered decline in the nineteenth and twentieth centuries due to locational constraints and the emergence of newer methods of industrial production and transport (Morgan 1995). The Valley, once home to these industries and to a considerable residential population, had, by the 1970s, due to industrial decline and residential clearance, become an area of cheap land, home to a number of light manufacturing businesses, breakers' yards and garages. The Valley that had also been used as a tipping ground in the 1930s underwent extensive landscaping in the postwar era, leading to a greening of the area which is still valued today (Ouseburn Trust 2008).

The dilapidation of the Valley led both to low rental values of large exindustrial spaces and to an overgrown and fairly empty space that appealed to the financial realities and romantic sensibilities of early 'settler artists' in the 1980s. This period saw the emergence of the Valley's oldest and most well-known studio – 36 Lime Street Artists' Cooperative and Studios (Ouseburn Trust 2012) (see Figure 9.2). The period also saw the opening of a recording and practice studio and by this time a city farm – Byker Farm – was already located in the Valley (Ouseburn Trust 2012). The late 1980s saw the formation of the East

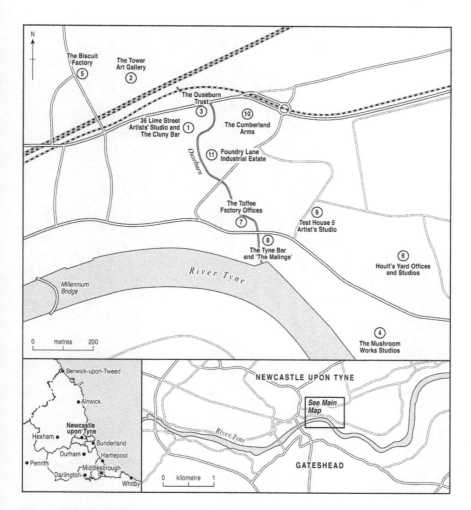

Figure 9.1 Map of the Ouseburn Valley.

Quayside Group in 1988 that was an amalgam of local residential, church and artistic interests aimed at protecting the industrial heritage, greenery and character of the Valley in response to the large-scale regeneration of the adjacent Quay-side area of the city (Langley and Robinson n.d.). The East Quayside Group eventually changed into a more organised governance group – the Ouseburn Trust – a charitable organisation that was formed in 1995 to head a bid for Single Regeneration Budget funding for the Valley, eventually winning £5 million in funding for infrastructure and heritage developments in the Valley; the early 1990s also saw the establishment of a heritage group in the Valley, that would soon be complemented by the Ouseburn Trust's own heritage organisation.

Figure 9.2 36 Lime Street Artists' Cooperative and Studios (source: authors).

The period from the millennium onwards has seen many developments in the Valley that has made it a prime location for leisure use and for creative working in the North East of England and the largest and most important of four creative economy clusters identified in the Newcastle and Gateshead urban area (EKOS 2012) (see Figure 9.3). Around the turn of the millennium, the Ouseburn Trust coordinated a number of public art projects in the Valley including outdoor sculptures and a 'bottle trail' symbolising the glass-making heritage of the area (Ouseburn Trust 2012). Theoretically these developments can be read as signifying that the 'artistic mode of production' (Zukin 1989) had arrived in the Valley and that it was now ready for further development. The year 1999 saw the establishment of the Cluny bar and art gallery that also houses a performance space, mainly for musical acts, and this central venue (both geographically and socially) in the Valley was expanded in 2004. The year 2000 witnessed the beginning of a greater interest in the area on behalf of the local authority, and in this year, due to the industrial architecture and greenery of the area, the Ouseburn Valley was awarded conservation status.

This period also saw the opening of the Mushroom Works, an art gallery and studio in 2004, and in 2006 the Biscuit Factory studios and gallery opened, alongside the Artworks Gallery (the latter has subsequently closed due to financial difficulties). The Valley has borne witness to many other developments in this period including the opening of the Centre for the Children's Book (2006), the redevelopment and reopening of Byker City Farm as Ouseburn Farm (2006), the creation of a barrage over the Ouseburn River, and in 2012, the opening of the old Maynard's toffee factory as 'The Toffee Factory' – a large space on the west bank of the Ouseburn River dedicated to digital and creative industries (Ouseburn Trust 2012) (see Figure 9.4).

Figure 9.3 View of the Ouseburn Valley from Byker Bridge (source: authors).

Figure 9.4 The Toffee Factory (source: authors).

Developments in this part of Newcastle upon Tyne, as well as marking the area as a place of creative production, have also signified the growth of the Ouseburn Valley as a space of leisure and tourist consumption. The area, due to its association with early industry in Tyneside, has become a centre for industrial heritage. The Victoria Tunnel, previously used as a coal tunnel in the nineteenth century to transport coal from the west of the city to the Valley and then to the Tyne, underwent redevelopment in 2008 from a state of dereliction through Heritage Lottery funding, and in 2010 was taken over and run as a toured visitor experience by the Ouseburn Trust. The Victoria Tunnel was voted the Gold Award Winner in the 2013 North East Tourism Small Attraction Awards, and currently, at the time of writing, is recommended as the number one visitor attraction in Newcastle upon Tyne on Trip Advisor (ouseburntrust.org). The industrial age heritage of the Valley is also signified by the general architectural style of the area and by the publication of the *Ouseburn Heritage* journal by the Trust as well as an on-going oral history archive of the area, also run by the Ouseburn Trust.

As well as heritage aspects of the Valley's leisure and tourism product an annual festival is held in July, known as the Ouseburn Festival. This festival has grown from being a small, semi-spontaneous event organised by local artists and nearby residents in the late 1980s, to being a larger and more structured festival that now includes a variety of events from poetry reading and dance performance to musical acts and children's activities. As such the event now provides an important contribution to the Valley's visitor economy. The creative working of the Valley is also entwined with the leisure offerings of the Ouseburn, with the Valley conducting the Open Studios event biannually that allows visitors behind the scenes of artists' workshops and gives artists themselves a promotional opportunity for their work (ouseburnopenstudios.org). A broader Newcastle and Gateshead cultural event, 'The Late Shows', also features many facilities in the Valley including 36 Lime Street Artists' Cooperative and the Victoria Tunnel, and this annual event, in a similar vein to the Open Studios events, allows visitors views into, and creative experiences within, the workshops and studios of the Valley's artists and creative businesses (thelateshows.org.uk).

As well as heritage offerings and discrete events, the Valley has a clear location in Newcastle's nightlife scene, being described as far back as 2001 as an 'alternative' leisure scene in the city (Chatterton and Hollands 2001). The Valley is home to six pubs and bars: the aforementioned Cluny and the Tyne Bar, the Ship Inn, the Free Trade Inn, the Tanners Arms and - most iconic of all – the Cumberland Arms, that describes itself as a traditional pub, and offers real and craft ales and a variety of entertainments from folk and blues music to comedy nights to traditional Northumbrian Rapper dancing. The Valley is also home to a volunteer-run cinema, the Star and Shadow, and to a horse riding stables, and these leisure facilities are complemented by, as previously mentioned, the Centre for the Children's Book, Ouseburn Farm and the general green ambience of the area.

The above descriptions give us some insight into the ways in which the Ouseburn Valley has changed in the last two decades, but we also need to discuss the role of the local state in this process to more fully understand how a previously marginal area has been incorporated, in recent years, into strategic economic planning for the city. The local authority, Newcastle City Council, had up until the turn of the Millennium generally viewed the Ouseburn Valley as an area in need of residential clearance and small-scale industrial development (Newcastle City Council 2003). The remaining residents of the Valley had by the 1970s been moved to social housing developments in other parts of the city, and the main infrastructural development in the area was the creation of the Foundry Lane Industrial Estate in 1983 (Ouseburn Trust 2012) – a concrete and corrugated steel development that would now struggle for planning permission under the Valley's conservation area status.

The local authority, although supporting Single Regeneration Budget (SRB) applications for infrastructural developments in the Valley in 1995, did not until 2003 produce a formal policy document in relation to the Ouseburn Valley as a strategic element in the city's overall development. The *Regeneration Strategy for the Lower Ouseburn Valley* (Newcastle City Council 2003) represents a significant focus on the area as a growth node for the city due to the clustering of creative and cultural businesses located there, and also due to its potential as a tourism and leisure hub outside the city centre of Newcastle upon Tyne. The document states that the local authority's vision for the Ouseburn Valley was that by 2010 it will be a

> thriving sustainable urban village ... the best heritage features of the area
> will have been preserved [and] a wide range of businesses, especially those

relating to creative, innovative, multimedia and cultural activities will be prospering. A wide variety of service and leisure offerings will be available for residents, employees and visitors to the area.

(Newcastle City Council 2003, p. 3)

The same year also witnessed the publication of a joint DEMOS and Royal Institute of Chartered Surveyors report on urban regeneration in the city which suggested that placeness and 'gritty authentic' (Minton 2003) urbanism, as opposed to the large-scale developments of 'traditional' waterfront regeneration projects, was the key to urban growth, through creative economies (see Figure 9.5). These documents clearly reflect the increasing interest on the part of local

Figure 9.5 The 'gritty and authentic' Ouseburn Valley? (source: authors).

authorities and urban policy groups in creativity as a force of urban development. As such these documents reflected the growing interest in the creative
industries at the time found in national policy (DCMS 2001) and academic economic development theory (Florida 2002). Perhaps just as important a signifier
of the local authority's interest in the Ouseburn Valley as a growth engine was
the naming of a new 'Ouseburn' ward in the city in 2004; this name had not previously been used in the electoral boundaries of the city.

In 2012 Newcastle City Council published a second planning document for
the Valley entitled the *Ouseburn Regeneration Investment Action Plan*. This
document noted the development of the Valley in the nine intervening years
since the first regeneration plan and suggested that residential development in
the Valley would be a major keystone of further regeneration of the area. The
document suggested that the Valley had now become a centre of creative industry with 400 businesses employing around 2,000 workers, mainly in the creative
industries (Newcastle City Council 2012). This statistic, however, belies the fact
that the North East Region of England currently has the lowest proportion of
creative economy employment in England (DCMS 2015), with only 5.4 per cent
of jobs in the region coming from this sector. Regardless, the Valley is seen to
be the prime location for the wider Tyneside conurbation's creative economy
growth and it is proposed that the creative economy strategy on Tyneside should
concentrate on building networks and communities of practice between the
Ouseburn Valley and the area's smaller creative clusters (EKOS 2012).

The leisure offerings of the Valley were also strongly highlighted in the 2012
local authority planning document and by 2012 the Ouseburn Valley had become
'one of 3 main concentrations of leisure, culture and tourism in Newcastle and
Gateshead' (Newcastle City Council 2012, 30). The 'alternative and smaller
scale arts, music, heritage and particularly children and family orientated attractions' (Newcastle City Council 2012, 30), alongside the character of the Valley's
pubs and the events held in the area, were outlined as the main drivers for a
visitor economy now numbering 400,000 visits (Newcastle City Council 2012)
per year.

Recent years have seen, in line with the 2012 plans, further residential development in the Valley with a mixture of social and private housing schemes
receiving planning permission. One such development, the Malings, is currently
under construction and when completed will provide 'a new sustainable
community in the heart of Newcastle's historic Ouseburn Valley consisting of
76 low energy, eco-friendly homes with a choice of 1, 2, 3 and 4 bedrooms'
(themalings.co.uk) (see Figure 9.6). A new development at James Place, next to
the Valley's iconic Cumberland Arms pub is also intended to preserve the creative ethos of the Valley in combination with 10 artists' workspaces and 16 residential units, begin development in the near future (Ouseburn Trust 2015).
Residential, creative enterprise, tourism and leisure developments are also
reflected in the *Core Strategy and Urban Core Plan for Gateshead and Newcastle upon Tyne*, adopted in March 2015 after examination by an inspector
appointed by the Secretary of State for Communities and Local Government

Figure 9.6 The Malings residential development (source: authors).

(Newcastle City Council and Gateshead Council 2015). These three aspects of the Ouseburn Valley's development are respectively the three main priorities of the Core Plan that proposes how Newcastle and Gateshead should aim to develop themselves up until the year 2030.

The description above has illustrated how the Ouseburn Valley in Newcastle upon Tyne has emerged from post-industrial dilapidation in the 1970s to become a vibrant cultural hub: a centre of creative industries, leisure use and tourist visitation. This process has occurred due to initial locational preferences of artists, drawn to the area through low rental costs and a desire to inhabit a marginal space, that was, in the 1980s and early to mid-1990s, largely unregulated by the local state and lacking in commercial interest from outside parties. The interest of the local state in the area can be seen to coincide quite clearly with the emergence of the 'creative cities' discourses of the early 2000s, and the desire to maintain and promote a creative sector within Newcastle upon Tyne is clearly articulated in the local authority's support for infrastructural developments in the area, for funding bids, and through the inclusion of the Ouseburn Valley as a distinct aspect of the urban conurbation's overall strategic planning priorities. The importance of tourism and leisure to the Valley and the wider city is also clear. Heritage, alternative nightlife, urban greenery and events, all within a 'creative ambience', are clear pull factors, and the success of the Open Studios and Late Shows in the Valley are testimony to the increasing importance of 'creative experiences' for contemporary leisure users and tourists (cf. Richards 2011; Richards and Wilson 2007).

This discussion of the development of the Ouseburn Valley is now complemented by a discussion of the views of resident artists and leisure users of the

Valley. We discuss how the Valley offers opportunities for 'creative leisure' and networking for creative workers in the area. We also consider how the travel desires of many artists and users of the Valley often look towards creative districts and other bohemias in different cities as travel and tourism destinations.

Community perspectives on the Ouseburn Valley and issues of creative consumption

In-depth semi-structured interviews, as well as a process of participant observation, were conducted over an 18-month period and the findings from these interviews and observations are highlighted as below:

1   The Ouseburn Valley was seen by resident artists and broader users to be an area of leisure opportunities distinct from the rest of the city. It was viewed as a zone that allowed for creative leisure and creative tourism experiences.
2   Travel biographies and future travel intentions revealed a concern for authenticity of experiences and for a continuation of creative experiences when away from the home environment. For many respondents these experiences were to be found in bohemias and cultural districts of other cities, particularly major creative centres such as New York.

The Ouseburn Valley as a centre for creative leisure

The Ouseburn Valley was viewed as a space in which creative leisure experiences could be had, and importantly many respondents suggested that these experiences were not as easily accessible in other areas of the city. Many people were active in the production of self-authored creative practices during their leisure time. One user, not a working artist in the Valley in terms of their primary employment, suggested that their spare time was often taken up with pursuing art and painting, and this creative aspect of their leisure time was afforded by having a studio in the Biscuit Factory art gallery in the Valley. Another individual was also involved in stand-up comedy and music production, and their comedy interests were supported by performing self-authored shows in the Cumberland Arms in the Valley. This same respondent suggested that the Valley was a place where people were more receptive to new and innovative artistic and cultural performances, people who inhabit the Valley's pubs being 'perhaps a little bit more open-minded' than those who may have preferences for bars and pubs in the city centre. A different frequenter of the Valley suggested that although they were in fact a photographic technician they often defined themselves as a 'musician' as the creation of music in time outside work was a key point of their leisure practice and self-identification. For this person the Valley was a space that allowed the rehearsal and performance of their musical production.

Music and the performance of group sessions for aspiring guitarists were also important to another respondent, and again these group sessions were allowed a space within the Cumberland Arms in the Valley. The creative ambience of the

Cumberland Arms was also commented on by two other regulars of the pub who suggested, respectively, that the bar was a place that was defined by 'creativity ... difference and authenticity' where networking with other "creative" individuals was possible. Further to this, another respondent suggested that, as well as allowing for self-expressive performances to be given by patrons, the Cumberland Arms was a place where the creativity of others could be experienced in a spontaneous manner: 'It's great cos it's totally independent and that's quite rare ... and it has traditional music and a culture of people coming together to play music ... you know you'll be sitting there and they all come in with their fiddles' (and start playing).

Another contact, the lead singer in a well-known Newcastle-based alternative music band, suggested that visual art and painting had increasingly taken up her leisure time, an interest in a different creative field to her music and singing. Similarly, a resident of 36 Lime Street Artists' Cooperative and Studios suggested that even though his main employment was as a puppeteer, music still informed an important part of his creative self-expression outside puppetry. He commented that the Valley was a space where musical creativity was a central aspect of leisure practices. This interviewee commented that the Valley was a space where spontaneous self-expression was possible: 'I can go out and walk around and play my mandolin and nobody bats an eyelid ... my wife can walk around wearing fairy wings and a tutu and that's acceptable here where maybe it isn't in the outer world.'

Again, the idea of an outer world suggests that the Valley affords self-expressive and creative experiences that may not be, in the perception of this person, possible in other parts of the city. Other examples of leisure-based creativity can be seen in the suggestion that, although one interviewee was a photography lecturer, photography was more of a vocation than a job, with spare time often being spent on taking photographs and attempting to get them exhibited in gallery spaces in and around the Valley. Further examples of creativity in putatively non-working time were given by a number of respondents in relation to interactions with the landscape of the Valley and the wider city. Two respondents suggested that they were involved in 'guerrilla greening', involving the greening of urban spaces, and the creative transformation of neglected areas of land into garden spaces. A number of other respondents suggested that the Ouseburn Valley Festival was (more so in the past as it was seen to have become more 'commercialised' and 'regulated' in recent years) an opportunity for both the creative production of experiences and experiencing the creativity of others; examples of spontaneous creative practice in this regard involved the spray painting of one artist's car and its conversion into a 'flower box', the spontaneous setting up of sound equipment to have impromptu shows and parties, and the lighting of fires in the area to celebrate the summer solstice.

Travel and tourism experiences of respondents

We have seen above that the Ouseburn Valley acts as an arena for creative leisure experiences within Newcastle upon Tyne. The Valley, through the increase in visitor numbers that it has witnessed in recent years, is also a testament to how these creative experiences within leisure and tourism practices are becoming more popular with broader segments of the population. The respondents often shared accounts of their travel and tourism experiences that pointed to the fact that, for many, creative districts and creative experiences in other places were often motivating factors for travel and tourism. Experiencing other creative districts and other artistic cultures was seen as an integrated practice, strengthening the respondents' vocation of 'artist' or 'creative'.

One interviewee suggested that leisure time activity pursued in the environs of the Ouseburn Valley was often complemented by trips to the Edinburgh Festival to perform comedy routines, and trips to Berlin to interact with and learn from other practising artists, this being an important part of time away from work. Another respondent suggested that they disliked 'generic' urban environments and that one of their favourite places was 'Tacheles (in Berlin) that was once an art squat but now has been turned into a cultural hub where people can just come and chill'. For this individual, travel experiences were a means to increase their knowledge of artistic practice through interacting with artists and their work at other locations. This desire to experience other creative districts was also echoed by respondent 3 who suggested that if she visited New York it would be 'the MOMA and the Guggenheim [that would be of interest] but I would also be interested in going to some of the galleries on the Lower East Side ... I'd go to Brooklyn and to Williamsburg.' The same respondent suggested that if she were to go to Liverpool for a weekend she would be more interested in visiting the Bluecoat Centre, a 'creative hub' that she described as a 'better-resourced version of 36 Lime Street', than anywhere else in the city.

The allure of New York's creative districts was also promoted by two other respondents. One of these interviewees suggested that a visit to the city in the past had been influential in terms of him working with other sculptors in the city and the other suggested that New York, and particularly its creative districts, were places that were 'buzzing' and that afforded inspiration in areas of artistic practice. The desire to experience 'elsewhere bohemias' was also raised by another respondent who suggested that

> I like cities all over really ... I like to go into the centre of cities but I also like to find all of the other interesting places I suppose ... Ouseburn type of areas of cities that are slightly more diverse places.

Venice, as a source of artistic inspiration and learning, was also outlined by interviewees as being an important destination.

The purpose of travel and tourism was importantly, for nearly all of the respondents, bound up with the desire to expand their knowledge and techniques of their particular artistic practice and to generate contacts and opportunities in these cities and creative districts. A musician in the Valley commented that, although it was not his primary means of employment, as a musician he wished to experience the music scenes and everyday creative practices of musicians in other European cities. Other respondents commented that travel and tourism experiences, far from being a total break from their values and behaviours in their home environments, involved 'trying to absorb as much as you can ... and being inspired by these places', 'always looking for new work and new artists [when travelling or on holiday]', and that being an artist is

> what you do all of the time, so it would be quite weird if you didn't take that interest away with you ... it tends to be in your mind all of the time so it's not like you can switch off.

Similar sentiments were also raised by another respondent who suggested that an attempt to differentiate home and travel experiences would be 'really difficult, as part of me's always thinking about work ... I love to go to Brussels cos my brother lives there but I love it cos it's got a fantastic art scene and the architecture's amazing.'

Conclusions

This chapter has discussed how the Ouseburn Valley in Newcastle upon Tyne has been transformed from a marginal space of dereliction and post-industrial decay to a centre for creative industries and leisure and tourism experiences in this city. This transformation has been brought about through initial settlement of artists in the area, who were drawn to the Valley by its marginality, unusual aesthetic of combined green spaces and industrial-age architecture, and its affordability. We have discussed how the political economy of 'creativity', at both the national and the local level, from the millennium onwards fostered a much deeper involvement on the part of the local authority in the area. The desire to nurture the Ouseburn Valley as a creative hub for the city and the wider region was also complemented by the growth of the area as a prime 'alternative' leisure and tourist resource for the city, and as such, the Valley in part can be seen to appeal to the desires of newer tourist motivations that prize creative ambiences and involvement within creative practices as paramount (Richards 2011; Richards and Wilson 2007).

Our study has also demonstrated, at the qualitative level, how workers and leisure users in the Ouseburn Valley desire creative leisure experiences, and how the Valley is seen to be uniquely placed in Newcastle upon Tyne to provide these experiences. The chapter has also reviewed how many of the mobile practices of the artists and users of the Valley search for creative experiences in the elsewhere while travelling or on holiday. As such, the Ouseburn Valley can be seen as a quite specific generating area for other creative destinations. These findings also point to the dedifferentiation or integration of the home lives and the tourism and travel biographies of the respondents, as creativity and a desire to engage with artistic practices are often prime motivating factors for use of the Ouseburn Valley and for travel and tourism experiences.

References

Brooks, D. (2000). *Bobos in Paradise: The New Upper Class and How They Got There.* New York: Simon and Schuster Paperbacks.

Chatterton, P. and Hollands, R. (2001). *Changing our 'Toon' – Youth, Nightlife and Urban Change in Newcastle.* Newcastle upon Tyne: University of Newcastle upon Tyne.

Cohen, E. (1972). Towards a Sociology of International Tourism. *Social Research.* Vol. 39. No. 1: pp. 164–189.

Cohen, E. (1979). A Phenomenology of Tourist Experiences. *Sociology.* Vol. 13: pp. 179–201.

Curran, W. (2007). From the Frying Pan to the Oven: Gentrification and the Experience of Industrial Displacement in Williamsburg, Brooklyn. *Urban Studies.* Vol. 44. No. 8: pp. 1427–1440.

DCMS (2001). *Creative Industries Mapping Document.* London: HMSO.

DCMS (2015). *Creative Industries: Focus on Employment, June 2015.* London: HMSO.

Edensor, T. (2007). Mundane Mobilities, Spaces and Performances of Tourism. *Social and Cultural Geography.* Vol. 8. No. 2: pp. 199–215.

EKOS (2012). *The Creative Sector in Newcastle and Gateshead: Report for Newcastle City Council.* Glasgow: EKOS.

Evans, G. (2009). Creative Cities, Creative Spaces and Urban Policy. *Urban Studies.* Vol. 46. No. 5: pp. 1003–1040.

Florida, R. (2002). *The Rise of the Creative Class: And How it's Transforming Work, Leisure, Community and Everyday Life.* New York: Basic Books.

Forkert, K. (2013). The Persistence of Bohemia. *City.* Vol. 17. No. 2: pp. 149–163.

Hall, P. (1998). *Cities in Civilization.* London: Weidenfeld and Nicholson.

Kauffmann, E. P. (2004). *The Rise and Fall of Anglo America.* Cambridge, MA: Harvard University Press.

Krivy, M. (2013). Don't Plan! The Use of the Notion of 'Culture' in Transforming Obsolete Industrial Space. *International Journal of Urban and Regional Research.* Vol. 37. No. 5: pp. 1724–1726.

Landry, C. (2000). *The Creative City: A Toolkit for Urban Innovators.* London: Earthscan.

Langley, B. and Robinson, P. (n.d.). *Sustainability and Regeneration in the East End of Newcastle.* No publisher or place of publication.

Long, J. (2009). Sustaining Creativity in the Creative Archetype: The Case of Austin, Texas. *Cities.* Vol. 26: pp. 210–219.

Markusen A. (2006). Urban Development and the Politics of a Creative Class: Evidence from a Study of Artists. *Environment and Planning A.* Vol. 38. No. 10: pp. 1921–1940.

Medeiros, W. (2005). Mapping San Francisco 1965–1967: Roots and Florescence of the San Francisco Counterculture. In Grunenberg, C. and Harris, C. (eds) *Summer of Love: Psychedelic Art, Social Crisis and Counterculture in the 1960s.* Liverpool: Liverpool University Press, pp. 303–348.

Minton, S. (2003). *Northern Soul: Culture, Creativity and Quality of Place in Newcastle and Gateshead.* London: RICS/Demos.

Morgan, A. (1995). *Bygone Lower Ouseburn*. Newcastle upon Tyne: Newcastle City Libraries and Arts.

Newcastle City Council (2003). *Regeneration Strategy for Lower Ouseburn Valley*. Newcastle upon Tyne: Newcastle City Council.

Newcastle City Council (2012). *Ouseburn Regeneration Investment Action Plan*. Newcastle upon Tyne: Newcastle City Council.

Newcastle City Council and Gateshead Council (2015). *Planning for the Future: Core Strategy and Urban Core Plan for Gateshead and Newcastle upon Tyne (2010–2015). Adopted March 2015.* Newcastle upon Tyne: Newcastle City Council.

Ouseburn Open Studios (2015). *The Open Studios.* Available at: www.ouseburnopen studios.org. Accessed 1 May 2015.

Ouseburn Trust (2008). *Ouseburn Trust Annual Report 2007–2008.* Newcastle upon Tyne: Ouseburn Trust.

Ouseburn Trust (2012). *A Celebration of 30 Years of Ouseburn Regeneration.* Newcastle upon Tyne: Ouseburn Trust.

Ouseburn Trust (2015). *Newsletter.* February. Newcastle upon Tyne: Ouseburn Trust.

Ouseburn Trust (2015). *The Ouseburn Trust.* Available at: https://ouseburntrust.org.uk/victoria-tunnel/. Accessed 4 May 2015.

Peck, J. (2005). Struggling with the Creative Class. *International Journal of Urban and Regional Research.* Vol. 29. No. 4: pp. 740–770.

Ray, P. H. and Anderson, S. (2000). *The Cultural Creatives: How 50 Million People are Changing the World.* New York: Three Rivers Press.

Richards, G. (2011). Creativity and Tourism: the State of the Art. *Annals of Tourism Research.* Vol. 38. No. 4: pp. 1225–1253.

Richards, G. and Wilson, J. (2007). Tourism Development Trajectories: From Culture to Creativity? In Richards, G. and Wilson, J. (eds) *Tourism Creativity and Development.* London: Routledge, pp. 1–34.

Seigel, J. (1986). *Bohemian Paris: Culture, Politics and the Boundaries of Bourgeois Life 1830–1930.* Baltimore: Johns Hopkins University Press.

The Late Shows (2015). *The Late Shows.* Available at: www.thelateshows.org.uk/home.html. Accessed 1 May 2015.

UKTI (2014). *UK Creative Industries – International Strategy.* London: HMSO.

Urry, J. (2002). *The Tourist Gaze* (2nd edn). London: SAGE.

Wilson E. (2000). *Bohemians: The Glamorous Outcasts.* London: I.B. Tauris.

Zimmerman, J. (2008). From Brew Town to Cool Town: Neoliberalism and the Creative City Development Strategy in Milwaukee. *Cities.* Vol. 25: pp. 230–242.

Zukin, S. (1989). *Loft Living: Culture and Capital in Urban Change* (2nd edn). New Brunswick: Rutgers University Press.

10 The gamer as tourist

The simulated environments and impossible geographies of videogames

Michael Salmond and Jacqueline Salmond

With the increase in graphical fidelity of computers and the advances in screen and virtual reality technologies, new worlds have opened up for tourists. These virtual spaces, those that exist on gaming consoles and computers, are designed in much the same way that physical spaces are designed by those with a focus on tourism. In recent decades, countries and their populations have constantly manufactured cities, open spaces, parks and even wildernesses such as Yellowstone National Park to entice and serve tourists. International entertainment corporations have created environments with infrastructure and areas as large as small cities purely for tourists to enjoy (Walt Disney World, Universal Studios, etc.), Along with the entirely created environments are locations which are artificially enhanced to create a hybrid space, part real and part fake. The trapped aesthetic of Veniceland, the idealized tourist trope of Venice, Italy (Davis and Marvin, 2004), or Stratford-upon-Avon with its focus on Shakespeare (Hubbard and Lilley, 2000), are examples of such hybrid locations. These altered and created geographies are as fake and virtual as any digital realm created for a videogame. These spaces are removed from our realities and are cultivated to remain in an altered state for the benefit of tourists. This chapter argues that the creation and exploration of the digital realm can be considered alongside the more traditional types of tourism.

Videogames as an industry bring together a number of sub-areas of the creative industries, such as visual arts, music, software engineering, advertising and marketing, and are therefore a large and growing sector of the creative industries. We would argue that videogames are also part of the creative industries from a theoretical perspective; games can enable their players to be creative and generate new or unique virtual experiences which can be shared and circulated. Similarly within the physical tourism industry there is a practical connection to the creative industries through graphics, advertising, marketing, etc. and there is a theoretical connection to tourism through the exploration of physical environments. It is this overlap of the connection to tourism which this chapter will explore: how videogames allow the gamer to enact a touristic lifestyle within a virtual environment and create feedback loops between physical and virtual realities.

The gamer tourist

Within the tourism literature how and why people travel has been considered in a variety of ways (Theobald, 2005). There is also a rich body of literature exploring the identification of the tourist, and whether this is the best term, or traveler, or backpacker, or some new identity (McCabe 2005). One enduring thread which crosses much of the tourism literature is that people travel to *experience*. The scale, scope, depth, style, quality, and quantity of experience may vary across and within groups, but experience is a constant which separates the tourist-traveler from the business traveler. It is the desire for experience which most closely links physical travelers with digital travellers, as Endensor states: "tourism is extraordinary rather than mundane ... it concerns 'play' rather than 'work'" (2001: 2). Gamer-tourists have much the same rationale for "visiting" a digital space as real-world tourists: a desire for experience, adventure, fantasy fulfilment, and exploration. Along with touristic motivations, gamer-tourists enact touristic behaviors; they collect locations and souvenirs, take photographs, record video, and tell stories about their travels.

Videogames have borrowed tourism-based terminology and actions and incorporated them within games. To encourage players to explore an environment the most commonly used reward is the "tourism" achievement. The videogame Halo 2 (Bungie, 2004) has an achievement called "tourist" which is obtained when a player has "visited" and played eight different multiplayer maps. The videogame Crysis 2 (Crytek, 2011) has a "tourist" achievement for collecting in-game "souvenirs". The game Borderlands (Gearbox Software, 2009) has a tourist achievement which is gained by interacting with statues of one of the characters which are dispersed around various locations in the game. These achievements are linked to the gamer's profile and are viewable by friends or others dependent on their profile settings. The achievements become souvenirs to be shown to those outside of the game and are a way to show where the gamer-tourist has "travelled" and the experiences they have had. These achievements, trophies or souvenirs are part of the game-developers' reward system which is used to encourage certain modes of play and experimentation within the game. They also fulfill the "collector" mentality common in game culture of wanting to complete as much of the game as possible and prove it to those outside of the game (Graft, 2009). These reward systems are used by the developers to encourage particular modes of play and experimentation or to introduce aspects of the games' system. This in-game behavior and enactment parallel those of a tourist updating their Facebook streams or blogs with images of themselves on vacation and sharing videos and photos of experiences for consumption by others (White and White, 2007). A gamer displays the depth of their interaction with the game space; a tourist uses social media to broadcast their interactions with their destination.

Along with souvenir collection, mediation through photography, and recording, the tourist experience has been adopted by the videogame creators and players too. Duncan Harris of deadendthrills.com does not play games in the traditional sense; instead he captures images and records their beauty, action or moments in exactly the same way as a tourist visiting Paris would. In a similar vein James Pollock has a blog called "virtual geographic" which is dedicated to his photography of game environments, events, and landscapes. These creative individuals are part of a larger in-game photography community of tourists and aesthetes who are using videogames as destinations. Videogame developers such as Naughty Dog took up this trend and developed a specific in-game "photo mode" for its remastered version of "The Last of Us" (Naughty Dog, 2014). Whilst playing the characters, this photo-mode enables the player to create their own imagery within the game environment, posing characters and recording landmarks, environments, or actions (as one of the in-game characters you can even take selfies). This shift from playing to a more measured experience which allows for meditations on a virtual environment is symptomatic of a shift within the gaming mindset away from visceral thrills and toward habitation and reflection within virtual worlds.

In a videogame the player is immersed in an overlaid universe which explores alternative versions of reality and this allows for the deployment of touristic modalities of exploration of the virtual space. Players can enact touristic behaviors by "collecting" locations, by recording and broadcasting their game play or by accumulating in-game 'souvenirs'. In the videogame Animal Crossing (Nintendo, 2001) players can link with others and visit the lands they have created as part of the game play, creating tourists out of other players as they explore the player-crafted environments. Many Role Playing Games (RPGs) within the fantasy genre use quests and narrative (in the form of maps and historical and/or geographical information) to enhance the player's connection to the place, in effect becoming "tour guides" for the player. This is especially true of the genre of open-world games where there is no set path or experience that directs the player toward specific events and outcomes. The openness of the world enables the player to explore the environment in much the same way as its real world analog. Open-world games (examples would be the Grand Theft Auto series from Rockstar Games, the Assassin's Creed Series from Ubisoft, and The Elder Scrolls series from Bethesda Game Studios) reward the players for exploring their environment and have in-built serendipitous moments where a player may encounter something unexpected and remarkable (creating memorable experiences), as they would when exploring a real environment. This chapter will explore several different aspects of videogames operating as tourism destinations including representations of real environments (e.g., Fallout 3 and The Last of Us), fictional spaces (e.g., Skyrim and Mass Effect), historical explorations (L.A. Noire and Assassin's Creed) and impossible spaces (Katamari Damacy).

Real spaces and manufactured reality

There are a number of ways in which videogames generate spaces that can be visited and experienced. Videogames utilize "real" and "unreal" spaces to allow for a multitude of explorable environments. The game spaces can be representations of existing present-day cities (London in the game The Getaway, Team Soho, 2002), natural environments (the underwater environments of Endless Ocean, Arika, 2007), historical representations (1947 Los Angeles in L.A. Noire, Team Bondi, 2011), potential realities (the nuclear wasteland of Washington DC in Fallout 3, Bethesda Game Studios, 2008), or the fantastic (the mystical worlds of Final Fantasy X, Square, 2001). Each created environment allows for or encourages touristic behaviors; this is especially true in the open-world mechanic which was created as an escape from previously more confined and restrictive game-play models. In these previous mechanics players could only follow a predetermined path toward completing a game (known as "on rails" game formats, for example Doom, ID Software, 1993). Even within this model there is a connection to tourism modalities: the "on rails" format is not dissimilar to the predetermined path of a package tour. There is little or no deviation from the main path in the game or the tour in these models. The open-world system is the opposite; these games have enormous maps that cover a large area or areas where the player can wander from town to town or location to location. The creation of the mechanic of the open-world videogame came about not just due to improvements in computer technology and graphical fidelity, but from the wish of developers and gamers to be able to "reach the mountains you can see in the distance".

The open world game translates to the tourist real-world analog: a player and their character are free to roam the created landscape. There are limitations that do not necessarily exist in the real world of course: a player cannot dive into the ocean and swim to an island or new continent, or even take a boat there unless the game permits it. This restriction is not untrue of the real world either as passage between borders or areas is often controlled in some way. Within the rules of the game world the player is free to travel, explore, and discover. This is where the closest analogy with tourism lies: the player enacts the modality of a tourist. Open-world games still retain the familiar components of many genre games, giving the player quests and mini-quests to complete but there is often no set order in which the quests have to be completed. Players in open-world games such as Skyrim, Grand Theft Auto V, and Fallout 3 can choose to do quests or not. If they choose to, the player could just wander around the game space looking at and interacting with the environment for no purpose other than to explore. Because they are games, there are triggers within the worlds which are there to encourage specific behaviors or choices for the player which in turn drive the narrative or action of the game forward. This is paralleled with inter-actions with other tourists and tour guides which can encourage a tourist to explore particular places or objects. Effectively a tourist can be given quests by others to complete their tourism narrative of being fully immersed in a foreign place; this is not unlike what occurs in many RPGs.

Interactions within open-world games usually occur through quests (or tasks) a player is given by a Non-Player Character (NPC). The NPC exists in the world to advance the player to a particular point and experience. The concept of being sent on a quest is not specific to tourism terminology, but the trips that tourists do take can be thought of as quests. The parallels are close enough for us to suggest the definition of gamer-tourist: one who enacts the same behaviors within a game world as they would in the real world. A gamer-tourist can seek out quests of their own by interacting with NPCs (other tourists, tour guides, etc.) or reading travel blogs and seeking previous visitors' advice. A quest could be as innocuous as being told by a friend that they should "should check out the Eiffel Tower, it's amazing," when visiting Paris, and the individual can choose whether or not to succumb to that peer pressure and indulge in that experience. In the game Skyrim an NPC can ask the player to find a lost item; then, if the quest piques the interest of the player they may undertake it knowing that there will be some form of reward at the end. Quests can be self-imposed by player-tourists too; this can range from looking at an in-game map and wondering what a temple looks like, to trying to find a particular monument, store, or interesting location within the game world.

A quest-giver NPC is the equivalent of a tour guide, having a predetermined concept of what the player-tourist should and should not see (pre-programmed in the case of the videogame) and offering an experience within those restrictions. The tour guide is there to establish the most important and must-see elements of the land you are visiting and their job is to get you to these monuments or experiences regardless of whether you had that much interest in the quest originally. Grand Theft Auto V (Rockstar North, 2013) and Sleeping Dogs (United Front, 2012) reflect directly on the player-tourist in the virtual cities of the game. One example of a tourist quest comes from the videogame Sleeping Dogs which is set in contemporary Hong Kong. The player's character Wei Shen meets an American student, Amanda Cartright, and if the player chooses to talk to this character they can agree to meet her for a date in Victoria Park, a real location in Hong Kong. Once there, Amanda asks the player to take photographs of her for her blog, directly enacting the role of NPC quest-giver and focusing the narrative as well as enacting touristic behavior. This is an example of a real-world analog to that of a young tourist of a similar age "hooking up" whilst traveling. In Grand Theft Auto V, the fictional city of Los Santos (which is very much based upon Los Angeles) crosses over realities in that it is fully explorable on a version of Google Maps and has its own in-game tourism board that supplies the player with quests focused on player-tourist exploration. In both of these videogames player-tourists are collecting images, memories and different experiences from these locations. The gamer is performing the role of a tourist, consuming created landscapes in the virtual world.

In addition to the processes of photographing, interacting with or collecting locations, videogames can recreate particular understandings of place. Game developers use the backdrops of real cities as deliberate aesthetic link that build upon familiarity and borrow the authenticity of a real city. Players have an internal model of how a city works, even if they have not visited this particular one, because they have learned about cities from other media such as film or television. This internal model allows the game developer to use stereotypes as cognitive shortcuts for the player that will make the space more believable and therefore more immersive (Madigan, 2010). If Japanese players have never visited London or New York it is likely they have experienced a version of that city in another media format such as film or television. They know that the location exists in the real world and thus this connection makes the digital version that much more believable. Although the realities of the actual locations may be altered in videogames, knowing that the game space is built upon a real space adds authenticity and a sense of realism in regard to presence for the player. Much as in the tourism mindset, this authenticity is an important part of experiencing place and is a valued aspect of the game experience. A virtual version of New York City or London can be as accurate or fantastical as the developer sees fit. Videogame developers can layer over a real city to create an alternate or fanciful version whilst maintaining the essence of that city space. The player internalizes the map of the location using landmarks and geographies in the same way as they would in the real world. Games enable creative connections with real-world spaces that can fire the imagination of players in much the same way that J.K. Rowling layers a fantasy wizard world on top of our reality, creating an impossible but imaginative Harry Potter version of London. The Harry Potter series has been very useful for the British Tourist Board in being able to promote itself to individuals who have grown up with the boy wizard and now want to connect with that world as much as possible (Topham, 2003). This same leverage could be brought to bear from the videogame industry.

Sleeping Dogs is set in contemporary Hong Kong but its fiction is grounded within Hong Kong martial arts cinema popularized by actors and directors such as Jackie Chan and Jon Woo. When a player is running or driving through Hong Kong in Sleeping Dogs, they are aware that this is a version of a real city, but (unless they reside in Hong Kong) they will have no idea how accurate the rendition is. The closeness to reality is less important than the generation of a particular sense of place: a feel of a location rather than an actuality. What occurs is an internal generalization of the depiction of the foreign space, a feeling that it is close enough to get a sense of the city. The experience of the gamer-tourist is related to their level of trust in the development team. If the setting is modern-day Hong Kong, London or Tokyo, the player may have a reasonable expectation that the developers are going to create a faithful rendition of that location if that is what the game aesthetic demands. There are now several channels on YouTube dedicated to "game versus real world comparisons" (IGN, Mr McKane, Roosterteeth). The comparison video may focus on the historical accuracy, the physical mapping, or the architectural correctness of a game's location. These videos are shot by tourists as well as locals and directly link videogames to tourism; people go out of their way to experience a real location based upon their experiences in a videogame. There has been a considerable amount of crossover from the virtual game world to the real world (merchandise, cosplaying, conferences, etc.) and tourism is becoming the newest incarnation of this trend. For example in the game Resistance Fall of Man (Insomniac Games, 2006), a virtual and alternate reality version of the cathedral of Manchester (UK) was used. The in-game representation was realistic enough to concern the cathe-

dral's owners who brought a lawsuit charging the game's developers with dese-
cration (the suit was subsequently dropped). As a by-product of its inclusion in
the videogame, the cathedral experienced an upswing in visitor numbers (Arendt,
2007). People who had played Resistance Fall of Man became gamer-tourists
eager to see the real space they had only witnessed in their game.

Reality reimagined

As well as the virtualization and re-rendering of the real word, videogames
create impossible or unlikely spaces. Some of these spaces may be based on
existing reality, tweaked a little to create a new experience (for example, the
Grand Theft Auto IV and V reinterpretations of New York City and Los Angeles
respectively). When playing games such as Fallout 3, The Last of Us and Skyrim
it is understood by the player that although the space is based on a semblance of
our reality the game space operates within the narrative rules of a world that
could exist if a nuclear explosion occurred in the USA (Fallout 3) or an infection
created mutated citizens in Boston (The Last of Us), or the Vikings' mythologies
and magic were real (Skyrim). Videogames are always fantasy environments,
and they are often impossible spaces. This is one of the reasons why videogames
are so engaging to players: they perform the function of wonder, and they fire the
imagination, offering possible futures or pasts based upon our own experiences.

The videogame Fallout 3 creates a post-apocalyptic area known as "the
wasteland, where anarchy reigns, survival is tough and hardship is very real."
The physical location for the wasteland is based on Washington DC, thereby
allowing the gamer as tourist to experience the location in a way not possible in
reality. The gamer-tourist can be visiting a space they would not actually wish to
visit but through the game they are able to experience an alternative version of a
space which can influence their understandings of the real world. The impossible
environments of the videogame space perform a very specific tourist function:
they give us access to possibilities and spaces formed from others' imagination.
As well as fantasy or future possibilities, there are historical environments which
would be impossible to visit without a time machine. A stand-out in the recreation of historical environments is the Assassin's Creed franchise (Ubisoft).
The series begins with the first game set in the twelfth century (Assassin's Creed,
2007) and has its latest installment (Assassin's Creed; Syndicate, 2015) set in
the nineteenth century. The main focus of these games has been historical as the
settings move from the twelfth-century Middle East focusing on the cities of
Masyaf, Jerusalem, Acre and Damascus, to fifteenth-century Florence to colonial
Boston and New York. The eighteenth-century setting was geographically
located in the Caribbean and revolutionary Paris, with the nineteenth-century
setting of a stylized Victorian London. Ubisoft, the creators of the Assassin's
Creed franchise, have sunk enormous resources into crafting accurate versions
of these geographies for the player to experience (Stuart, 2010).

These games produce an historical space through the generation of historical
façades and architecture of their period setting. The immersive environments can

be "visited" from the ground to the rooftops, with many objects and locations carrying historical facts that are overlaid in the game. The on-screen "guides" of historical places are written much like a tourist guide book would be; they include characters from the world that the player may have met and their history, as well as historical context and back-story for the landmark or building. For example, in Assassin's Creed 2, the developers created fifteenth- and sixteenth-century versions of parts of Florence, Venice, Forli and Tuscany. When a player encounters a location of historical importance such as the Basilica di San Lorenzo, an in-game prompt offers historical context for the location and land-mark. This is the game performing the role of a tour guide, providing additional historical and contextual information to the gamer-tourist, enriching their experience and understanding of a particular location (the player can decline the prompt if they so wish, the main focus of the game being action). This guide book approach was especially prominent in the early incarnations of the game franchise, Assassin's Creed 1, 2, and 3. The fifth game, Unity (2014), was developed by 10 studios and took seven years to create an almost one-to-one scale model of revolution-era Paris. Because of the nature of the open-world game, the player is free to roam the city or landscape without having to engage with the game narrative or action. When playing as Altaïr ibn-La'Ahad in twelfth-century Jerusalem or as Ezio Auditore da Firenze in fifteenth-century Florence, the player can wander around as a gamer-tourist. The non-player characters are, for the most part, accurately dressed and the cities accurately mapped from original plans, sketches, and historical record. Assassin's Creed 2 takes specific pains to engage the player with the socio-political landscape of Renaissance Italy. This set of games has specifically focused on historical accuracy and has been leveraged in some small part by Italian tourism entrepreneurs, some of whom offer Assassin's Creed tours of Florence which match the game's content with real-world history, context, and surviving locations. The cultural overlap that occurs in 3D game versions of geographies enables historical and immersive interactions to take place. These overlaps make the virtual world of the game seem more real and add depth. They also serve as a knowledge function for the player. The gamer-tourist is able to experience a location in a unique way in a different context than the physical tourist.

Unreality

There are also digital spaces that have no real-world analog. In 2011 a UK-based game developer, nDreams, created a floating archipelago within the online space of Sony's PlayStation Home. Aurora, the digital archipelago, received over a million visitors in its first six weeks of opening, which according to the press release was more "than the Taj Mahal and the London Eye combined" (IGN, 2011). The success of Aurora goes some way to proving that there is a very real interest in "traveling" to digital spaces and operating as a tourist within that space. The ease of "travel" to Aurora was a factor in its initial success (all that was required to visit the island was an internet connection and a PlayStation 3 console) with visits to the digital island continuing for six years and amassing over 18 million visits by 1.8 million unique "players" over the lifetime of Play-Station Home (IGN, 2011). Unlike many real-world tourists, digital tourists revisited often and created communities, effectively becoming natives of a new land. Some visited Aurora once, and some came back multiple times, which enabled them to then act as guides for new visitors. The message boards for the Aurora community had many active members who became greeters, police and citizens of the new land, moving from tourists to locals (essentially migrating).

Another example of unreality which also incorporates cultural signifiers and souvenir collection is the videogame Katamari Damacy (Namco, 2004). In this Japanese-developed videogame the player has to collect items from the game world to repopulate the universe with stars made from 'stuff'. The items that are collected are Japan-centric and offer a sociocultural crossover opportunity for Western players. The game's settings are fantastical but also uniquely Japanese in origin, from a tatami-matted house to a city populated with Japanese school children, sushi, Power Rangers-style action figures and other items that reflect Japanese identity and popular culture. The game world of Katamari Damacy makes no literal sense but it has a strong aesthetic and is not just reflective of creative Japanese videogame development but also connects non-Japanese players with aspects of Japanese culture. The fantasy environment fulfills many stereotypes but also provides the possibility of insights into how the Japanese see their own cultural artifacts as well as creating an impossible space that is totally unique for the player. Each level in Katamari Damacy is different and comprises a series of "lands" that are whimsical and imaginative. The gamer-tourist is able to explore and interact with these unique environments. The first game in the series became a cult hit and this created spill-over into our own reality with merchandise, cosplay, and makers who created their own artifacts based upon the game. Fans of the game were in effect creating their own souvenirs of a place that does not exist in our own reality, but the connection was so strong that the players wanted to take something from the virtual world and bring it into the real world as a way to remember and connect with that space. This enactment of souvenir creation and relation to an experience is taken directly from the language of tourism, the need to connect and reconnect with a space and a time (Collins-Kreiner and Zins, 2011).

Player and tourist fantasy fulfillment – enacting versions of self

Tourism for some involves a process of self-transformation (Bruner, 1991) or an opportunity to enact a different version of the self (Tucker, 2005). Many touristic behaviors are pre-defined by certain actions, or performances, which encourage particular behaviors (Endensor, 2001) or are activities not performed at home (Urry, 2002). An example could be a young female tourist who is far more promiscuous on vacation in Ibiza than she would be at home. It could be a 40-something male who wants to been seen as more "cultured" and "knowledgeable" and so visits wineries and art galleries, an act he does not perform at home. Tourists may also change their physical appearance; this could be weight loss, fake tans, haircuts or highlights and so on. They may also wear different clothing to that of home, sometimes due to necessity (beachwear etc.), sometimes due to affectation (Panama hat or particular brand of backpack). In all these ways the tourist "shell" allows individuals to enact different versions of themselves, what are essentially fantasy selves.

Similarly, videogame scenarios and playable characters in a videogame allow for an alternate self to be created. This could be action hero, savior of the universe or mass murderer with no judicial penalty; it could be a different gender or an animal. RPG and open-world videogame characters can also change their physical appearance, clothing, hairstyles, and accessories. For example, Skyrim allows players to customize their in-world character look: their race (not just human), skin color, size, weight, and other visual qualities. The character customization occurs before the game begins and enables the player to begin to connect with the avatar and to transfer or play out personality traits the player/ author feels are relevant to the new character. Avatar customization is a performative act, one that enables the player to imbue traits into their avatar and this can directly affect in-game decisions and interactions. Videogames therefore offer a more extreme version of self-creation than physical tourism, but they perform the same function. They allow the individual to experiment with a different self-identity and to experience interactions and experiences in a different way.

Conclusion

Tourism is no longer just realized in the physical world; gamers as tourists are visiting imagined, impossible, and artificial versions of our own world. Allowing the player to enact touristic behaviors creates a new form of experience that generates different understandings. As the digital becomes more immersive and "real" there are increasing crossovers between the real and the unreal. Individuals become attached to their digital self or avatar as they see this projection as a more appropriate representation of (their) self. Gamers travel and share stories of experiences in much the same way as traditional tourists. The slippage between real and virtual continues unabashed in Japan where virtual locations are now being mapped onto real locations to make them tourist destinations. A Japanese game developer, Capcom Entertainment, has capitalized on similarities between rural locations and the locations of its hit series Monster Hunter (2004–). A spa resort in Yamanouchi, Nagano Prefecture, held a Monster Hunter-themed event which brought fans of the game as new tourists to a location that was previously unremarkable and lacking in visitors (Dutton, 2011). Konami, another Japanese videogame developer, has created events in different locations across the country based on fabricated location from their dating sim Love Plus. Game developers in Japan have partnered with a botanical park in Mimata to cross-promote a game Colony na Seikatsu Plus and have marketed it and the location through merchandise; fans' reactions and visits to the park ramped up considerably (Westbrook, 2011).

Videogames which are set in particular locations draw on an ideal (and/or dystopian) image of an environment or space, utilizing fantasy elements which could increase interest in physical travel to a location. As part of the creative industries, videogames could be used to promote real-world locations to people who would have previously had little or no interest in them. Entertainment in any medium makes connections with audiences. Another approach could be for tourist agencies to work with videogame developers. So, for tourists who desire authenticity and more depth when seeking a location and who wish to become more immersed in that culture, videogames could enable that connection to occur before a trip takes place. Videogames such as the Assassin's Creed franchise allow a historical engagement with a city that no longer exists or still exists in part as a tourist destination. Those who play the game would connect with its settings in a way that is nuanced and to an extent knowledgeable. What is clear is that the new medium of the videogame is creating a new form of tourist: on the one hand, the gamer-tourist, who views visiting a virtual world in the same way they would view a real-world location; and the informed and engaged gamer-tourist who having seen a location in a videogame is driven to experience its real-life counterpart. Embracing the medium of videogames for tourism whenever possible will drive a new form of tourism experience. Clearly there are opportunities to utilize videogames as cultural connectors to countries, cities or cultures in the same way that television and film are utilized to promote or brand locations (New Zealand's connection to the *Lord of the Rings* film franchise, Tunisia's connection to the *Star Wars* films and the London of *Sherlock Holmes*, etc.). However, whenever a location and/or culture is presented and packaged, particular understandings of people and places are generated, some of which may not represent all community members or the desired development of a location. Both videogames and tourism do this, and therefore it is important to be aware of the understandings which are being created when a location is utilized, whether digital or physical.

References

Andrews, M. (1989). *The Search for the Picturesque: Landscape Aesthetics and Tourism in Britain, 1760–1800*. Stanford, CA: Stanford University Press.

Arendt, S. (2007). Church of England Finally Forgives Sony for Resistance, *Wired*, October 24, www.wired.com/2007/10/church-of-eng-1/, accessed March 12, 2015.

Assassin's Creed 2 Tours, www.tripadvisor.com/ShowUserReviews-g187895-d2181 488-r181628319-Guided_Tours_of_Florence-Florence_Tuscany.html, accessed April 18, 2015.

Bruner, E. (1991). The Transformation of Self in Tourism. *Annals of Tourism Research*, 18(2), 238–250.

Collins-Kreiner, N. and Zins, Y. (2011). Tourists and Souvenirs: Changes Through Time, Space and Meaning. *Journal of Heritage Tourism*, 6(1), 17–27.

Davis, R. and Marvin, G. (2004) *Venice, the Tourist Maze: A Cultural Critique of the World's Most Touristed City*. Berkeley: University of California Press, eBook Collection (EBSCOhost), accessed May 27, 2015.

Desforges, L. (2000). Traveling the World: Identity and Travel Biography. *Annals of Tourism Research*, 27(4), 926–945.

Dutton, F. (2011). Monster Hunter Helps Japanese Tourism: Rural Resort Ships in Gamers, July 1, www.eurogamer.net/articles/2011-01-07-monster-hunter-helps-japanese-tourism, accessed April 20, 2015.

Edensor, T. (2000). Staging Tourism: Tourists as Performers. *Annals of Tourism Research*, 27(2), 322–344.

Edensor, T. (2001). Performing Tourism, Staging Tourism: (Re)producing Tourist Space and Practice. *Tourist Studies*, 1(1), 59–81.

Graft, K. (2009). Analysis: The Psychology Behind Item Collecting and Achievement Hoarding. May 29: Gamsutra.com, accessed April 27, 2015.

Grand Theft Auto, GTA V Google Map of San Andres, http://gta-5-map.com/, accessed May 27, 2015.

Hernandez, P. (2014). The Last of Us: Remastered's New Photo Mode is Fantastic. *Kotaku*, August 4, http://kotaku.com/the-last-of-us-remastereds-new-photo-mode-is-fantastic-1615795216, accessed March 12, 2015.

Hubbard, P. and Lilley, K. (2000). Selling the Past: Heritage-tourism and Place Identity in Stratford-upon-Avon. *Geography*, 85(3), 221–232.

IGN (2011). New Virtual Archipelago Gets More Visitors than the Taj Mahal and London Eye Combined, *IGN*, accessed May 14, 2015.

McCabe, S. (2005). Who is a Tourist? A Critical Review. *Tourist Studies*, 5(1), 85–106.

MacCannell, D. (2013). *The Tourist: A New Theory of the Leisure Class*, 4th edn, Berkeley: University of California Press.

Madigan, J. (2010). The Psychology of Immersion in Video Games, July 27, Psychology-ofgames.com, accessed April 20, 2015.

Pine, J. and Gilmore, J. (1998). Welcome to the Experience Economy. *Harvard Business Review*, July 1, accessed April 28, 2015.

Rath, R. (2015). How Accurate is Hong Kong in Sleeping Dogs? The Escapist, February 12, www.escapistmagazine.com/articles/view/video-games/columns/criticalintel/12969-Examining-Hong-Kong-Through-the-Lens-of-Sleeping-Dogs, accessed March 12, 2015.

Richardson, B. (2008). Resistance Fracas a Blessing for Church. *GamerRadar*, February 14, www.gamesradar.com/resistance-fracas-a-blessing-for-church/, accessed March 12, 2015.

Selwyn, T. (1996). *The Tourist Image: Myths and Myth Making in Tourism*. Chichester: John Wiley.

Sleeping Dogs Reality Comparison Forum, http://forums.sleepingdogs.net/viewtopic.php?f=2&t=1524, accessed March 12, 2015.

Stuart, K. (2010). Assassin's Creed and the Appropriation of History. *Guardian Games Blog*, November 19, accessed May 14, 2015.

Theobald, W. (2005). The Meaning, Scope, and Measurement of Travel and Tourism, in Theobald, W. (ed.), *Global Tourism*, 3rd edn, London: Taylor and Francis.

Topham, G. (2003). Harry Potter is a Wizard for Tourism, *Guardian*, April 24, www.theguardian.com/media/2003/apr/24/pressandpublishing.theharrypotterfilms, accessed March 12, 2015.

Tucker, H. (2005). Narratives of Place and Self: Differing Experiences of Package Coach Tours in New Zealand. *Tourist Studies*, 5(3), 267–282.

Urry, J. (2002). *The Tourist Gaze*. London: Sage.

Westbrook, L. (2011). Videogames Boost Tourist Trade in Rural Japan, *Japanese Magazine*, January 1, www.escapistmagazine.com/news/view/106733-Videogames-Boost-Tourist-Trade-in-Rural-Japan, accessed April 20 2015.

White, N.R. and White, P.B. (2007). Home and Sway: Tourists in a Connected World. *Annals of Tourism Research*, 34(1), 99-104.

Yin-Poole, W. (2014). Assassin's Creed Project Widow Paris Vs Unity Paris, *Eurogamer*, September 25, www.eurogamer.net/articles/2014-09-25-assassins-creed-unitys-project-widow-is-an-interactive-tour-of-paris-with-andy-serkis, accessed April 20, 2015.

11 Travel and transformation in the fantasy genre

The Hobbit, A Game of Thrones and Doctor Who

Warwick Frost and Jennifer Laing

Introduction

The Opening Ceremony of the 2012 London Olympics presented two distinctive images of industry and cultural heritage in Britain. The first represented the Industrial Revolution. Under the direction of Isambard Kingdom Brunel (played by Kenneth Branagh) and 50 top-hatted industrialists, an idyllic village was rapidly transformed into a smokestack landscape. Such an emphasis on Britain as the birthplace of industrialisation was also reinforced through the Olympic mascots (Wenlock and Mandeville) being cartoon drops of iron, rather than the usual practice of utilising endemic animals.

As the Opening Ceremony moved from the nineteenth to the twentieth century, a new production image came to the fore. Instead of heavy manufacturing, the image was of creative industries. Peter Pan, Sherlock Holmes, Mary Poppins and Harry Potter represented literature. Appearances were made by James Bond (Daniel Craig), Mr Bean (Rowan Atkinson) and Doctor Who's Tardis. Popular music featured with performances of the Beatles, the Rolling Stones, Queen, the Who and Madness.

Over the last few years we have shown a Youtube compilation of the Opening Ceremony to our undergraduate students and followed up with a general discussion of who and what were being used to represent Britain's identity. The results have been consistent. Even though these were Business students, the story of the Industrial Revolution had little resonance or relevance. None of them pointed out that this was a dumbed-down version of history (Brunel didn't build smokestacks and lived after the main period of change). Nor did any student mention the lack of references to mercantilism or colonialism. In contrast, they did understand the creative industries, recognised many of the references and understood how they contributed to the formation of a cultural identity.

While this example refers to Britain, the juxtaposition between the old and the new economies could be played out for a wide range of Western countries. Coal and steel are the past, whereas literature, music and film are seen as the signifiers of a modern, sophisticated country. Cool Britannia has replaced industrial Britain.

Our interest is in the production of fictional stories and what they tell us about travel and tourism experiences. Conventionally, this has been seen in terms of tourists visiting places connected with stories. Seeking to satisfy this demand, attractions and sites have been developed that feature and interpret fictional works and characters. In London, for example, the tourist can visit Sherlock Holmes's residence at 221B Baker Street, pose in front of the statue of Peter Pan in Kensington Gardens or drive for a while to Charles Dickens World or the Harry Potter Studio Tour. Emphasising the modern shift from heavy industry to creative industries, Detroit – formerly the Motor City – has sought to reverse its decline through the construction of a statue of Robocop to attract tourists. Research into media-induced tourism has identified how destinations are being reconstructed as new forms of cultural landscapes (Jewell and McKinnon 2008) or 'places of the imagination' (Reijnders 2011). This touristic interest even applies to cases of fantasy worlds, such as the increased tourism to New Zealand resulting from the films of *The Lord of the Rings* (Buchmann *et al.*, 2010; Buchmann and Frost 2011; Jewell and McKinnon 2008).

While fictional stories generate tourism flows, they also tell one something about the nature of travel. Fiction often focuses on journeys, with movement and changing environments providing drama. Such stories make a promise that the reader or audience can also have an exciting or magical experience through travel. Indeed, the promise is often made of personal transformation through travel. Fiction provides one with an inspiration to travel, sometimes to a specific place, but also quite generally.

Our research has focused on what fictional stories have to say about travel and personal development. We have explored this issue across a range of media and genres. For literature, we have argued that tropes of travel as life-changing appear in fictional genres as diverse as historical, crime, children's, westerns and fantasy (Laing and Frost 2012). In later works we have focused on stories of *katabasis* (a descent into hell) and explorer fiction (Frost and Laing 2012; Laing and Frost 2014). Considering film, we have examined how travel in the Australian Outback is portrayed (Frost 2010), the imagining of rural villages as places for alienated urbanites to escape to (Frost and Laing 2014) and as the major influence on how tourists see the American West (Frost and Laing 2015). As this body of work grows, it reinforces our view that fiction – whatever the form or genre – emphasises ideas that travel provides the potential for personal growth and transformation.

In this chapter, our aim is to explore messages of transformation in fantasy fiction. We have touched upon this earlier in a brief consideration of travel to *impossible worlds* in novels, utilising examples such as *Gulliver's Travels*, *Alice in Wonderland*, *His Dark Materials* and *Harry Potter* (Laing and Frost 2012). In that study, we were mainly concerned with the journey of a hero from the real world to a hitherto hidden fantasy or alternative place. In this chapter, we want to go further and examine the construction of complex and detailed fantasy worlds that characters journey through. Our interest here is fuelled by the modern rise in interest in fantasy, particularly this construction of worlds across series of books or television series.

Our three case studies are *The Hobbit* (Tolkien 1937, filmed by Peter Jackson 2012–2014), *Doctor Who* (BBC, 1963–1989 and 2005 to present) and *A Game of Thrones* (Martin 1996, with the series *A Song of Fire and Ice* continuing and produced for television by HBO, 2011 to present). While the novels by Tolkien and Martin are clearly fantasy, *Doctor Who* occupies a greyer area. Sometimes characterised as science fiction, it contains narrative elements that are way beyond the normal parameters of that genre. Chapman (2006: 39) argues that 'it would probably be more accurate to describe *Doctor Who* as science fantasy rather than pure science fiction, in that its plots did go beyond what was scientifically or technologically plausible'. In line with that argument, we have chosen to place it within the fantasy genre.

All three cases are immensely popular. They are characterised by their large scale (*Doctor Who*, for example, constitutes over 800 episodes) and complexity of characterisation and representation of places. Furthermore, apart from being successful productions by creative industries, they are characterised by intensive and active fan bases, whose engagement is manifested widely through social media, conventions and fan-based productions. The scale and intensity of these productions make them particularly apt for analysis, as they present complex and sometimes provocative notions of what it means to travel and the possibilities of travel experiences.

This chapter is structured in five parts. The first three consider each of the case studies. With *The Hobbit* and *A Game of Thrones*, our focus is on the original novels rather than the film and television productions. The fourth section examines issues relating to fandom, including consideration of fan culture as a creative industry in its own right. The final section draws the analysis together, identifying key themes.

The Hobbit (J.R.R. Tolkien, 1937)

Bilbo Baggins is the eponymous hero. He lives in the rural idyll of the Shire, a romanticised version of the English Midlands that had disappeared by the time Tolkien wrote. Hobbits are:

> A little people, about half our height.... There is little or no magic about them, except the ordinary everyday sort which helps them disappear when large stupid folk like you and me come blundering along.... They are inclined to be fat in the stomach; they dress in bright colours ... [and] wear no shoes.
>
> (Tolkien 1937: 12–13)

One morning Bilbo encounters Gandalf the Wizard. At first he doesn't recognise him, but then remembers: 'not the Gandalf who was responsible for so many quiet lads and lasses going off into the Blue on mad adventures ... you used to upset things badly in these parts once upon a time'. When Gandalf suggests an adventure for Bilbo, the hobbit replies, 'Sorry! I don't want any adventures, thank you' and shuts the door (Tolkien 1937: 17).

The next day, Bilbo is unexpectedly visited by 13 dwarves. This has been arranged by Gandalf, who also returns. After a chaotic dinner, Thorin, the leader of the dwarves, gets down to business. Gradually a tale of a lost treasure is revealed. Years earlier the dwarves had accumulated great wealth, but they were attacked by the great dragon Smaug, who now guards their ruined city. Gandalf has acquired a map and a key and the dwarves have decided to attempt to reclaim their heritage.

Gandalf suggests that Bilbo be recruited. Small and used to hiding, he could be their 'burglar', helping them into the lost city. The dwarves are sceptical ('he looks more like a grocer'). As they talk, Bilbo gets excited with the quest. The next morning, however, he has doubts: '"Don't be a fool, Bilbo Baggins!" he said to himself, "thinking of dragons and all that outlandish nonsense at your age!"' (Tolkien 1937: 43–44). Then Gandalf comes again, telling him the dwarves are waiting and chivvying him to hurry and get going. Bilbo departs, 'to the end of his days Bilbo could never remember how he found himself outside, without a hat, a walking-stick, or any money' (Tolkien 1937: 45). His adventurous journey has begun.

Tolkien introduces Bilbo as decidedly unheroic. Small and fussy, he is the epitome of domestication. Wearing an apron, he dispenses food and drink to his guests. Why he decides to go – and indeed why Gandalf wants him – is left vaguely unexplained. This critical introduction brings to mind the concept of the Hero's Journey developed by folklorist Joseph Campbell (1949). He argues that most myths have common elements and those involving a heroic journey have clear stages. Bilbo's encounter with the dwarves and Gandalf suggests the *Call to Adventure*. Bilbo is essentially minding his own business when he is drawn into this adventure. Perplexed, the hero is initially reluctant and holds doubts.

The group of adventurers journey across the varied landscape of Tolkien's fantasy world of Middle Earth. Leaving the safety of the Shire, they venture into wilder and more dangerous lands. In a series of episodes they encounter different beings – Trolls, Goblins, Orcs, Elves and Men. Accordingly, the geography of Middle Earth is mapped out and explained to the reader through these unfolding adventures.

Bilbo has doubts as the going gets harder and harder. Pushing into the Misty Mountains:

> It was a hard path and a dangerous path, a crooked way and a lonely and a long. Now they could look back over the lands they had left ... Bilbo knew there lay his own country of safe and comfortable things.
>
> (Tolkien 1937: 75)

Now the atmosphere has changed. This is no longer a simple children's book. Bilbo is homesick and the danger is increasing. There is an intense foreboding that they are hurrying towards their doom. The disgruntled dwarves are no longer friendly travelling companions. When Bilbo gets lost, 'the dwarves wanted to know why he had ever been brought at all ... and why had the wizard not chosen someone with more sense' (Tolkien 1937: 119).

Here the story turns on Bilbo's encounter with Gollum in the dark tunnels under the mountains. This is akin to a *katabasis*, a descent into hell that transforms the Hobbit. The merciless Gollum wants to kill and eat Bilbo and the hero is only able to survive through using his wits – a quality that has hitherto been hardly apparent. Bilbo tricks Gollum into showing him the way out and in the process acquires a magic ring that allows him to become invisible. Being tested through intense danger, Bilbo emerges as a trickster – a common theme in many heroic tales. He now has special powers and the confidence to use them. Instead of being a burden, Bilbo now emerges as the most important member of the party. In later adventures he leads the escape from an Elvish dungeon and infiltrates the Dragon's lair.

At the end of his adventures, Bilbo returns home. However, rather than a hero's welcome, he finds that he has been away so long that he has been 'presumed dead' and his property is being auctioned. Furthermore, once settled in, he finds that he has a new reputation, that he is considered by many to be no longer respectable. Gandalf tells him that 'you are not the hobbit that you were' (Tolkien 1937: 361). Certainly he has proved himself an adventurer and will in the future restlessly make more journeys. In addition, however, his *katabasis* leading to gaining the ring has affected him. Bringing home the ring is a curse; while Bilbo lives happily, it will continue to trouble him.

Doctor Who (BBC, 1963–1989 and 2005 to present)

The Doctor is a Time Lord. An alien from the planet Gallifrey, he is able to travel through time and space in a craft (the TARDIS) that is disguised as a 1960s police box. When mortally wounded, he is able to regenerate into a different body and persona, a plot invention designed to explain changing actors in the lead role. His travelling companions are mainly drawn from Earth.

Initially, stories alternated between the past and the future. Aimed at children, they were intended to be educational. Reinforcing that intention, the Doctor's first companions included both a science and a history teacher who could provide exposition as needed. Famously, BBC executives originally insisted that the producers 'do not include Bug-Eyed Monsters ... [and that the] central characters are never Tin Robots' (quoted in Chapman 2006: 17). However, such instructions were ignored and the introduction of the Daleks in the second story ensured that the series was a ratings success. Merciless robotic killers, the Daleks became a re-occurring adversary, as did another race of alien robots in the Cybermen.

The historical stories presented the Doctor and his companions as tourists, observing historical characters and incidents, but pursuing the Doctor's rule of no intervention. As set out by a BBC executive, 'the characters cannot make history. Advice must not be proffered to Nelson on his battle tactics when approaching the Nile nor must *bon mots* be put into the mouth of Oscar Wilde' (quoted in Chapman 2006: 20). In *The Aztecs* (1964), history teacher Barbara unsuccessfully tries to stamp out human sacrifice in fifteenth-century Mexico. As the Doctor explains, 'you can't rewrite human history – not one line, what you are trying to do is utterly impossible. I know. Believe me, I know'. In response Barbara complains, 'What is the point of travelling in time and space? You can't change anything – nothing'. Such a narrative suggests one of the paradoxes of modern Western travel: while the tourist fantasises about immersion in an exotic culture, they cannot do very much to assist the place they are visiting – and if they do there is the risk of irrevocable change, even damage (Laing and Frost 2014).

In *The Time Meddler* (1965), they encounter another Time Lord, who wants to change the result of the Battle of Hastings. That story introduced the idea that history could be changed. After that, the historical episodes diminished in number and nearly always concerned the Doctor defeating alien invaders in the past. From around 1967 onwards, the stories alternated between modern-day alien invasions and futuristic travels to other worlds. Such narratives recall Leo Tolstoy's adage that 'there are only two stories – a man goes on a journey and a stranger comes to town'. In such stories, political allegory was strong. While it was possible to see critiques of current politics (Dipaolo 2010), there was also a more general Orwellian commentary on the corruption of absolute power. As in much fantasy – particularly time travel fantasy – journeys to other and alternative worlds are a common literary device for commentary on the contemporary world.

The Doctor's companions function as mediators between the stories and the audience. It is notable that since the series recommenced in 2005, they have all been contemporary and English (and attractive females). The first in the reboot was Rose Tyler (Billie Piper, 2005–2006). Living on a public housing estate, she has few prospects and is bored with her life. Meeting the Doctor opens up opportunities for travel and adventure. In contrast, her mother and boyfriend are disapproving and warn her not to go with the Doctor. Rose creates the template for future companions as people having something missing in their lives. Travel is both an escape from and an antidote to their malaise. This is further emphasised with Donna (Catherine Tate, 2008). Initially obnoxious and boorish, she is the epitome of a 'chav'. However, as she travels with the Doctor, she is transformed, becoming more caring and humane. Unfortunately, when she returns home, her travel memories are wiped and she reverts to her former unpleasant self.

Travel with the Doctor is dangerous and his appearance is usually the trigger for a range of violent deaths. Even companions die, for example Katarina (1966) and Adric (1982). In *The Family of Blood* (2007), the Doctor invites Joan to travel with him. She responds with one question, 'If you hadn't come here, would any of these people have died?' The instance of Sarah Jane Smith (Elizabeth Sladen) further demonstrates the potential negative legacy of travel with the Doctor. From 1973 to 1976, she was one of the most popular of the Doctor's companions. When it was time to leave the series, she was provided with an unusual departure. At the conclusion of *The Hand of Fear* (1976), the Doctor drops her off in a suburban London street. He is returning to Gallifrey and cannot take her with him. However, he doesn't tell her that. She expects him to come back for her. It is not until 30 years later – in *School Reunion* (2006) – that Sarah Jane meets the Doctor again. Their reunion is bittersweet. She is 30 years older. The Doctor has now regenerated and is nothing like the Doctor she knew. There is a strong sense that her life has drifted, that the adventurous travel she had in her twenties has never again been matched. Nonetheless, she does not regret her time travelling with the Doctor. For the Doctor's current companion Rose, there is the dawning realisation that she too will be abandoned sometime in the future. That the Doctor promises that he will never do this reinforces the inevitability of it occurring. For all the companions, the curse of these fantastic travels is that they are only temporary. Someday the travel will stop.

The early incarnations of the Doctor were strong and inscrutable. Even though they sometimes hid their true nature through dithering and childishness, underneath they were powerful entities. Unlike the companions, they were alien rather than human. However, when the series was resurrected in 2005, the Doctor was given a new dimension. In his recent past he had destroyed the Daleks, but in doing so he had also obliterated Gallifrey. All his friends and family were dead and he was now the last of his kind. Gibbs refers to the 2005 series as providing the 'post-traumatic Doctor', who is 'a battle-hardened and traumatized survivor ... more ruthless and less pacific ... [whose] forced jollity indeed masks a traumatized psyche' (2013: 958–959). Returning to Earth, he looks for human companionship. As he engages in new adventures, travel becomes something that it has never been before for him. In addition to curiosity and adventure, he is now motivated by the need for healing through travel.

A Game of Thrones (George R.R. Martin, 1996)

This is a medieval fantasy world of knights and battles. It could be Europe with some fictionalised geography. Certainly the interplay between warring factions ('the game of thrones') is partly based on real conflicts such as the Wars of the Roses. However, around the edges there are unworldly elements. While this is a story about humans and there are no hobbits, orcs or elves, there are dragons and ghostly entities (the Others). Interestingly, these fantasy elements are placed at the edge of the known world, so that while the reader knows they exist, from time to time various characters dismiss them as travellers' fanciful tales.

Our focus is on the first book in the series (which roughly equates to series one on television). The main characters are introduced as engaging in journeys that will change their future. Though only some realise it, they are all engaged in 'playing the Game of Thrones'. Like chess pieces, they move – which in turn requires other pieces to move. Accordingly travel is part of the game and they have little control over what is happening.

Being displaced and seeking to return home is a major theme. The story starts with King Robert arriving at Ned Stark's Winterfell castle. He asks Ned to accompany him to his capital and take the position of King's Hand (chief minister). When initially asked, Ned is 'filled with a terrible sense of foreboding. *This* was his place, here in the north' (Martin 1996: 45). Later Ned confides to his wife, 'the south is a nest of adders I would do better to avoid ... my father went south once to answer the summons of a king. He never came home again'

(Martin 1996: 60). This is no hero's call to adventure, but rather a call to travel to his doom. He later has the chance to come home, but hesitates. In the capital he is accused of treason and executed.

Across the sea are other claimants to the throne. Brother and sister Viserys and Daenerys are in exile. Viserys dreams of a vengeful return, but the younger Daenerys has no memory of a home: 'she had never seen this land her brother said was theirs.... These places he talked of ... they were just words to her' (Martin 1996: 27). Wandering from place to place:

> as the years passed and the Usurper continued to sit upon the Iron Throne, doors closed and their lives grew meaner ... they called her brother 'the beggar king'.... 'We will have it all back someday, sweet sister' he would promise her ... Viserys lived for that day. All that Daenerys wanted back was ... the childhood she had never known.
>
> (Martin 1996: 28)

To return home, Viserys marries his sister to a Dothraki prince. The promise is that he will gain an army to invade the kingdom. Now they travel with the nomadic horde. Impatiently, Viserys waits for the promise to be fulfilled. He has no interest in the Dothraki, save for their military might. In contrast, Daenerys slowly changes as they travel. She starts to learn their customs and language. She begins to see the Dothraki as her people and her home.

Tyrion is the brother-in-law of King Robert. A dwarf, he is often marginalised. Intelligent, curious, thoughtful and witty, he is a popular character with readers. With wealth and position, he can choose to be a tourist. After visiting the Starks at Winterfell, he announces he is going north rather than returning to the capital. Some of the Night Watch are heading to the great wall that protects them all from the unknown horrors of the icy north. Tyrion has 'a mind to go with them and see this Wall we have heard so much of ... I just want to stand on top of the Wall and piss off the edge of the world' (Martin 1996: 87). Tyrion then is an exception; his travel is discretionary and only motivated by wanderlust. Nonetheless, it will lead him into danger and he will be drawn off in directions he did not anticipate.

Fandom and co-creation

Fictional narratives – particularly on television – often develop a cult status and intensive fan communities. Manifesting originally through fan clubs and conventions, in recent years fan groups have embraced social media, forming virtual communities. This phenomenon may be seen from two perspectives (Kozinets 2001). First, they constitute a *social world* with its own rules, rites and values. Second, they provide an example of *co-creation*, whereby the fans as consumers of creative productions are not merely passive, but through their activities and interaction become part of the production process. It is this second approach that we concentrate on here. Due to space restrictions, our focus is on the fan communities for *Doctor Who*.

While originally conceived as a children's show, *Doctor Who* immediately gained a sizeable adult following. Catering for multiple audiences often led to tensions. For example, there is a long history of debate over the levels of violence, sex and adult concepts in the series (Chapman 2006). From the beginning, the series attracted fans who wanted to go deeper into this fantasy world. The intensity of this fandom is not surprising, for the series contained an addictive mix of an enigmatic hero with a hidden backstory, unresolved sexual tension with the companions and iconic villains.

The influence of fans came to the fore after the series was discontinued in 1989. Rather than fan interest diminishing, it grew. A parallel may be drawn with *Star Trek*, which also returned once a new generation of television executives realised the possibilities of reinvigorating a powerful heritage brand. In both cases, ceasing production of the series bound fans together, united in a sense that they were 'true believers', a small group who truly understood how good the show was. While it is easy to categorise such groups as small, marginal and ineffective, in the case of *Doctor Who* the opposite was true. The resurrection of *Doctor Who* in 2005 was primarily due to commercial reasons. The BBC realised that sales of merchandising and videos were growing, indicating a strong market for a return. While a group of producers pushing for a reboot were fans themselves, the decision to create a new series – and to provide high-quality production values – was based on the economic power of the fans.

A decade on, this commercial dimension is still obvious. Whereas fans in the past were satisfied with photos next to police call boxes (Figure 11.1), there are now a wide array of experiences and merchandising. One of us visited the Doctor Who Up Close Exhibition in Cardiff in 2009 which is now known as the Doctor Who Experience. It featured sets of the TV show, as well as representations of iconic characters like the Cybermen (Figure 11.2). In Christmas 2014, we visited the Doctor Who Pop-Up Shop. What was particularly noticeable were the demographics of the customers in this crowded shop. We were certainly the oldest. Perhaps most surprisingly, the Generation Y clientele was overwhelmingly female.

The new iteration of *Doctor Who* corresponded with the rise of the internet and social media. Fan discussion groups and blogs dissected plots and characters and speculated on meanings and future developments. For the producers, this high level of engagement was often trying (Dipaolo 2010). In at least two instances, this co-creation manifested itself in references to obsessive fans within the plots. The first was the episode *Love and Monsters* (2006). In an unusual plotline, it focused on a group who have become obsessed with the Doctor and are trying to track down his whereabouts. Tellingly, nearly all of them are destroyed (Gibbs 2013). An even more explicit message related to the character Osgood. A bespectacled and nerdy scientist, she wears a long coloured scarf in the manner of Tom Baker's Doctor from the 1970s. Highly popular, as she represented a quintessential obsessive fan, she was unexpectedly killed off in 2014. This may have been a demonstration of power or frustration directed towards the fan base, a sign of the producers' annoyance with fans (we are grateful to Anne Buchmann for bringing this to our attention).

Figure 11.1 A tourist poses next to the Tardis, an old police phone box in Earl's Court, London.

Figure 11.2 Cyberman, forming part of the Doctor Who Up Close Exhibition, Cardiff, 2009.

Conclusions

The conventional view of media and tourism is that readers and viewers are inspired to travel to places represented in the media they have consumed. The creative industries of film and literature then beget spin-off tourism operations. In the cases considered here, this leads to the Hobbiton attraction in New Zealand, the Doctor Who Experience in Cardiff and the Game of Thrones Tours in Northern Ireland.

However, this is only part of the story. Fiction also inspires people to consider travel in more general ways. Travel becomes something they want to undertake, a possible rite of passage, a pleasing and educational experience, something that defines them, an experience that transforms them. The three fantasy case studies considered can all be seen in this way. Travel is at the heart of these stories. Through travel, the main characters (and the audience) are moving through a fantasy landscape, seeing new places and interacting with exotic characters. Travel may be simply to satisfy curiosity or wanderlust, or to escape from drudgery or oppression. In the cases considered, it is invigorating and wonderful, but it comes with potential dangers. An Odyssey may also be a *katabasis*.

The fantasy element is important to the promise of travel. These stories dwell on the magical element. They begin with ordinary people in everyday circumstances, yet their journeys take them to or through extraordinary places and experiences. The fantasy genre allows full play with the idea that travel can take one to another world.

References

Buchmann, A. and Frost, W. (2011) 'Wizards Everywhere? Film Tourism and the Imagining of National Identity in New Zealand', in E. Frew and L. White (eds) *Tourism and National Identities: An International Perspective* (pp. 52–64), London and New York: Routledge.

Buchmann, A., Moore, K. and Fisher, D. (2010) 'Experiencing Film Tourism: Authenticity and Fellowship', *Annals of Tourism Research*, 37(1), 229–248.

Campbell, J. (1949) *The Hero with a Thousand Faces*, London: Fontana (rept. 1993).

Chapman, J. (2006) *Inside the Tardis: The Worlds of Doctor Who*, London and New York: I.B. Tauris.

Dipaolo, M.E. (2010) 'Political Satire and British-American Relations in Five Decades of *Doctor Who*', *The Journal of Popular Culture*, 43(5), 964–987.

Frost, W. (2010) 'Life-Changing Experiences: Film and Tourists in the Australian Outback', *Annals of Tourism Research*, 37(3), 707–726.

Frost, W. and Laing, J. (2012) 'Travel as Hell: Exploring the Katabatic Structure of Travel Fiction', *Literature and Aesthetics*, 22(1), 215–233.

Frost, W. and Laing, J. (2014) 'Fictional Media and Imagining Escape to Rural Villages', *Tourism Geographies*, 16(2), 207–220.

Frost, W. and Laing, J. (2015) *Imagining the American West through Film and Tourism*, London and New York: Routledge.

Gibbs, A. (2013) '"Maybe That's What Happens if You Touch the Doctor, Even for a Second": Trauma in *Doctor Who*', *The Journal of Popular Culture*, 46(5), 950–972.

Gregg, P.B. (2004) 'England Looks to the Future: The Cultural Forum Model and *Doctor Who*', *The Journal of Popular Culture*, 37(4), 648–661.

Jewell, B. and McKinnon, S. (2008) 'Movie Tourism – A New Form of Cultural Landscape?', *Journal of Travel and Tourism Marketing*, 24(2/3), 153–162.

Kozinets, R.V. (2001) 'Utopian Enterprise: Articulating the Meanings of *Star Trek*'s Culture of Consumption', *Journal of Consumer Research*, 28(1), 67–88.

Laing, J. and Frost, W. (2012) *Books and Travel: Inspiration, Quests and Transformation*, Bristol: Channel View.

Laing, J. and Frost, W. (2014) *Explorer Travellers and Adventure Tourism*, Bristol: Channel View.

Martin, G.R.R. (1996) *A Game of Thrones*, London: Harper Voyager, 2011 reprint.

Reijnders, S. (2011) *Places of the Imagination: Media, Tourism, Culture*, Aldershot: Ashgate.

Tolkien, J.R.R. (1937) *The Hobbit*, London: Harper Collins, 1998 reprint.

12 Conclusions

Philip Long and Nigel D. Morpeth

It might be anticipated that the concluding section of a book on the creative industries and tourism would extol the virtues of a grouping of sectors which are viewed as producing economic benefits for nation-states globally (and significantly through tourism) and in the process be reified as part of a 'solution' to the deindustrialisation of Western societies and as a basis for economic development globally. However, advocacy is of course not the role of an academic text and, as we highlighted in the Introduction above, there are inherent tensions in attempting to conceptualise 'creativity', 'tourism' and 'industries' in combination, and these present a challenge to policy-makers and also to our understanding of creative practice.

In relation to these tensions, renowned UK musician and artist Brian Eno recently critiqued the concept of the creative industries being underpinned by the central elements of culture and the arts and their incommensurability with industry (Eno, 2015). He observed that 'I found myself writing something about the creative industries and started to wonder about the genesis of the term and understand why people working within the creative arts are desperate to get a bit of money from government.' He went on to say that

> apparently the way of getting money is to persuade them that you are an industry and if you are an industry you are part of an economic framework and everything you do can be expressed as a single number like the contribution to GNP or the number of jobs you help create.

He laments how in quantifying the value of creativity it can be diminished, stating that 'I thought this is the beginning of the end of the arts if we try to make everything expressible by a single number', adding 'what we also do by the same token is that things which can't be evaluated in that way are not worth anything.' Eno further noted that the UK Government Education Secretary

> thought it was a good idea for students not to go into the Arts and Humanities because they did not offer such good job prospects as the STEM (Science, Technology, Engineering and Maths) subjects. The idea that those are the important things which are part of the economic mill and that art is a bit of a luxury.

Eno went on to speculate that this has implications for how art and artists are viewed – as 'untamed and unfettered individuals who are not part of the affairs of the state'. We hold these tensions in mind as we conclude this book through considering its contributions, along with proposing topics relating to creative tourism that require further research.

This book has illustrated critical issues in research on the connections between the creative industries and tourism through a range of international examples focused on component sectors and also in relation to creative tourism policy and practice across this disparate field. These contributions have added to the literature in an emerging area of academic enquiry, policy intervention, and professional and tourist practice. However, this book is far from exhaustive in its coverage of the field. Here we recognise gaps in knowledge about aspects of creative tourism and suggest areas where there is a need for further research. Some component sectors of the creative industries as defined in the UK by DCMS (2001) and CCS (2013) and recognised internationally have received considerably more scholarly attention than others in the tourism literature. We briefly consider this in the following order:

- advertising and marketing
- architecture
- design and designer fashion
- film, TV, video, radio and photography
- IT, software and computer services
- publishing
- music, and the performing and visual arts.

Marketing is a very well-established sub-field within Tourism Management Studies and industry practice. However, there has been limited attention to the critical application to tourism of theory and practice from the specialised 'creative marketing' fields of advertising, public relations and nation-branding (Aronczyk, 2013; Dinnie, 2008). Examples of topics that warrant further research in these contexts include the ethics and history of nation-branding campaigns that are directed at attracting tourists, particularly in the context of representations of socially and politically repressive regimes (see, for example, Rosendorf, 2014 on the origins of nation-branding aimed at restoring the reputation through tourism of Franco-era Spain). How tourism advertising campaigns may be evaluated for their effectiveness, and also semiotically in their representations of women, families and 'the other' and in cases of intermediation and inter-textuality, are additional areas that require more research.

Architecture is rarely addressed directly in the tourism literature, usually being implicit within the field of tourism planning and development (Mugerauer, 2009; see also Strange, Chapter 6 in this volume). The aesthetic quality, appeal and safety of the built environment are clearly of fundamental importance for both tourists and 'host' communities. Other topical concerns in architectural studies that warrant more attention regarding their implications for tourism and local communities include the privatisation and reconfiguration of publicly owned space to privilege consumption and attract the much sought-after and stereotypically 'high-spending' cultural or creative tourist (and exclude others). Associated with this are controversies surrounding architectural interventions that are aimed at attracting the 'creative class': the 'gentrification' of formerly artistic neighbourhoods and displacement of communities in places that are promoted as 'destinations' for tourists. Managing the behaviour of tourists in the 'night-time' visitor economy in urban space in UK and some European town/ city centres is a further topical issue with architectural and design dimensions. The architecture of tourist resorts, hotels, theme parks, etc. is also of historical and contemporary transdisciplinary research and specialist professional interest.

Limited tourism research has also been afforded to design and designer fashion. We suggest that there is a need for research to address issues such as the ethics and sustainability of the fashion industry in the context of 'luxury' consumerist tourism; the globalisation of fashion brands and tastes; and cultural and aesthetic sensitivities that may be provoked among 'hosts' concerning tourist dress. The representation of national identities as reflected in fashion tastes and the commodification of 'national dress' as intangible cultural heritage also warrant further study.

The tourism connections of the 'screen media' of film and, to a lesser extent, television and video have received considerably more theoretical and methodological research attention than other sectors of the creative industries (Beeton, 2015; Chambers and Rakić, 2010). Photography as visual culture and research methodology in tourism has also been addressed (Palmer *et al.*, 2010). However, the historical and contemporary aural representations of places and tourists through radio and audio channels are much less covered in the tourism field. We also suggest that research is lacking on the implications of the digital manipulation of screened locations for tourist experience and place image (e.g. New Zealand 'adapted' as Mordor and the Shire in the *Lord of the Rings* and *Hobbit* film series). Intermediated connections between screen and other media, such as print literature and the web and the phenomenon of tourist and amateur forms of film making and distribution through social media, are also important emergent issues. We suggest research into the semiotic and tourism dimensions of diverse film genres (such as documentaries, outdoor screenings, dramas and comedies with tourism storylines such as *The Beach, Paradise Love, Carry on Abroad, Les Vacances de Monsieur Hulot*, etc.). There is also a need for interprofessional learning and understanding between film/TV and tourism practitioners, though this point applies across creative industry sectors.

There is an understandable and burgeoning interest in the relationships between tourism and information technologies, software and computer services expressed in the notion of digital or 'e-tourism' (Egger and Buhalis, 2008). However, we suggest that the characteristics and consequences of tourism 'cyber cultures' would benefit from research attention to their historical, offline antecedents as expressed for example in the figure of the *flâneur* and analysed through psychogeographical perspectives on 'playful' or 'radical tourism

(Antony and Henry, 2005; Coverley, 2006; Debord, 2009; Garrett, 2014; Lynch, 1960; Self and Steadman, 2007; Solnit, 2006). In Chapter 10 above, Salmond and Salmond eloquently highlight the metamorphosis from the tourist as gamer to the virtual tourist becoming an e-citizen who colonises virtual community spaces which they dubbed unrealities. Issues of the 'digital divide' the pervasive role of the major social media corporations, and generational and gender experiences and behaviours online as regards tourism warrant further research. Questions of online tourism data security and the surveillance of tourist activity online by governments in the contexts of mass migration and the 'war against terror' are also clearly of key concern both theoretically and in policy and practice.

We interpret publishing here as being concerned with fictional and travel literature and also application of literary critical analysis to the stories that authors tell about tourism explicitly or by implication and those that are read by people as tourists. There is widespread creative 'packaging' of literary associations between the tourism and publishing sectors centred on historical and contemporary authors, book launches, festivals, 'book towns', the anticipation of opportunities linked with forthcoming publishing 'events' (e.g. anniversaries, the release of screen adaptations), etc. There is considerable interest among tourism practitioners such as destination marketing organisations (and guide book publishers) in articulating potential tourist places, activities and experiences with a strong narrative, indicating the critical importance of language in tourism and literary texts. Finally, there is a need for more study of non-English-language literary associations with tourism.

Links between musical genres, performing and visual arts and tourism have been subject to some research and policy interest (Bennett, 2000; Connell and Gibson, 2003; Long, 2014; UK Music, 2015). Further research in this field might be concerned with how local music 'scenes' come about, along with their appeal to tourists (Cohen, 1999). Research attention might also usefully be directed to the dynamics of music and arts (sub-cultural, fan) tourist audiences; networks of musicians, artists and related tourism practitioners; art tourism destination socioeconomic environments; strategies of urban development, city marketing, tourism and artistic infrastructure in the context of the creative industries; and the extent of local and national/international media coverage of the arts (Johansson and Bell, 2009: 220–225). Relationships between tourism, world music and non-Western arts genres as intangible cultural heritage also require further study (Church, 2015).

Government policies that address tourism and the creative industries at various levels of governance are outlined in Table 1.1 in the Introduction above. We suggest that further research and policy consideration are given to the extent to which tourism and creative industries policies converge (are 'joined up' across government departments). Contrasting professional and political ideologies and discourses underpinning creative industries and tourism policies may also be examined. We note that the policy discourse surrounding the 'visitor economy' often fails to include adequate recognition of the role of the creative industries.

Parallel policy discourses about the 'creative', 'cultural' and 'knowledge' economies usually fail to mention tourism. Furthermore, creative industries are
typically included, if at all, in tourism policies and strategies as part of the loose
and vague term 'attractions'. However, creative industries may play a much
more important and defining though subtle and complex role in shaping a destination's socio-cultural *milieu* (whether one subscribes to the existence of the
'creative class' or not).

The contributions to this book suggest that different policies and strategies for
the creative industries are prevalent in different countries, reflecting contrasting
interpretations of culture and creativity. Ambrosino, Guillon and Sagot-
Duvauroux (Chapter 8) and also Whiting and Hannam (Chapter 9) highlight the
role of the creative city in having the capacity to engineer distinctive strategies
and policies for creativity (and in the absence of a French national strategy for
creativity) at a city level. Both chapters focus on the importance of creative *animateurs* who are able to generate political and policy initiatives to mobilise
resources for creativity. In the case of Newcastle upon Tyne in the UK, Whiting
and Hannam locate communities which have the capacity to create bohemian
communities of creative production and this would warrant further research in
other contexts.

Ambrosino, Guillon and Sagot-Duvauroux also highlight how design has
been central to the industrial past of Saint-Etienne as a designated Cite du
Design and how it has become central to narratives of creativity being embodied
within objects and images both in a historic and a contemporary sense and promoted for tourism. This is partly reliant on creating an atmosphere of *distinctiveness* in the city and reconnecting with the historical lineage in design based on a
metal industry as well as weaponry and fabric industries. There is a parallel with
the city of Sheffield in the UK which has used creativity and design as a central
strategy for economic regeneration through the branding of the 'Steel City' as
'Authentic and Independent'. A further parallel between the two cities is the way
in which development of creative practice has been initiated at a local level on a
city scale unfettered by national interventions (and in the case of Sheffield in the
1980s, having to operate a local political administration within diminished
national resourcing of local budgets). The driving force for this initiative for
design in Saint-Etienne was to enlist the support of the higher education sector
through the École des Beaux-Arts and the schools of Engineering and Design
which worked with the city authority to provide student placements on urban
design projects. Furthermore, the creation of a biennale of design positioned
Saint-Etienne on a world stage for design. The role of higher education in creative industries and creative tourism leads us to reflect on practice and professional development.

Creative tourism as practised by 'creatives' as workers and 'performed' by
tourists in their co-creation of experience requires more research. *Creative
labour* is eulogised by policy-makers and advocates (stereotypically) as 'driving'
innovation and wealth-creation throughout the economy (Bakhshi and Windsor,
2015). However, there are huge differences in the nature of employment across a

spectrum of the creative industries from, for example, the global technology and commercial media industry to self-employed artists. There are also very mixed findings from research on the relationships between employment within the creative industries and subjective well-being which broadly reflect this divide. It is suggested that positive characteristics associated with (some) creative occupations that correlate with life satisfaction, 'worthwhileness' and happiness include:

- personal autonomy and control of working time and processes;
- opportunities for mobility;
- self-actualisation through pride in creative outputs;
- freedom of expression;
- the development of competencies;
- a sense of usefulness to society;
- openness to new ideas and tolerance of unconventionality.

(Fujiwara *et al.*, 2015: 4–5; see also Kong, 2005)

While it is important to recognise that on a macro level policy-makers extol the economic virtues of the creative industries there are also concerns about the quality of employment in some creative occupations, involving self-exploitation ('flexploitation'), casualisation and precariousness as being typical features of creative industry labour markets, with self-employment and project-based working becoming more widespread in the economy as a whole (Comunian *et al.*, 2011, Comunian *et al.*, 2010; Hartley *et al.*, 2013: 51). Bigsby (2015: 27) expresses the economic reality facing many creative practitioners in the UK starkly and as follows,

> in this country [the UK], the median income for professional authors in 2013 was £11,000.... Ten years ago, 40 per cent of writers earned their money solely by writing. In 2013, it was 11.5%. The average income of an artist in 2014 was £10,000, down £6,000 in real terms since 1997. Musicians in a major orchestra earn, on average, a little over a third of what they would in the US. Half of Actors' Equity members earn less than £5,000 a year while nearly half have worked for no pay ... the average salary of a director working in the subsidised theatre is £10,759, and have worked for nothing.

The romantic notion of creative labour is also challenged by the paradox that 'much value creation in the creative industries is due to "mundane" or "humdrum" labour, the work of accountants, lawyers and a range of technical staff, located on the boundary where commerce meets art' (Hartley *et al.*, 2013: 68). There may therefore be an exaggerated celebration of the liberationist potential of 'creative' labour as a benign narrative.

Tourism and the Creative Industries are parallel domains of further and higher education and professional development programmes (Ashton and Noonan,

2013; Cooke, 2002; Fisher, 2012; Hughes *et al.*, 2008). For Hartley *et al.* (2013: xi), courses in Creative Industries (or 'Cultural Industries Management') typically include coverage of:

- communication technologies and media studies;
- business, economics and policy applied to the creative industries;
- creative arts management (music, visual and performing arts);
- media production (film, television, digital);
- design (fashion, architecture, graphics);
- law (copyright and intellectual property);
- education and training (for creative practitioners).

The study of tourism is therefore marginal at best in the creative industry curriculum. We also note that in the UK, the subject benchmark statement for tourism (QAA, 2008) makes scant reference to the creative industries. Furthermore, there is no single curriculum benchmark statement guiding course developers in the UK for the creative industries, with separate coverage of, for example: Communication, Media, Film and Cultural Studies; Art and Design; Languages, etc. As regards skills-based apprenticeships, further education and professional development programmes, we also note that there are parallel sector skills agencies in the UK, with 'Creative and Cultural Skills' focused on the creative industries and 'People 1st' responsible for tourism and hospitality.

Creativity and tourism have thus been traditionally separated in different scholarly domains and if these dichotomies are to be more effectively transcended then the fusion of creativity and tourism through pedagogy suggests that the tourism destination managers of tomorrow require a better understanding of the ways in which tourist experience may be informed and enhanced by different aspects of creativity. This can only come about through dialogue across the fields of tourism and the creative industries and reflection on how each may inform the other in developing the critical, reflective practitioners of the future. Such 'co-creation' of knowledge and creative capacities is also pertinent to the consideration of the consumer/tourist who effectively labours, and is perhaps exploited at times, in the design and distribution of creative tourism products, processes and networks. However, for individuals, the possession of or the ability to develop the capacity to 'be creative' is viewed as a highly desirable state that may be taught/learned and applied in everyday life as well as in commercial and policy contexts including, of course, in tourism.

References

Antony, R. and Henry, J. (2005). *The Lonely Planet Guide to Experimental Travel*, Footscray, Australia: Lonely Planet

Aronczyk, M. (2013). *Branding the Nation: The Global Business of National Identity*, New York: Oxford University Press

Ashton, D. and Noonan, C. (eds) (2013). *Cultural Work and Higher Education*, Basingstoke: Palgrave Macmillan

Bakhshi, H. and Windsor, G. (2015). *The Creative Economy and the Future of Employment*, London: NESTA

Bakhshi, H., Hargreaves, I. and Mateos-Garcia, J. (2013). *A Manifesto for the Creative Economy*. London: National Endowment for Science, Technology and the Arts

Beeton, S. (2015). *Travel, Tourism and the Moving Image*, Clevedon: Channel View

Bennett, A. (2000). *Music, Identity and Place*, London: Macmillan Press

Bigsby, C. (2015). A precious commodity: What price will we pay for taking the arts for granted? *Times Higher Education Supplement*, 6 August, p. 27

Boden, M. (1994). What is creativity? In M. Boden (ed.), *Dimensions of Creativity*, pp. 75–117. London: MIT Press/Bradford Books

Bohm, A. (1998). *On Creativity*. New York: Harper and Row

CCS (2013). *Classifying and Measuring the Creative Industries*, London: Creative and Cultural Skills

Chambers, D. and Rakić, T. (eds) (2010). *An Introduction to Visual Research Methods in Tourism*, London: Routledge

Church, M. (2015). *The Other Classical Musics: Fifteen Great Traditions*, London: Boydell and Brewer

Cohen, S. (1999). Scenes. In B. Horner and T. Swiss (eds), *Key Terms in Popular Music and Culture*, pp. 239–249. Malden, MA: Blackwell

Comunian, R., Faggian, A. and Jewell, S. (2011). Winning and losing in the creative industries: an analysis of creative graduates' career opportunities across creative disciplines, *'A Golden Age?' Reflections on New Labour's Cultural Policy and its Post-Recession Legacy*, *Cultural Trends*, Vol. 20 (3–4) Special Issue, pp. 291–308

Comunian, R., Faggian, A. and Li, Q. (2010). Unrewarded careers in the creative class: the strange case of Bohemian graduates, *Papers in Regional Science*, Vol. 89(2), pp. 389–410

Connell, J. and Gibson, C. (2003). *Sound Tracks: Popular Music, Identity and Place*, London: Routledge

Cooke, P. (2002). *Knowledge Economies: Clusters, Learning and Cooperative Advantage*, London: Routledge

Coverley, M. (2006). *Psychogeography*, London: Pocket Essentials

Davies, R. and Sigthorsson, G. (2013). *Introducing the Creative Industries: From Theory to Practice*, Los Angeles: Sage

DCMS (2001). *The Creative Industries Mapping Document 2001*, London: Department of Culture, Media and Sport

Debord, G. (2009). *Society of the Spectacle* (trans. Knabb, K.), Eastbourne: Soul Bay Press

Dinnie, K. (2008). *Nation Branding: Concepts, Issues, Practice*, London: Butterworth Heinemann

Egger, R. and Buhalis, D. (eds) (2008). *E-Tourism Case Studies: Marketing and Management Issues*, Boston: Elsevier and Butterworth Heinemann

Eno, B. (2015). *BBC Music John Peel Lecture*, London: BBC, available at http://downloads.bbc.co.uk/6music/johnpeellecture/brian-eno-john-peel-lecture.pdf, accessed 13 November 2015

Fisher, S. (2012). *The Cultural Knowledge Ecology: A Discussion Paper on Partnerships Between HEIs and Cultural Organisations*, working paper, London: Arts Council England

Fujiwara, D., Dolan, P. and Lawton, R. (2015). *Creative Occupations and Subjective Wellbeing*, London: NESTA

Garrett, B. (2014). *Explore Everything: Place Hacking the City*, London: Verso

Gretzel, U. and Jamal, T. (2009). Conceptualizing the creative tourist class: technology, mobility, and tourist experiences, *Tourism Analysis*, Vol. 14, pp. 471–481

Hartley, J., Potts, J., Cunningham, S., Flew, T., Keane, M. and Banks, J. (2013). *Key Concepts in Creative Industries*, London: Sage

Hennessey, B. (2003). The social psychology of creativity, *Scandinavian Journal of Educational Research*, Vol. 47(3), pp. 253–271

Hughes, T., Tapp, A. and Hughes, R. (2008). Achieving effective academic/practitioner knowledge exchange in marketing, *Journal of Marketing Management*, Vol. 24(1–2), pp. 221–240

Johansson, O. and Bell, T.L. (eds) (2009). *Sound, Society and the Geography of Popular Music*, Burlington, VT: Ashgate

Kong, Lily (2005). The sociality of cultural industries, *International Journal of Cultural Policy*, Vol. 11, pp. 61–76.

Long, P. (2014). Popular music, psychogeography, place identity and tourism: the case of Sheffield, *Tourist Studies*, Vol. 1, pp. 48–65

Long, P. and Morpeth, N. (2012). Critiquing creativity in tourism. In M. Smith and G. Richards (eds), *Routledge Handbook of Cultural Tourism*, pp. 304–310, London: Routledge

Lynch, K. (1960). *The Image of the City*, Harvard, MA: MIT Press

Mugerauer, R. (2009). Architecture and urban planning: practical and theoretical contributions. In T. Jamal and M. Robinson (eds), *The Sage Handbook of Tourism Studies*, pp. 49–180, London: Sage

O'Brien, D. (2014). *Cultural Policy: Management, Value and Modernity in the Creative Industries*, London: Routledge

Palmer, C., Lester, J. and Burns, P. (eds) (2010). *Tourism and Visual Culture, Vol. 1: Theories and Concepts*, Wallingford: CABI

QAA (2008). *Hospitality, Leisure, Sport and Tourism – Subject Benchmark Statement*, London: The Quality Assurance Agency for Higher Education

Richards, G. and Wilson, J. (eds) (2007). *Tourism, Creativity and Development*, London: Routledge

Rosendorf, N. (2014). *Franco Sells Spain to America: Hollywood, Tourism and Public Relations as Postwar Spanish Soft Power*, London: Palgrave Macmillan

Sandbrook, D. (2015). *The Great British Dream Factory: The Strange History of our National Imagination*, London: Allen Lane

Self, W. and Steadman, R. (2007). *Psychogeography*, London: Bloomsbury

Solnit, R. (2006). *A Field Guide to Getting Lost*, London: Canongate Books

Sternberg, R.J. (2006). Introduction. In J.C. Kaufman and R.J. Sternberg (eds), *The International Handbook of Creativity*, pp. 1–9. Cambridge: Cambridge University Press.

Tan, S., Kung, S. and Luh, D. (2013). A model of creative experience in creative tourism, *Annals of Tourism Research*, Vol. 41, pp. 153–174

UK Music (2015). *Wish You Were Here 2015: UK Music's Contribution to the UK Economy*, London: UK Music

Warwick Commission on the Future of Cultural Value (2015). *Enriching Britain: Culture, Creativity and Growth*, Warwick: University of Warwick, UK

Weiner, R.P. (2000). *Creativity and Beyond: Cultures, Values, and Change*, Albany, NY: State University of New York Press

Index

Page numbers in *italics* denote tables, those in **bold** denote figures.

190   *Index*

Taylor & Francis eBooks

Helping you to choose the right eBooks for your Library

Add Routledge titles to your library's digital collection today. Taylor and Francis ebooks contains over 50,000 titles in the Humanities, Social Sciences, Behavioural Sciences, Built Environment and Law.

Choose from a range of subject packages or create your own!

Benefits for you

» Free MARC records
» COUNTER-compliant usage statistics
» Flexible purchase and pricing options
» All titles DRM-free.

Benefits for your user

» Off-site, anytime access via Athens or referring URL
» Print or copy pages or chapters
» Full content search
» Bookmark, highlight and annotate text
» Access to thousands of pages of quality research at the click of a button.

REQUEST YOUR FREE INSTITUTIONAL TRIAL TODAY

Free Trials Available
We offer free trials to qualifying academic, corporate and government customers.

eCollections – Choose from over 30 subject eCollections, including:

Archaeology	Language Learning
Architecture	Law
Asian Studies	Literature
Business & Management	Media & Communication
Classical Studies	Middle East Studies
Construction	Music
Creative & Media Arts	Philosophy
Criminology & Criminal Justice	Planning
Economics	Politics
Education	Psychology & Mental Health
Energy	Religion
Engineering	Security
English Language & Linguistics	Social Work
Environment & Sustainability	Sociology
Geography	Sport
Health Studies	Theatre & Performance
History	Tourism, Hospitality & Events

For more information, pricing enquiries or to order a free trial, please contact your local sales team: www.tandfebooks.com/page/sales

For Product Safety Concerns and Information please contact our EU
representative GPSR@taylorandfrancis.com
Taylor & Francis Verlag GmbH, Kaufingerstraße 24, 80331 München, Germany

www.ingramcontent.com/pod-product-compliance
Ingram Content Group UK Ltd.
Pitfield, Milton Keynes, MK11 3LW, UK
UKHW021611240425
457818UK00018B/508